# ENVY IS NOT INNATE

# ENVY IS NOT INNATE
## A New Model of Thinking

*Patricia Polledri*

# KARNAC

First published in 2012 by
Karnac Books Ltd
118 Finchley Road
London NW3 5HT

British Library Cataloguing in Publication Data

A C.I.P. for this book is available from the British Library

ISBN-13: 978-1-78049-002-1

Typeset by V Publishing Solutions Pvt Ltd., Chennai, India


www.karnacbooks.com

# CONTENTS

ACKNOWLEDGEMENTS                                                    vii

ABOUT THE AUTHOR                                                    ix

FOREWORD                                                           xi
by Patrick Gallwey

INTRODUCTION                                                       xix

CHAPTER ONE
Historical background: a brief overview                            1

CHAPTER TWO
Literature review                                                  8

CHAPTER THREE
Encapsulated containerlessness                                     49

CHAPTER FOUR
Shame and envy                                                     83

*CHAPTER FIVE*
Self envy                                                                          98

*CHAPTER SIX*
Perverse relationships in pathological organisations          126

*CHAPTER SEVEN*
Womb envy                                                                     137

*SUMMARY AND CONCLUSIONS*                              154

*REFERENCES*                                                             159

*INDEX*                                                                         183

# ACKNOWLEDGEMENTS

It seems as if I have been writing this book for all my professional life and many people have contributed to my thinking, more than I could possibly name or thank in this short space. The early development of my ideas about the psychopathology of envy was greatly facilitated by the insightful comments and support of several inspirational teachers, mentors, and supervisors who range across the whole spectrum of the human sciences.

One of my deepest debts, and certainly the most specific one, without which this book absolutely could not have been written, is the many women and the few men I have treated who were detained in various prisons and psychiatric hospitals in the United Kingdom. Where I have quoted, paraphrased, or summarised what they have said, I have changed their names and all identifying information in order to protect their privacy.

I would like to thank most particularly Professor Vicky Lebeau, for suggesting I write this book in the first place. She encouraged me to draw on the whole range of clinical experiences I had with forensic patients, to speak from my deepest self and to write in my own voice. Dr Patrick Gallwey and Dr Arthur Hyatt-Williams supervised the clinical cases and, along with Dr Estela Welldon, provided the inspiration.

Caroline Ball has added enormously to the quality of the text with her expert editing skills.

Most of all to my family—to speak merely of gratitude for the encouragement they have given me is an understatement that is justifiable only because of the inadequacy of any words to express their generosity toward me, and the strength their support has given me.

Permission is given by Faber and Faber to use the quote from Sylvia Plath's poem in the text.

Permission is given by the *British Journal of Psychotherapy* to use material previously published in an article entitled "Envy Revisited" which is quoted from in the text and the References.

Permission is given by Valerie Hornby to use her art image from Flickr for the book cover designed by Luke Polledri.

*Note on terminology*

In spite of their identity in sound and in ultimate etymology, *fantasy* and *phantasy* tend to be apprehended as separate words, the predominant sense of *fantasy* being "caprice, whim, fanciful invention", while *phantasy* is "imagination, visionary notion" (Rycroft, 1968). Since the psychoanalytical concept is more akin to imagination than to whimsy, I have used the spelling *phantasy*—as opposed to *fantasy*—throughout.

# ABOUT THE AUTHOR

**Patricia Polledri, PhD**, is a forensic psychotherapist in London, who has spent many years developing the further understanding of developmental psychopathology in order to produce a workable model that is relevant to clinical practice. She has developed her ideas both from clinical experience and from academic research at University College London Medical School, Department of Psychiatry and Behavioural Sciences, and at the University of Sussex, School of Law, Politics and Sociology.

# FOREWORD

*Patrick Gallwey*

> *For the apotheosis of Reason we have substituted that of Instinct, and we call everything instinct that we find in ourselves and for which we cannot trace any rational foundation. This idolatry ... will probably hold its ground until it gives way before a sound psychology, laying bare the real root of much that is bowed down to as the intention of Nature and the ordinance of God.*
>
> —John Stuart Mill, *On Liberty* (1859)

In this book Patricia Polledri puts forward a challenge to a long-standing psychoanalytic tradition, namely the use of instinct as the major primary source of psychopathology, with traumatic experiences secondary to the point of being unconsidered. She focuses in particular on the Kleinian concept of envy, which Klein held to be a manifestation of Freud's concept of what he called the "death instinct". This, he held, opposed the "life instinct" and was a drive to passivity and, *inter alia*, resulted in sadomasochism and aggression. She acknowledges the importance of Klein's contention that intra-psychic destructive attacks in phantasy on the good qualities in others (which Klein called "envy"), particularly the feeding mother, are a source of grave mental disturbance. However,

Polledri sets out with great erudition her view that envy is a reaction to adverse nurturing experiences and is not an instinctive drive, and is not therefore a universal human trait that needs to be overcome to establish sanity and mental stability. Polledri explores the concept of envy as a profound reflection of traumatic psychopathology, using clinical illustrations to show how it affects individuals she has treated, the scope over and above attacks on the feeding breast, and the implications this has for society in its propensity for creating harmful, even horrific, behaviour.

The psychoanalytic reliance on instinct as a primary source of psychopathology is typical of an habitual misuse of the concept to explain evil as a universal human characteristic. After Darwin, instinct became understood as a biological vehicle for inherited traits that improve the chances of survival of a particular species. It has, however, continued to be misused to enable quick pseudo-explanation of complex phenomena. In psychoanalysis, this misuse has resulted in a tradition that makes mental disturbance a central and universal trait of human nature. Perhaps surprisingly, considering the strong Jewish roots of the discipline, this is more on a par with the Christian concept of original sin, which is even more starkly reflected in Klein's concept of innate envy of the infant towards the goodness and love of the feeding mother and her breast.

During my days as a trainee analyst, I was very interested in infant observation, but I was rather rattled when my supervisor, an eminent Kleinian, voiced praise at a Catholic mother who had reacted to her infant crying by saying, rather than picking it up, "Oh it's only his original sin." This, she maintained, enabled the mother to remain unworried and unruffled by her infant's distress, and advanced it as parallel to the use of the concept of innate envy in psychoanalytic work. This was not a very encouraging start in my attempt to take the training seriously.

Psychoanalysis as a discipline has the disadvantage of being unable to subject its hypotheses to vigorous testing, and as a result it suffers from an excess of theory. It is rescued when the theories are rational and based on *empirical observation* as a starting point, but their hypothetical nature is often forgotten and too often presented as factual. This has traditionally been the case with psychoanalytic theories of instinct.

Freud's use of instinct began with his need to *avoid a clinical observation*, instead of following it through to see if it had an empirical reality. He had been following the hypothesis, so richly continued by Janet, that hysterical illness was the result of traumatic experiences that were too painful to recall. In this work, sexual abuse of his female patients by their fathers became a frequent revelation, and he was quite unable to accept what he was being told. Freud first of all published his findings but disguised the identity of the abusers, calling them uncles or some other male relative. Finally, as a way out, he claimed the accusations were phantasy and a reflection of infantile sexual wishes. This was Freud's point of departure. From then on, the idea of a traumatic source of mental disturbance was abandoned. Instead, he developed his theory of polymorphously perverse infantile sexuality and the Oedipus complex as innate, universal sources of mental conflict, resulting in neurotic disorder through repression of essentially asocial appetites by pressure from the social environment. Although he elaborated on his theory of infantile sexuality, he always presented it as the major instinct to which the "ego instincts" such as the "instinct for self-preservation" were subject. From this, it followed that the needs of infants were subordinated to a secondary level of importance, and Freud's theories of innate conflict with the social environment dominated.

In the chapter entitled "History of Trauma in Psychiatry" in the book he edited (*Traumatic Stress*, 1996), Bessel van der Kolk gives his view on this theoretical stance of Freud's. He records how Janet's work on the effects of traumatic experience on the integration of mental functioning was gradually forgotten and "the acceptance of psychoanalytic theory resulted in a total absence of research of the effects of real traumatic events on children's lives. From 1895 until very recently, no studies were conducted on the effects of childhood sexual trauma."

Of course, had Freud been able to face what his patients were reporting, not only would it have enhanced research into the effects of trauma, including sexual trauma on children, but it would have given impetus to the late nineteenth-century concern for the welfare of children. In the UK, the NSPCC had been formed as a response to the realisation of the plight of orphans and the abuse of children. Freud could have been responsible for the uncovering of sexual abuse in wealthy and middle-class families some three generations earlier than the late twentieth-century revelations, and the lives of many children could have been protected (*The Assault on Truth*, J. Masson (1984) and *Father–Daughter Incest*, J. Hernan (1981)). This would have meant that psychoanalysis would have taken a very different shape. Freud's innovative description of transference and free association as a technique for exploring the historical subjective life of his patients would not have been developed as it has, so psychotherapy would be the poorer. His formulation of transference as a clinical phenomenon was built on inferences drawn from a direct *observation* of the well-known incident of Breuer's flight in alarm from his patient's embraces. I have no doubt the importance of the transference derives from Freud's ability to draw conclusions of a clinical kind from the implications of an observation that he could have easily dismissed as of no clinical relevance.

Freud's later formulation of the id, ego, and superego was bound up with his introduction of the death instinct, but also rested on his inventive idea, presented as a "discovery", that the Oedipus complex was finally resolved by taking possession of the desired father in phantasy by incorporation into the self. This idea forms the basis for the notion of *introjective identification*, which was adopted later by Melanie Klein as a basis for the achievement of sanity by the developing infant.

Melanie Klein's model of psychopathology derives importantly from an original *observation* while working with disturbed children, using a play technique to study the early transference. She observed her child patients would subsequently show fear towards a toy that had been the subject of their aggression. This observation led to many of her ideas on mental development and disorder of the mind. It is not part of my brief to attempt a complete review of her work and ideas, but for the purpose of Polledri's work with Klein's concept of envy, it is the case that Klein stuck to the tradition of attributing a primary instinctual source of the death instinct to explain the cause of primitive envy. She postulated mental mechanisms of an ultimately psychotic nature, with projective and introjective identification playing universal developmental roles in the aetiology of mental disorders and sanity, thereby paralleling Freud's concept of regression.

Projective and introjective identification are omnipotent phantasies that destroy the difference between self and the other and obliterate the gap in time and space, as well as the difference in function, and are therefore incompatible with individual identity and self-determination. They produce profound confusions of identity and symbol formation, and personal growth of the self is hampered to the extent of their operation. Klein's formulations on primitive envy have led to a greater understanding of psychopathological conditions including psychotic states. She held them to be universal, needing to be overcome by everyone through a primitive process of atonement, and this she called the depressive position. Her belief in these positions or stages in normal development was not the result of observation on normal and disturbed individuals but derived, it seems, from data gathered in analytic work with disturbed children, which she then ascribes to universal human developmental hurdles. In addition, because of the emphasis on instinct as the primary cause of envy, which she held lay at the root of these primitive mechanisms, traumatic experience becomes a secondary consideration. Sometimes deprivation is held to make envy worse, but reconstructions of adverse childhood experience are rarely an important consideration in Kleinian analyses.

In spite of variation in particulars of Freud's basic theories, which he tended to call "discoveries", a generally accepted stance in later psychoanalytic theories remained: that of attributing psychopathology observed in disturbed patients to stages in the normal development of the mind. Primitiveness is equated with psychological dysfunction, so the human infant is envisaged as born in a state of mental disorganisation amounting to a psychotic state. From this point of view, all infants have to overcome their innate instinctual strivings; they will fight stages of development in conflict with the parents and only achieve sanity and adaptation at the expense of forgoing their natural appetites. Ronald Fairbairn advanced a more up-to-date critique of Freud's view of instinct, in which the central ego represents a sane object-relating mental structure. This was finally developed by John Bowlby, who concentrated on the effects of maternal deprivation, neglect, or abuse of infants as primary causes of mental disturbance.

The traditional emphasis on psychopathological instincts that began with Freud represents a very old-fashioned type of dualism between body and mind. There is every reason to believe all subjective experience has a physical counterpart in the body, mostly in the brain and central nervous system, but also ubiquitously.

In normal circumstances, infants are born with healthy, well-functioning bodies and, provided things continue without mishap, will progress in healthy growth to maturity. There are complex natural functions within and between cells, tissues, and organs so that the whole human organism, like all living things, is a naturally integrated, busy, thriving entity. Stages in development come about through innate processes that initiate anatomical, physiological, and functional changes, which do not have to be learned. Babies turn and feed from the breast without instruction, they crawl naturally when they are ready, and secondary sexual development is automatic. Physical illness is common enough but, with the exception of genetic mishap and malignancy, can almost always be ascribed to malnutrition, infection, trauma, or another agent that interferes with the natural state of the body. With time and maturity come resistance and immunity; it is in the early years that there is greatest vulnerability to permanent damage, and the earlier this occurs the more widespread will be the adverse consequences. The young need especially careful protection so that they can thrive and grow. This protection not only guards against harm but also aids development, so there are high levels of cooperation between the young and the parents. This nurturing behaviour is an innate characteristic of the parents of many higher organisms, especially the more complex genera, and, roughly speaking, lasts until the offspring acquire self-sufficiency. In humans, the period of dependency on the parents is particularly long and complex.

Any theory of the mind that rejects dualism between the body and the mind must start with a parallel picture of an expected normal, genetically based development. It should begin with the hypothesis that, given standard conditions of care and freedom from interference, the mind will, like the body, show fundamental integration and a pattern of innate, complex, self-perpetuating development. Mental disorder, like physical disability, must be approached as being due to interference with developmental needs through neglect, deprivation, trauma, genetic mishap, or noxious agent.

Some years ago, in a radio talk about his work as a psychoanalyst, Edward Glover asserted that the discipline needed a theory of normal development. I have tried in recent years to construct a theory of normal intra-psychic development, starting with observations on the behaviour of newborn infants that could not have been learned. Instincts emerge as positive drives to aid survival, growth, and the development of creative cognitive and emotional capacities. It is, however, necessary in any such enterprise to attempt an explanation for the existence of widespread human badness, especially institutional badness, without resorting to the notion of bad *instincts*. Polledri explores with her customary erudition the concepts of penis and womb envy, using her extensive experience in the forensic field. She offers the following thoughts:

> Rather than resorting to the idea of a death instinct, one could take it a step further and relate it to a universal urge to return to the safety and security of the womb, to a period in man's life when passivity

reigned, when no response was required, no demands were made. I am suggesting that this "paradise lost" evokes such rage and murderousness as to engender the wish to destroy anything that represents its absence—life, consciousness, and reality itself. This would imply that violence and destructiveness are a fundamental hostility to otherness and separatenes. (p. XX)

Earlier, Polledri suggests that the idea of envy to a bodily organ such as the penis or the womb is more likely to be of its function rather than its morphology.

I have approached this area in which Polledri advances such interesting ideas from a somewhat different angle, but am at one with her point about the pertinence of universal experience. The fulfilment of adequate attachment relies on a reciprocal instinctive response between infant and mother, in which the relative helplessness of the infant presages a threat to its existence if it cannot mobilise an appropriate response in the mother. The extent to which the nurturing figure, usually the mother, has lost touch with the instinctive maternal responses will be directly proportional to the experience of threat to the infant and its sense of helplessness. In my view, it is the consequences of this helplessness that result, in later life, especially in men, in a drive to be powerful, for them to be the victors in competition and to quickly resort to aggression to avoid the terrifying memory of their early helplessness. Female infants knowing, at depth, that they are heirs to the provision of maternal safety for babies have a greater capacity to buffer any shortfall in the maternal response they have experienced. As a result, women are less reliant on aggressive competition and social supremacy but pay a dreadful price of being seen by many men as representative of the source of their once needy helplessness and become the targets in various ways of male retaliation. Of course, the memory of the intra-uterine state when no such sense of helplessness existed would heighten the sense of a lost paradise and fuel revenge.

When the attachment experiences between infant and mother have been positive and reciprocal, this will result in the development of a capacity for love and empathy of others, for the development of rational thought and positive imaginative speculation. Primitive successful mother–infant interdependency forms the drive for the creation of interdependent social groups and the amazing human capacity for the construction of artefacts both material and mental.

A fuller view of normal mental development can only increase our understanding of the real nature and cause of human mental abnormality and destructive behaviour, as Polledri has done so successfully. Thanks to Bowlby's work, attachment theory is now becoming more widely used, especially among child psychologists and child psychiatrists, as a basis for understanding aetiology and the construction of treatments. With this book, Patricia Polledri has added to this creative development, and it deserves a place in all psychiatric and psychological facilities and will be of great interest to the intelligent lay reader.

# INTRODUCTION

In the 1950s, Melanie Klein developed her theory of envy based on the mother's breast and its creativity; she claimed envy to be innate and to be the cause of all mental illnesses, as well as causing the infant's difficulties in overcoming its innate ambivalence towards the feeding breast. In doing this, Klein assumed that a baby has a very expressive phantasy life. She construed her theory of ego disintegration as a consequence of envy's innate destructiveness, rather than as resulting from any lack in external environmental factors.

This book explores the subject of envy from a fresh perspective and argues that envy is not simply a straightforward result of constitutional forces, but rather the end result of a very complex process. The concept of envy needs to incorporate new objective findings not only from the psychological, psychiatric, and social sciences, but also from the biological sciences.

## Aims and intentions

Psychoanalytic models of the mind provide metaphors for how the mind works, but all have a limited value: there is no ego or id in the brain. Certain types of projective identification are ways of describing what we observe and experience as empathy, but can also impose unreal restrictions. Indeed, such models have been abused by clinicians who distort them, and patients are sometimes made to fit into the analyst's preferred model of the mind, which may have unfortunate treatment consequences.

The best models open up new areas of exploration by introducing fresh concepts of mental development, the mechanisms that derive from them, the way psychopathology develops, and the way such problems can be understood in psychotherapeutic treatment. The more major contributions, because of their heuristic value, attract a large following and are usually further developed as a result. There comes a time, however, when the heuristic potential begins to run out. Adherents of the particular school almost always deny this. They adopt an increasingly proselytising stance so that the main tenets of the model are endlessly rehearsed, the limitations increasingly denied, and extensions of them introduced to prop up the faults in the concepts (Polledri, 2003).

Melanie Klein's contribution was a major innovation but has for some time been undergoing the same fate. Her challenge to sexual instinct as the principal source of psychopathology, by her emphasis on destructive drives leading to ego splitting and projective identification, resulted in a workable model for the analysis of psychotic states of mind through their identification in the primitive transference. She relied on Freud's theory of the death instinct to explain the dominance of early unconscious destructive and aggressive phantasies and embodied this in her concept of envy. She postulated that the infant, from birth, was subject to intense anxiety deriving from spoiling attacks in phantasy on the feeding breast stimulated by envy of its goodness. This, she held, prevented introjection of the breast as a good object, threatening the survival of the ego, so this bad aspect of the self was split and projected into a split object. The infant was seen therefore as dominated by mechanisms of a psychotic kind in what she called the "paranoid-schizoid position" (Klein, 1932, 1946).

The most powerful objection to Klein's theory of envy hinges on archaic thinking—that the infant envies the available breast and "the very ease at which the milk flows", that they are not within the orbit of omnipotent control, and so are "unattainable". Klein's concept of phantasy relied for its very sense on the Freudian idea of hallucinatory wish fulfilment, made possible through omnipotent processes (Klein, 1957). The term "omnipotent phantasy" is based on Freud's paper "Mourning and Melancholia" (1917), in which he said that the melancholic was demonstrating a pathological identification between self and object. So to give up being the central object of your parent's love is achieved through an omnipotent phantasy of incorporating the abandoned love object into the ego and setting up the object there as part of the structure of the self. Freud's thinking results in an omnipotent phantasy coming into play as part and parcel of normal development.

Although Klein stated that acceptance of the death instinct was not a necessary condition for utilising her theories on infantile aggression, it has played a large part in the writings of her followers and supports her belief that destructive attacks on the early good object are of a primary nature (Klein, 1932, p. 284). The innate variability of envy meant that the intensity of its attacks determined the gravity of the paranoid-schizoid position rather than the severity of bad experience being the crucial factor. Psychopathology, within this hypothesis, is caused essentially by the extent of the individual's negative nature (Polledri, 2003).

One advantage for analytic work is of course that such an approach prevents the analysis being used as a vehicle for evading responsibility for the perpetuation of strife. However, it also allows analysts to evade responsibility for failures in their understanding by seeing resistance or worsening in the patient's condition as the result of unresolved envy. All setbacks become negative therapeutic reactions.

However, Freud and Klein did not have access to new research on the interaction of nature and nurture. I will argue that Klein used the word "instinct" incorrectly and underplayed the environmental contribution to the normal and pathological development of the psyche.

This study engages with a crucial debate within psychoanalysis concerning the question of the constitutional aetiology of primitive envy in the Kleinian model, as opposed to a model that recognises deprivation in the external environment as the fundamental root of envy, destructiveness, and psychotic pathologies. Can one refer to a death *instinct* as such, or is this a destructive urge, or a death wish that is secondary to environmental influences? And what are the implications for treatment? If a clinician is influenced by his or her view of destructiveness as innate, that is, as a death *instinct*, will they see envy as being constitutional and independent of environmental influences? Will they treat the psychoanalytic models as concrete?

The main topics of investigation in this study are relevant to both the theory and practice of psychoanalysis. It aims to liberate clinical practitioners from the intellectually invalid position of sticking to one model, and to facilitate *thinking*, in the best sense of the word, and the use of the clinician's countertransference in the therapeutic setting. If it is accepted that these models are symbolic of experiences that are difficult to describe otherwise, then apparent contradictions need not be stumbling blocks.

Towards achieving this aim, I present Patrick Gallwey's 1996 model of development as a useful clinical tool, a development of the Freudian and Kleinian model of instinct, which is based on a sinful view of human nature and is incompatible with Darwinian theory. Darwin (1872) stated that "certain primary emotions arose through genetic dictate, but that they matured and were shaped by environmental influences through personal experiences throughout the lifespan" (Hart, 2008, p. 4). Gallwey's model is an attempt to give an intra-psychic account of infant attachment needs. The crucial environmental experience is the parent's instinctual response to the infant's needs and a counterpart of the primary instincts of attachments which are crucial in the development of mental health.

A fundamental principle of the discipline of developmental psychopathology is that it is important to understand normal healthy development in order to understand abnormal development. The Gallwey model is presented as a *paradigm* to develop a fresher approach to the bridging of attachment theory and psychoanalysis. The model is one in which environmental influences are given a more balanced emphasis in our understanding of infantile development, especially in developing the notion that external deprivations must be of greater consideration in forming an aetiology of envy. It is posited as a more productive model to be applied clinically and theoretically to enhance our understanding of the origins and vicissitudes of envy and destructiveness.

As psychoanalysis is currently seeking an expanded theory of interaction, organising principles of interaction can be discerned when mother and infant are viewed as a system. These organising principles describe a self-interactive *process*, not dynamic content. Recent neuroscientific research, mainly that of Beebe and Lachmann, Schore, and Seigel, supports the case for the environmental contribution (Beebe & Lachmann, 2002; Schore, 2003a; Siegel, 2007). These neuropsychoanalysts have extensively researched the idea that the development of the infant is dependent upon the healthy attachment to the mother/caregiver, and that disturbed attachments results in anatomical, physiological, and psychological disturbances. If explored from a neurological basis, splitting may not be a mental phenomenon alone, but may have a parallel in the neurophysiological development of the central nervous system (Schore, 2003a).

Melanie Klein opened up the psychoanalytic study of psychosis in so far as she believed that the infant was quite naturally capable of forming a loving relationship with the mother from the beginning (Klein, 1946, pp. 1–24; 1952, p. 98). However, she believed this primary bonding was *both* dependent upon omnipotent phantasy *and* threatened by innate destructiveness. She linked this destructiveness to Freud's belief in an inborn form of passivity, which he named the death drive (Freud, 1920 g), and, as I will show, her thinking on the question of inborn envy is in line with Freud's dismal view (Klein, 1957).

I am suggesting that the roots of envy are embedded, rather, in a situation characterised by an individual's failure in attachment to their primary object (most usually the mother). Envy can be understood if we examine what fails in the nurturing environment—envy is a reflection of object loss, related to symbol formation, in the development of the self. This has been described by Gallwey (1996, p. 160) as a failure in "primary linking functioning". Gallwey's model is useful, especially in adult treatment, when we examine the relationship between a patient's inability to think about relationships and traumatic events from the past and his or her current difficulties in sustaining stable relationships in the present.

Freud's important contribution was that if a person cannot recall emotionally laden events in a way that can be *thought* about, then the person has to repeat those events as a substitute for remembering (Freud, 1914 g, p. 150). Gallwey has developed our understanding of how these traumatic events are lived out in patterns of relationship that seem self-defeating or strongly repetitive and driven in quality. In each case, "thinking about" is replaced by some other form of mental and behavioural expression. I cite Gallwey's model and Freud's psychoanalytic perspective on mental development in order to demonstrate how classic psychoanalytic ideas and attachment theory can be bridged, as early patterns of development are already becoming established in the first year of life.

The elaboration and development of Gallwey's model has been of particular interest to me, both in the forensic setting and in clinical practice, in trying to understand disorders of thought, in terms of the individual's success or failure in experiencing early linking activities. For example, during assessment, an individual may demonstrate an inability to use logical connectives or the inability to conceptualise an existential quantifier. Quantifiers in logic are about general statements, and an existential quantifier connotes the nature of *some* objects; for example: "*Some* people are psychoanalysts" (existential quantifier), as distinct from: "*All* psychoanalysts have a theory of mind" (universal quantifier). An inability to recognise the difference can often be understood in terms of specific failures in all three early linking functions that Gallwey identified as completing the process of primary identification (Gallwey, 1996, p. 161). In Gallwey's model, distinguishing the vital experience from other experiences establishes an important mental function which, apart from providing a crucial perception on which to build value judgements and the distinguishing characteristics of objects and feeling states, is reflected later on in the ability to understand the validity of the logic of predicates.

One of the major contributions to this book is the inclusion of clinical material to support the theoretical argument that envy is not constitutional and independent of environmental influences. The clinical material adds to our understanding of how the psychotic process arises as a result of the very earliest disruptions in communication and illustrates how the fractured development of such disturbed individuals can be traced from very early childhood onwards.

I have always been concerned about why the concept of envy is rarely considered in the assessment of individuals who pose a risk to others, mainly in the field of forensic psychotherapy, as well as in other social sciences. I agree with Gallwey that envy is an important concept and that "It has great explanatory value for borderline perverse and psychotic states of mind and has proved enormously important in the analysis of destructive forces within the individual personality" (Gallwey, 1996, p. 159). Integral to this research, therefore, has been my work with women who have found themselves caught up in the forensic psychiatric services and who have been diagnosed by those services, at one time or another, as suffering from a psychotic episode, usually diagnosed as "a borderline personality disorder" and severe depression. In relation to the case histories, I will discuss how envy can be understood if we explore how the lack of certain forms of interpersonal experience has a profound impact on the developing mind. The case histories will be my most important examples from developmental psychopathology (that is, the consideration of normal and abnormal development alongside one another). They describe anonymised but real individuals who not only have difficulties in thinking about relationships, but who have conflicting feelings about their sexuality, professional identity, and self-esteem. The major obstacle with which they struggle is in finding and defining themselves.

## Structure of the book

In order to present recent and current thinking in context, I begin with a brief history of forensic psychotherapy in the UK, followed by a literature review, which encompasses psychoanalytical theories past and present on the concept of envy. Here I discuss in detail how Klein constructs her theory of envy as an instinct, the theory from which I will depart in order to challenge Klein as the primary thinker on envy.

A major part of the literature review concentrates on the concept of envy by reviewing its original formulations, but it also covers ideas emerging from the work of neuropsychoanalysis and infant research. This research has much to offer attachment theory and is of importance in the development of our knowledge in the understanding of aggression and violence. The value of neuropsychoanalytic research is that its contribution is based on how severe traumatic attachments result in structural limitations of the early developing right brain, expressed in a number of enduring functional deficits, including a fundamental inability to regulate emotional states under stress. There is a wealth of neurophysiological research indicating that the environmental influences are of prime importance in infantile development (Beebe & Lachmann, 2002; Damasio, 1999; Fonagy, 2001; Hart, 2008; LeDoux, 1994; Schore, 1994, 1996, 2001, 2003; Siegel, 2007; Zulueta, 1996, 2000). An interpersonal neurobiology of human development enables us to understand that the structure and function of the mind and brain are shaped by experiences, especially those involving emotional relationships.

The literature review examines selected findings that have contributed to the development of attachment theory and psychoanalysis, and explores how attachment theory has had a bearing on its evolving relationship with psychoanalysis (Fonagy, 2001). I review here differences between attachment theory and what may be described as "traditional" psychoanalytic theory, with regard to the role of external versus internal factors in an individual's development, and how there is a common evolutionary basis for the different ideas of the unconscious in attachment theory and psychoanalytic theory. I compare and contrast the writings of Bowlby (1969, 1973), Winnicott (1984), Fairbairn (1951), and Gallwey (1985, 1992, 1995, 1996) with the writings of Klein, as it appears that as well as being Klein's critics, these writers were as much influenced by her work as were her followers.

Chapter Three, which I have entitled "Encapsulated Containerless-ness", is an extended commentary on Gallwey's 1996 model of development. I will present a case study to demonstrate the relevance of this model to clinical practice. This will be the first time his model has been utilised outside of the field of forensic psychiatry and psychotherapy.

Gallwey identified, from clinical studies, three basic linking functions which are, he suggests, present innately both in the infant and the nurturing environment as biological real requirements. I discuss each of these in turn. My focus will be on the consequences of a breakdown in symbol formation, which leads to the serious impairment of secondary phantasies; this is, as I will argue, incompatible with Klein's theory, which relies on a form of projective identification (Klein, 1946) in which the infant utilises the mother's capacity for managing anxiety and for thinking in the absence of its own equivalent capacity. I discuss how Gallwey (1996) examines this contradiction, with reference to the work of Bion (1961, 1962) and Segal (1957), and look at the relationships between Freud (1923b), Klein (1946–1963), Bion (1961), Winnicott (1984), and Gallwey (1996) on the issue of anxiety and death, the main concepts underlying my reconsideration of envy. I also discuss here Klein's term "projective identification" (Klein, 1946), another key concept in this book. The rationale for addressing the term at this stage is that projective identification implies a phantasy, and in order to phantasise, we have to assume that a capacity to symbolise is present. According to Kernberg (1975) and Gallwey (1996), this implies that there must exist a capacity for awareness not only of the difference between the self and the other, but also of how one feels—of one's subjective state—before it can be compared to other subjective states; only then does it make sense to attempt to get rid of it by expulsion.

Gallwey's model is original, but does not claim to be a new model of the psyche. I examine it in relation to the Winnicott model, which sees the child as evolving from a unity of mother and infant, and compare the similarities and differences between the two models. (For example, Gallwey's model is in line with Winnicott's three functions of this unity—holding, handling, and object relating—but Gallwey has taken the outcome of a failure in this process much further than Winnicott by developing a contrast between normal and abnormal development.) Importantly, both place great emphasis on what was avoided by both Freud and Klein; that is, the full implication of dependence, and therefore the importance, of the environmental factor: the history of the baby cannot be written in terms of the baby alone.

At this point, I introduce the first of my case studies to demonstrate how Gallwey's model can provide useful insights in clinical practice. A central theme of the clinical material is that both introjective and projective identification are, of course, omnipotent phantasies, and the core of my argument, which I develop in the discussions of my clinical examples, is that it is not possible to have a secondary phantasy, omnipotent or otherwise, until the self has been discovered and conceptualised as a separate entity.

The next chapter, "Shame and Envy", explores the genesis of shame and the defences against it, in particular envy. I discuss how psychoanalysis, specifically Kleinian psychoanalysis, has prioritised the oral and overlooked the importance of the eyes. Much emphasis has been placed on the mouth/breast as an early focal point of body image, but as a result inadequate attention has been given to the eyes and face in the mother–child interaction. I suggest here that, during the first six months of life, it appears that the subsequent development of a sense of shame is linked to the role the eyes play for the infant in constructing the mother's presence and forming the psychological centre of their relationship. This chapter describes how the eyes are the beginning of a psychic, rather than a biological, life. Visual stimulation, embedded in mutual gaze transactions between mother and infant, is an essential component of a growth-promoting environment. I explore the link between shame and visio-affective processes, validated in infant research, neurobiological and psychoanalytic writings of attachment theorists such as Ayers (2003), Beebe and Lachmann (2002), Broucek (1991), Kaufman (1992), Morrison (1989), Nathanson (1987), Robson (1967), Schore (1991), Stern (1974), and Tomkins (1987).

In "Self Envy", I use further case studies to demonstrate how envy can turn on the self, or at least an encapsulated element of the self, and explore how recognising this can be of assistance in clinical practice. In addition to Gallwey's, one of the theoretical models I consider to be highly relevant is that of Green's "dead mother syndrome", which I discuss in this chapter. I also introduce the concept of the transgenerational phantom, first described by Nicolas Abraham (1994), with a clinical example to describe how the transmission of psychopathology can pass from one generation to another. This remains deeply woven into the psychological fabric of the living, operating within the psyche as an unseen but potent conflict, residing within the internal landscape. The clinical material highlights how this can be understood as being a right-brain phenomenon and is never reflected upon by the observing self during treatment, as acknowledged by Shore (2003, p. 306).

The final two chapters, "Perverse Relationships in Pathological Organisations" and "Womb Envy", develop my view that the focus on drives and repetitions of early patterns of object relations does not always take into account the significance of the cycle in which a disturbed sense of self, from a failure in attachment, leads on to envy and the urgent need this generates (albeit in an obsessional and defensive fashion) to keep such painful feelings out of conscious awareness. The case studies in "Womb Envy" exemplify ways in which one form of perverse relationship can be acted out, and I address the cultural context of the phantasies described to make explicit the connections the clinical material has with questions of gender, penis envy, and womb envy in the context of both history and contemporary culture.

In conclusion, I summarise the reasons for reconceptualising the psychopathology of envy and various ways towards developing a greater understanding of this complex phenomenon.

## The use of clinical material

The rationale for structuring the book in this way is to provide a framework for the understanding of many crucial developmental links that run throughout the clinical material in the case studies. I am in agreement with Schore (2003a) that in addition to the subjective learning that evolves from many years of clinical experience, professional growth also involves a continual need to incorporate the new objective findings not only from psychological, social, and psychiatric, but also the biological, sciences.

Including clinical material permits me to explore the relation between trauma in infancy and early childhood and subsequent psychopathology, but it also raises certain fundamental issues regarding "truth" in a patient's reconstruction of the past, individual variance in interpretation of the same material, and how we, as psychoanalysts, learn.

In writing about the accrual of knowledge within psychoanalysis, Bion draws on H. Pritchard's *History of Knowledge* (1932):

> Pritchard … points out that in ordinary life when we are seeking knowledge, our interest is chiefly absorbed in the nature of what we are trying to know and not in the process by which we try to get to know it. It is probably true that psychoanalysts are similarly absorbed in psychoanalysis, rather than in the process by which we arrive at a knowledge of psychoanalysis. This preoccupation with the subject, to the overshadowing of the study of the process by which it is learned, is excusable; for the subject is vast and there is so much to learn. (Bion, 1992, p. 151)

As Bion says, "Psychoanalysis itself may be seen as born of a doubt about the realities of the knowledge we have, and of the process by which we obtain it" (Bion, 1992, p. 151).

## Epistemology, models of the mind, and metaphors

As epistemology refers to the theory of knowledge, especially with regard to its methods, validity, and scope (*Oxford English Dictionary*), it is important to address the philosophical and epistemological status of clinical material as being a particular body of knowledge that has its own specifications, problems, and implications with regard to theoretical questions concerning discourse, power, narrative, and representation. Therefore, throughout the book, I have gradually developed a sustained argument as to why Gallwey's model may be more helpful or original than Winnicott's in thinking about envy and destructiveness, and to this end, the clinical material provides examples of the major role the external environment plays in the development of psychopathology. However, as Dominique Scarfone (2008) points out, when clinical material is presented as evidence of any psychoanalytic theory, and selected perhaps for its correspondence with the theory that we hold as "true", we all know how much our clinical and theoretical views are resistant to competing points of view and how, after a debate, analysts usually adhere to their original ideas. Therefore, the inclusion of clinical material in this respect is not intended as evidence of anything. As Scarfone suggests: "Its aim is to provide a space where differences and commonalities are brought to the fore for the benefit of learning from another clinician's experiences" (2008, p. 5). Scarfone states that "such learning can happen regardless of agreement or disagreement about the theoretical underpinnings of a particular communication or of the technique and clinical style that is illustrated by clinical presentations, commentaries, and meta-narratives" (2008, p. 5). Scarfone believes that "From a more general standpoint, it is worth considering that, according to basic psychoanalytic wisdom, what we hold as our most rational choices are always *also* determined by reasons that our official 'reason' knows little about. As we are always exposed to the simultaneous occurrence of many converging, possibly contradictory, rational and irrational motives, there is no way round this" (2008, p. 5).

I agree with Scarfone that: "In the absence of what, in other positive sciences, is deemed the external validation of a theory through some 'crucial experiment' we have no choice but to keep listening to the over-determined communication that, for all its mixture of reason and irrationality, is, in psychoanalysis, not only tolerated, but actually sought for" (2008, p. 5). Communicating one's clinical experience in the traditional manner, as well as having colleagues express their opinions on what is presented, rests upon a logic that is specific to psychoanalysis. Gallwey is not being posited as the only theorist/clinician offering an alternative to the death instinct and innate envy. On the contrary, and in agreement with Scarfone: "the purpose of this section is to work towards favouring psychoanalytic communication *across* psychoanalytic schools and idioms" (2008, p. 5).

The importance of the inclusion of clinical material from the field of forensic psychotherapy in an academic study such as this has been to provide case material and a commentary from a totally different perspective which, it could be argued, has vast geographical, cultural, and theoretical distances from classical psychoanalysis. Yet, far from being a drawback, this makes things even more interesting if, for all the distances involved, we allow *something* in the narrated clinical material to somehow work its way through to us. Only then, from the presence of a shared psychoanalytic experience, can we foster the possibility of a "genuine psychoanalytic exchange", as suggested by Scarfone, and "profit from both our common reference to the analytic experience *and* our diversity in thinking" (Scarfone, 2008, p. 6).

## The question of truth

Hyatt-Williams and Cordess discuss how:

> All psychodynamic psychotherapy provides some sort of narrative to a life, as a particular type of biography. There is debate about the degree to which this is an historically true narrative and the degree to which it can aspire only to be an *emotionally* true reconstruction (Spence, 1982). Strict historical truth is not necessary for the healing process to evolve. Forensic psychodynamic psychotherapy emphasises the criminal act, or acts, as an important focus within this narrative. (Hyatt-Williams & Cordess, 1996, p. 14)

Modell discusses how André Green's "dead mother" "raises certain fundamental epistemological questions regarding the reconstruction of the past, and the relation between trauma in infancy and early childhood and subsequent psychopathology" (Modell, 2001, p. 76). He goes on to argue that it can be used as a paradigm and "a base from which we can explore the epistemology of trauma and the problem of reconstruction" (p. 76).

Winnicott touches on whether or not a distinction can be made when the "truth" about himself/herself that the patient is presenting must be treated as a type of transitional phenomenon, wherein the question of whether the patient's "truth" is reality or phantasy is never an issue (Winnicott, 1951). As with any transitional phenomenon, it is both reality and phantasy, subjective and objective, at the same time. The "truth" of the patient's feelings must be experienced by the therapist as emotionally true, just as the good-enough mother must be able to share the truth in her child's feelings about the comforting and life-giving powers of his "piece of cloth" (Ogden, 1979, p. 367). "We are not dealing with an 'all or nothing' phenomenon here and the handling of the feelings projected by the patient require considerable effort, skill, and 'strain' on the part of the therapist" (Winnicott, 1960).

De Shazer (1982) points to Bateson's (1979) cross-subjective ways of describing ideas as developing from two or more descriptions of the same process, pattern, system, or sequence that are collected differently—that is, the relationship between the two descriptions (cross-subjectivity) provides an idea that is similar to the depth of perception due to the differences between what the two eyes see. He goes on to say:

> Bion used the term "poly-ocularism" to describe the perception of knowledge; those that believe in the existence of one truth will inevitably ask: If you have different views, which one is right? Sight provides a useful metaphor, if we consider that in binocular vision it is irrelevant to raise the question as to which eye is correct and which eye is wrong. Binocular vision works not because the two eyes see different views of the same object, but because the *differential* between the two images enables the brain to compute the invisible, and more rounded, or fuller, dimension. (De Shazer, 1982, pp. 72–73)

By developing the Gallwey model in this book, I am proposing that a new way of conceptualising and learning can evolve by observing old problems, such as Klein's (1957) view of envy as an instinct, and re-examining the concept from an epistemological point of view. Gallwey's model has presented some steps towards a paradigm that is most useful in its contribution to attachment theory, based on the importance of the external environment in the understanding of normal and abnormal development in infancy. The use of the model in this book allows a different way of conceptualising the subject of violence and destructive behaviour as a change agent, and the clinical material viewed through the lens of this model can illuminate various elemental issues, epistemological and analytical, relevant to both the clinical practice and theory of psychoanalysis.

In line with Gallwey:

> I am sure the way forward lies in the ongoing development of a better understanding of why, in human violence, there is a failure of those mental mechanisms that ordinarily act as a brake on anger, hatred and sadism—mechanisms that result in perverse symbolic gratification of these drives, or produce neurotic or psychotic symptoms, but whose failure results in catastrophic or habitually destructive conduct. (Gallwey, 1997, p. 475).

# CHAPTER ONE

# Historical background: a brief overview

The UK has, from a very early stage, been at the forefront of pioneering the psychoanalytic understanding of criminology. More recently, the interest in forensic psychotherapy has taken on a new impetus, partly due to the recognition of forensic psychiatry as a sub-speciality of the Royal College of Psychiatrists. The following brief description of the development of forensic services in this country gives a background to the history of psychotherapeutic treatment, and provides the context in which Kleinian and other theories were formulated.

## From the Psychopathic Clinic to the International Association of Forensic Psychotherapy

The psychotherapy of those with criminal tendencies, or with a history of catastrophically dangerous behaviour, has its historical roots in this country in the appointment of visiting psychotherapists to the prisons under the auspices of the Home Office. This practice goes back prior to the Second World War and to the setting up of the Psychopathic Clinic in 1931 (renamed the Portman Clinic in 1937). This formed the clinical wing of the Institute for the Study and Treatment of Delinquency and was co-founded by Edward Glover. Glover was a pioneer in the combined field of psychotherapy and criminology, publicly remembered in the annual Glover lecture, delivered under the auspices of the Tavistock and Portman Clinic NHS Foundation Trust. He was also, as we shall see, vociferously opposed to some of Melanie Klein's ideas (Cordess, 1992; Polledri, 1997).

The 1976 Report of the Butler Committee on "mentally abnormal offenders" made many important recommendations for legal and administrative changes in relation to such offenders. The extent of the Committee's recommendations (140 in all) reflects its wide terms of reference, which included consideration of, first, the criteria on which "the law should recognise mental disorder or abnormality in a person accused of a criminal offence as a factor affecting his liability to be tried or convicted, and his disposal", and second, "what, if any, changes are necessary in the powers, the procedure and facilities relating to the provision of appropriate treatment, in prison, hospital or the community, for offenders suffering from mental disorder or abnormality, and to their discharge and aftercare" (cited in *British Journal of Law and Society*, 1976).

In the wake of the Butler Report, the NHS undertook during the 1980s a serious review of the role of psychotherapy, and the special and dedicated work of those at the Portman Clinic and the neighbouring Tavistock Clinic was organised under a special sub-committee of the Hampstead Health Authority (the clinics were, at the time, under the management of the Hampstead Health Authority). In 1985, the Seymour Report found that, despite opposition, psychotherapy did have a continuing role to play in the NHS. Because of their standing as providers of psychoanalytic psychotherapy services and training in the NHS, the Tavistock and Portman Clinics joined forces and, as part of the restructuring of the health services, jointly became an NHS trust in 1994, whilst maintaining their separate identities.

More recently, the Portman Clinic has renewed its endeavours by providing training programmes for psychotherapeutic treatment, largely as a result of the initiatives of Dr Estela Welldon, who helped to organise the International Association of Forensic Psychotherapy, which was set up in 1991 during the XVIIth Congress of the Academy of Law and Mental Health. The objectives of the association are, among others: to develop interest in and support for forensic psychotherapy internationally to provide a means for colleagues to co-operate more easily to facilitate the flow of information; to encourage communication with members of the legal profession and others involved in the management of offenders; to contribute, through further research, to the psychoanalytic understanding of violence, perversion, and delinquency. The association has developed well, with international contributions. As Cleo Van Velsen put it:

> Forensic psychotherapists are concerned with the psychodynamic understanding of the particular offender patient and, in this context, the crime becomes important as the means to understand better the psychopathology of the offender. Forensic patients uniquely demonstrate their internal worlds as with their crime they act out something of their internal object relations. (Van Velsen & Welldon, 1997, p. 5)

## Insights into human behaviour

In some ways, the idea of forensic psychotherapy as a separate discipline is somewhat artificial, as many patients who enter psychotherapy emerge as having problems of maladjustment or even violence. The request to treat dangerous and offender patients is easily made, but can be very hard to follow up with consistent work, since the anxiety, strains, and responsibility of trying to prevent acting out are very great indeed. Therapists may have to terminate treatment when the impact of childhood suffering or horrific neglect and abuse suffered by the patient during their developmental years becomes too difficult to deal with in the transference (Gallwey, 1997). As these patients have no sense of self, equally they cannot have a sense of self in relation to the other; therefore transference-based psychotherapy is limited as to its effectiveness as a therapeutic tool.

Psychoanalysis attempts an investigation of the nature and cause of psychopathology as an accompaniment to treatment. It uses the analysand's increasing contact with previously inaccessible feelings and phantasies, made available to them through the carefully controlled working alliance with their therapist, the facilitator of this undertaking. This approach to crime was one of the great new optimisms that derived from Freud's work and brought inspiration to the understanding of human behaviour.

Cordess describes how:

> Specific psychoanalytical models of disorders of conduct have been slow in coming. Freud gave the lead in his theories on acting out and his short paper, "Criminals from a Sense of Guilt" (1916), but these contributions were derived from observations on neurotic individuals. There had been several important psychoanalytic papers on the subject of criminality in the 1920s, notably Reik's "The Compulsion to Confess" (1925). In the course of a few pages, Freud put forward in his seminal 1916 paper the splendidly subversive hypothesis that some criminal acts are committed as a consequence of the individual's sense of (unconscious) guilt—that is, in order to assuage guilt, and not as a result of the absence of a capacity to feel guilt, as was generally assumed. (Cordess, 1992, p. 154)

He goes on to say (p. 154) that "guilt precedes the crime, rather than the other way round".

Freud's description of a similar relationship regarding phobia in "Inhibitions, Symptoms and Anxiety" (1926), which he describes as the work of *finding an object* for anxiety, had great influence and was later developed, most notably by Melanie Klein. The models for psychosis and borderline states developed by Klein (1946) in this country, and by Otto Kernberg (1975) and Heinz Kohut (1972) in the United States, have been accorded considerable explanatory force or status. I would argue, however, that this approach lacks an essential differentiation between intra-psychic and extra-psychic realms of pathological activity.

Theoretical concepts cannot always be relied upon when treating dangerous and disturbed individuals, perhaps due to the fact that their specific mental issues have to be explored and understood from their individual perspective and interpreted in their own right. The difficulties spring, in part, from the nature of the lives of many offenders, the exclusion of criminals from access to therapeutic facilities open to non-offenders, and the reluctance of trained therapists to involve themselves with this group of patients. This is perhaps due to the powerful transference and countertransference difficulties these patients mobilise during treatment and the tendency of those who have involved themselves with the treatment of this group to cling to their familiar models of psychopathology. The value of the "team" approach to management, especially in institutions, is that it facilitates the shared involvement of such "distributed transference"; this works for the benefit of the patients as well as making the emotional aspects of the job more manageable for staff, especially those in close patient contact throughout the day (Gallwey, 1997, p. 474; Polledri, 1997).

## Controversy and clinical developments

As mentioned earlier, Edward Glover was a pioneer of forensic psychotherapy in this country and his theories on problems of maladjustment and crime, particularly his ideas on the role of sexual perversion as a rationalisation of psychotic phenomena through sexualisation, added a new dimension to classical Freudian theory and the development of treatment in the combined fields of psychotherapy and criminology. Amongst his most obvious and lasting achievements—aside from his clinical work and extensive publications—are his roles as co-founder of the Portman Clinic and the Institute for the Study and Treatment of Delinquency, as joint founder of the *British Journal of Criminology* (he was co-editor until his death), and as co-founder of the British Psychoanalytic Society. However, he very publicly and controversially resigned from the society in 1944 (Cordess, 1992).

The battle that led to Glover's resignation was played out during 1941–45 in what became known as the "Controversial Discussions" (King & Steiner, 1991). As Cordess describes:

> The dispute arose from Klein's claims to have extended the scope of psychoanalytic work into the lives of very young children and, with later developments, into the theory and treatment of psychoses. Glover became the most vehement opponent of these views, and of Klein herself. He effectively cut himself off from the clinical and technical developments within psychoanalysis generated by Klein and the Kleinian group. He was therefore also largely divorced from the post-Kleinian evolution of ideas. However, the fact that Glover withdrew his energies from the Psychoanalytic Society in Britain meant that he had greater time and commitment for other activities. Most significantly, he applied some of the same energies to establishing a place for psychoanalytic thinking within the field of psychology and criminology. (Cordess, 1992, p. 516)

The post-Kleinian evolution of conceptual and clinical ideas has been most advanced in general by such psychoanalysts as Wilfred Bion (1957 through to 1992), Herbert Rosenfeld (1987), and Hanna Segal (1957, 1991, 1993, 1997), working with psychotic patients. Their particular influence and its application to forensic psychiatry and psychology in Britain are exemplified by the work of Arthur Hyatt-Williams (1964, 1975, 1998, 2002). In his work with sexual murderers serving life imprisonment, Hyatt-Williams introduced the concept of the simultaneous occurrence of external stressors, acting all at once, some by pure chance, on an individual already primed to lose control because of a failure in the developmental integration of primitive aggression (1964). The relative paucity of Hyatt-Williams' and Patrick Gallwey's publications in this field has not done justice to the quality of their teaching, clinical work, and thinking (Cordess & Cox, 1996). In relation to human violence, for example, Gallwey writes: "Most psychoanalytic theories of early mental life [including Winnicott's] view it as dominated by omnipotent phantasy. Psychosis tends to be seen as a regression to these primitive omnipotent states of mind" (Gallwey, 1996, p. 154). And in discussing the paradox that is experienced by those working with patients, both male and female, who, like many criminals, have endured very great abuse, neglect, and childhood suffering, Gallwey says:

> What impresses most is how well they have managed, and not so much how evil they have become. It is quite extraordinary how brave is the childhood spirit that can survive the extremes of abuse with some hope and sanity intact and keep going in spite of crippling damage during crucial periods of development. (1996, p. 154)

Donald Winnicott describes children as using omnipotent phantasy in the creation of a transitional object as part of their external reality (1989, pp. 54–55). For Winnicott, this places a different meaning on the word "omnipotence", in which the child needs to make the transition from omnipotent control of external objects to the relinquishment of control and eventually to the acknowledgement that there are phenomena outside one's personal control.

Winnicott's experience in the forensic setting was minimal compared to Hyatt-Williams' and Gallwey's, yet his model is of great importance in our understanding that the individual can only exist in relation to "the other". This finding is crucial in our understanding of human violence. What is clear from the work of Winnicott (1960) and John Bowlby (1988) is that human beings, like all mammals, are born with an innate predisposition to form intense attachments to their primary caregivers. Klein believed that primary bonding was reliant upon omnipotent phantasy and threatened by innate destructiveness (1952, p. 65). Winnicott's work on maternal bonding and the facilitating environment (1960, 1965) follows on from and develops the separation studies carried out on primitive infants and their mothers which reveals that attachment behaviour has a psychobiological structure. He concluded that an infant cannot be understood apart from its interaction with the mother. Similarly, these developmental concepts form the foundation of Gallwey's 1996 model.

# CHAPTER TWO

# Literature review

Starting with *Envy and Gratitude* (1957), I have reread Melanie Klein's work many times to facilitate my own thinking and its challenge to Klein as the primary thinker on envy. In particular, I could not really understand how any of the complicated theorising in relation to envy could be attributed to an infant. Fifteen years ago I found it impossible to present the paper I was requested to do, to a group of baffled international students with English as a second language, on the subject of psychoanalysis and attachment theory in relation to crime. Even from the copious notes I had made then, and had rewritten many times, I was struggling, and still do to this day, with the fact that there is no biological explanation to support a death instinct theory, which seems to me to be contrary to biological principles.

This view was first put forward by Ernest Jones (Rycroft, 1968), and the time has come for a review of the concept of envy from its original formulations and to present some fresh ideas about its relation to psychopathology.

## The psychoanalytical concept of envy and Klein's "constitutional envy"

Although the clinical importance of the psychoanalytic concept of envy had been well established since Freud's first account of penis envy, mentioned in many of Freud's papers, two themes came into special prominence, both being linked to the distinction between the sexes. In females, it was the envy of the penis and in males it was a struggle against passivity and femininity to another male; both of these Freud (1905d) attributed to the castration complex:

> The main factor in Freud's view of these phenomena as being bio-logically determined was a particular feeling of *lack*. The two most important and insurmountable obstacles to success were penis envy and masculine protest, which could be attributed to Freud's mascu-line-phallocentric vantage point, but did not do justice to later, well established clinical data. (Feldman & De Paola, 1994, p. 219)

The broader concept of envy does not concentrate solely on penis envy and hostility with anal-sadistic character traits as a background, which are the main factors described by Karl Abraham (1919), as a form of resistance to psychoanalysis. It was only with Klein's concept of "constitutional envy" (1957) that envy became "a quasi-nuclear concept, a cornerstone in the psychoanalytic process" (Feldman & De Paola, 1994, p. 217). Klein focused her thinking on the analysis of the anxieties and defences attached to envy, but did not envisage the possibility of analysing this complex feeling *in itself* (Masterson, 1999). In Kleinian psychoanalysis, "the envious attacks the patients made during analysis were brought to the fore without any apparent analysis of this complex feeling, probably because of its quasi-biological status in Klein's theory. In psychoanalytic work, envy became equated with penis envy in women and the repudiation of femininity in men" (Feldman & De Paola, 1994, p. 218).

Klein postulated that the feeling of envy was oral in nature, related to the primal scene, and based on the infantile theory that coitus is gratifying where mother incorporates orally the father's penis (Klein, 1952a, p. 56). The idea of a baby phantasising about its own origin is not "biological" in any simple sense.

As early as 1932, Klein had suggested that the child's feeling of envy is a reaction to the phantasy that its parents enjoy mutual sexual pleasures of an oral sort, while he/she gets nothing but frustration. In summary, the consequences for the little girl are that primarily she does not want to possess a penis of her own as an attribute of masculinity but to incorporate her father's penis as an object of oral satisfaction (Klein, 1932, p. 196). The little boy compensates for his feelings of hatred, anxiety, envy, and inferiority by reinforcing his pride in the possession of a penis, and displacing this pride onto intellectual activities, which assists in helping him to face his feminine phase (Klein, 1932, p. 250).

In 1957, Klein published *Envy and Gratitude*, a comprehensive statement of her concept of envy. In this, she reviewed envy in the light of her more recent experience and proposed an important shift in the concept, which was endorsed by her followers and disputed by opponents as well as some former collaborators. Klein's view of the infant's psychic conditions was that from the very beginning the newborn has an incipient ego, rudimentary and largely lacking coherence, *but* capable of performing some important functions, mainly defensive, such as: deflection of the death instinct, splitting, integration, projective and introjective identification, idealisation, omnipotent denial, and the capacity to deal with anxiety (Klein, 1957).

In spite of proposing a very elegant concept of envy, Klein did not maintain a consistent approach to the problem of its category. The main drawback in fully understanding the genesis of the psychopathology of envy is that there is insufficient data to produce a "provable" theory about when and what happens to the internal world of the newborn. However, I will continue to elaborate further on Klein's theory that envy is operative from the dawn of life, having a constitutional basis (Klein, 1957).

For Klein, the first object regarded as being envied is the feeding breast, which she posits is seen *from birth* as deliberately withholding gratification for its own benefit. The assumption that the distinction between self and object is present from birth is quite explicit. Klein believed that the intensity of the frustrations felt by the infant was linked from the beginning of life with the extent of sadism. In *Envy and Gratitude*, Klein states:

> I consider that envy is an oral-sadistic and anal-sadistic expression of destructive impulses, operative from the beginning of life, and that it has a constitutional basis. (1957, p. 176)

Innate envy of the mother's breast and its creativity is the primary cause of all mental illness because of the infant's difficulties in overcoming its innate ambivalence towards the breast. The infant is endowed with both innate envy of it and the need to use it as a recipient of its own projected death instinct. This theory assumes that the baby has a very vivid and violent phantasy life and that psychic functioning is characterised by displacement; destructive drives *find expression* in envy— that is, if envy is "constitutional" it is also a form of symbolisation, of representation.

Envy here is described as an expression of something else, the *destructiveness*, the urge to destroy the mother's breast, that is supposed to be logically prior, if only for a moment. The biological absurdity of this then begins to look like a retrospective construction; the infant's desire to destroy—based, presumably, on its frustrations—is harmless without real consequence for the breast, so is *not* a threat to psychic survival.

Klein (1946, p. 8) defined the process of "projective identification" as being a destructive aspect, starting from the beginning of life. This she described as an unconscious infantile phantasy by which the infant was able to relocate his persecutory experiences by separating (splitting) them from his self-representation and making them part of his image of a particular object. The phantasy of magical control (omnipotence) over the object may be achieved in this way.

Klein differentiates between projection and introjection: "One essential difference between greed and envy, although no rigid dividing line can be drawn since they are so closely associated, would accordingly be that greed is mainly bound up with introjection and envy with projection" (Klein, 1957, p. 181). Earlier, on the previous page, she elaborates:

> This book deals with a particular aspect of earliest object relations and internalization processes that is rooted in orality. I am referring to the effects of envy on the development of the capacity for gratitude and happiness. Envy contributes to the infant's difficulties in building up his good object, for he feels that the gratification of which he was deprived has been kept for itself by the breast that frustrated him. (Klein, 1957, p. 180)

For Klein, the majority of psychic life is determined by the conflict between the life and the death instincts, the general plan being based on the work of Karl Abraham. Added to this was the development of schizoid and paranoid phenomena, studied by Klein in great detail, which led on to her theory of instincts, notably the immediate manifestations of the instincts, their conflict, and their combinations of love, hate, greed, envy, and gratitude (Klein, 1975).

To evaluate the significance of these primal instinctual factors, it is important to understand how they make possible the most basic emotional experiences, those of pleasure and unpleasure. To understand this, it is necessary to consider the development of the Kleinian theory of gratification, deprivation, and frustration (Klein, 1927, p. 176; 1936, p. 295). "Klein's discovery of the intensity of the frustrations felt by the young child was linked from the beginning with the discovery of the extent of early sadism" (Petot, 1991, pp. 192–193).

### Gratification, deprivation, and frustration

In Kleinian psychology, all frustration or gratification is experienced in relation to an object; whether the object refuses it to the subject, or whether the subject refuses it to himself. Klein considered deprivation to be something more than mere frustration, especially as deprivation suggests an inter-subjective dimension of refusal on the part of the object (Klein, 1936). Frustration for Klein was felt as deprivation: "if the child cannot obtain the desired thing, he feels that it is being withheld by the nasty mother, who has power over him" (p. 295). Revenge was first described by Klein in her paper on criminal tendencies in normal children:

> The oral and anal frustrations, which are the prototype of all later frustrations in life, at the same time signify punishment and give rise to anxiety. This circumstance makes the frustration more acutely felt, and this bitterness contributes largely to the hardship of all subsequent frustrations. (Klein, 1928, pp. 187–188)

This is the central theme of Klein's theory of frustration, formulated well before the publication of *The Psycho-Analysis of Children* (1932). Deprivation produces an intense feeling of overwhelming pain. The intensification of this pain evokes anxiety about revenge, which is fuelled by the child's sadism.

There was no specific instinctual factor to describe the intensification of pain, as this model was conceived from Abraham's genetic theory

(1919) as being the phase of sadism at its peak. Klein did not choose between frustration and deprivation until she abandoned Abraham's genetic model in 1932, and introduced a special factor in the transformation from deprivation to frustration, the link being greed.

In 1952, Klein developed the theoretical concept of greed, which combined two independent themes. The first was the conceptual search for a factor intensifying the reaction to deprivation; the second was the result of infant observation practised by Klein to develop understanding of infant behaviour. In this way, she advanced her theories, which were criticised as being speculative rather than scientific (Holland, 1990).

Klein enhanced her views by stating that the infant's tendency to bite the nipple is associated with greed. This occurs much earlier, and appears relatively spontaneously, indicating that it is independent of a reaction of anger. Greed itself is a source of persecutory anxiety. The infant takes in the good milk and has the phantasy of union with the omnipotent good object, in which case greed is obvious. Alternatively, when persecutory anxiety is dominant, the infant is incapable of taking in an actual good object, refuses food, develops phobias, and withdraws into itself (Petot, 1991).

Klein associated a greed for food with the incapacity to be alone (1957, pp. 94–121). This incapacity to bear solitude is due to persecutory anxiety and a need to be constantly gratified, as this wards off fear of being attacked or abandoned. Thus greed is not only a primary instinctual factor it is also a defence against anxiety (Klein, 1957; Petot, 1991).

For me, Klein's definition of greed is very broad. In "Some Theoretical Conclusions Regarding the Emotional Life of the Infant", she states:

> In periods of freedom from hunger and tension, there is an optimal balance between libidinal and aggressive impulses, greed is the state of imbalance caused by the effect of privation: Whenever, owing to privations from internal or external sources, aggressive impulses are reinforced ... such an alteration in the balance between libido and aggression gives rise to the emotion called greed, which is first and foremost of an oral nature. (1952, p. 162)

This demonstrates Klein's displacement of the importance of *sources* of privation, internal or external. The instinctual process where oral-sadistic impulses predominate over oral-libidinal ones has as its primary psychic content, an emotion, which is greed (Petot, 1991).

This is characteristic of Klein's theory, to stress the emotion itself rather than its representations, because she was dwelling on the infantile. It should be made clear at this point that, for Klein, greed is inseparable from frustration with which it has a dual relationship. Greed is the psychic manifestation of an alteration of the quality of instinct resulting from privations, some of which are internal in origin.

Greed seems to derive from a phantasy of union with the omnipotent object—presumably *as phantasy*; this can be satisfied, even if only momentarily. The fact that, for Klein, some infants are incapable of enjoying the maternal care and breast when it is offered, is due to the predominance of innate aggression. She says: "Excessive aggressive impulses increase greed and diminish the capacity to bear frustration" (Klein, 1952a, p. 67). Greed and the incapacity to bear frustration are thus particularly harmful *because* they make the infant incapable of enjoying available satisfaction *because* they limit renewed contact with a good object. The genetic and clinical significance of greed derives directly, for Klein, from its instinctual nature. The combination of "instinct" and "nature" is misleading.

The notion of greed in relation to the Kleinian theory of the depressive position is an indication that a failure has occurred in the child's internalisation of the good object. Anxiety over this object loss tends to increase greed (Klein, 1952a, p. 73). The idea is that greed, despite its sadistic orientation, is closely connected with libidinal instincts.

Petot describes how, for Klein, "greed arises from an introjective tendency based on the sucking instinct, the positive evaluation of which remained a constant in Kleinian thought, as it did not lend itself to being the most active principle in the surfacing of painful emotions linked with frustration. It was supplanted by the notion of envy, which, in almost total obscurity since 1932, now reappeared in Klein's theory" (Petot, 1991, p. 199). From the moment Klein defined greed and began her attempt to make it the principal antagonist of object love, she began to employ the notion of envy, which she attached to greed by means of a double link. On the one hand, greed impels the infant towards the wish for everything desirable, and that which gratifies the object. In situations of deprivation, the infant attributes to the mother's breast, and later to the father, the unlimited satisfaction of which it felt deprived. Therefore, there is a link for Klein between greed and envy with regard to meaning: the first gives the second both motive and energy (Petot, 1991).

Additionally, there is a genetic relationship between the introjective technique of greed and the projective technique of envy. In fact, as the notion of envy becomes more precise for Klein, its link with projection becomes more and more evident (Klein, 1957, p. 181).

In 1952, Klein held the view that the aggressive form of projective identification was directly derived from the greedy attacks, accompanied by phantasy, in which the infant enters the mother's body. However, envy as a projective sadistic attack was only a consequence of greed.

An interesting distinction between greed and envy has been made by Colman, who describes how greed is interested only in incorporating what the object can provide, whereas envy wishes to incorporate the object itself: "the greedy person kills the goose that lays the golden eggs. The envious person wishes to *be* the goose and kills it in frustrated rage at not being able to lay the golden eggs himself" (Colman, 1991, p. 356).

### Death: a fear or a driving force?

For the Kleinians, the shape of envy is the death drive. It overshadows the life drives and is the ultimate source of paranoid, persecutory, and depressive anxieties, which will shadow the human subject throughout its life. However, extreme attention has to be paid to the tendency to accept that the death drive is the explanation for all aggression. What is termed as a "primary aggression" may well be a very primitive state of frustration.

It is crucial to distinguish between a fear of death, which is on the side of survival, and a drive towards death. Rosemary Gordon highlights the confusion between the fear of death, present in an ego whose existence would thereby be under threat, and Klein's death instinct theory: "The *fear of* death is a clinical reality and must be distinguished from a *drive towards* death" (Gordon, 1993, p. 166). Winnicott contends "that clinical fear of breakdown is the *fear of a breakdown that has already been experienced*, an existential 'dying', a cessation of the continuous sense of being, due to impingements in very early life before there was an ego able to integrate and remember this experience" (Winnicott, 1974, p. 104).

Masterson, discussing Klein's views on the existence of unconscious communication between mother and infant, states how Klein "ascribed all anxiety experienced by the infant as a result of persecution from its own death instinct, rather than allowing for the effect of negative feelings and ambivalence in the mother" (cited in Masterson, 1999, p. 125). Klein (1952a) asserted that the experience of good mothering is that it has a mitigating effect on innate destructive impulses, while Winnicott's critique of her in this regard was that she declined to explore how mothering itself could be a possible source of emotional pain and conflict.

Joyce McDougall describes her work with patients who, paradoxically, resort to apparently self-destructive behaviour or somatic states in order to survive psychically, in the face of "the double-bind messages and the forgotten pain and distress of the small child who had to learn to deaden liveliness in order to survive" (McDougall, 1989, p. 105). She writes of:

> Unsuspected death-like forces that are apt to pass from one generation to another, and may communicate, even to young infants, the conviction that their destiny is to accept non-existence as a separate being in their parents' eyes. (1989, p. 89)

Gordon sees a wish to return to a state of non-being and primitive union, aimed at the removal of boundaries, and at obliterating separateness (i.e., Freud's notion of a death drive), as totally *incompatible* with aggression which is, in contrast, aimed at creating separateness and difference from another (Gordon, 1993, p. 174; Masterson, 1999, p. 126). This is similar to Fairbairn's libidinal ego clinging to the exciting object.

In reviewing Ronald Fairbairn's writing about object relations theory (1952, 1955), Ingrid Masterson's view was that he saw "contact and relationship as essential to survival. Pathology is not due to excess of instincts, or to instinct-related conflict, but to distorted relationships. His concept of primary motivation rests on the stage of total infantile dependence" (Masterson, 1999, p. 132). She goes on: "Aggression, for Fairbairn, is a *potential*, not a primary drive; hate is a reaction to frustration of the need for contact through an attachment with others. Internalised objects are substitutes for unsatisfactory real others, perceived as outside of one's control, and are always attached to the split-off aspects of the ego which are in identification with them" (1999, p. 132). Fairbairn's view (1952) was that the individual's unconscious aim is to perpetuate these objects and to realise unfulfilled hopes in regard to them.

In *Envy and Gratitude* (1957), Klein states that "the struggle between life and death instincts and the ensuing threat of annihilation of the self and the object by destructive impulses are fundamental factors in the infant's initial relation to his mother" (p. 178), an indication that she believed that the death instinct referred to the ego. Klein attributes this to the infant's awareness of motivations and intentions on the part of the object.

I agree with Winnicott that "at the time of absolute dependence, with the mother supplying an auxiliary ego-function, it has to be remembered that the infant has not yet separated out the 'not-me' from the 'me'—this cannot happen apart from the establishment of 'me'" (Winnicott, 1974, p. 104).

This is where his good-enough mothering, the state of the child's narcissistic well-being (Winnicott, 1965), is radically affected through the constitutional strength of the oral drive and adequate environmental factors. If the maternal environment is not adequate in its holding, such early disturbances in the regulation of the well-being can lead to excesses of aggression being turned against the self.

Envy proper can be considered to be a complex object-related attitude or tendency made up of different component parts, but a certain level of ego development is necessary for its existence.

Envy may be triggered by frustration or inconsistent mothering or the child's inadequate capacity to appreciate time and space. However, aggression may not be inevitably linked to deprivation. The child may resent the inevitable limitations of maternal care, find it hard to tolerate the mother's control over it, and might prefer to destroy the maternal care rather than experience the frustration.

Historically, as early as 1921 Eissler referred to envy as "arising from the oral instinct. He considered envy to be a narcissistic side-stream arising out of the oral instinct, and as an important element in establishing a character based on this component instinct" (Eissler, 1921, p. 30). Eissler referred to a link between excessive envy and murderous phantasies and it would appear to be more to the point to say that Klein added the idea of a constitutional basis for envy (Joffe, 1969, p. 533).

*Defining the "death instinct"*

Expanding somewhat on Freud's life and death instincts in "Beyond the Pleasure Principle" (1920) in relation to the Kleinian theory of envy, the literature indicates that, historically, Freud's concept of the death instinct and Klein's 1957 concept of envy have been inextricably linked in the writings of psychoanalysis. To facilitate a clearer explanation as to whether or not we are describing innate drives when we talk of envy, the question of definition must be addressed, especially as, in the literature, there are more theoretical questions than answers surrounding the distinction between instinct and drive. Translation and mistranslation are exhaustively discussed by Laplanche (1976, 1999b). There are also disagreements as to whether Freud could himself differentiate between links with biology or metapsychology in his discoveries (see Barford, 1999, p. 37). Barford discusses how they are perhaps based on Freud's tendency to muddle scientific—that is, empirically based thinking— with metaphysical contemplation and understanding of the essence of reality, including epistemological and ontological elements (Barford, 1999, p. 26).

Instinct may well have been the wrong word to use for the English translation of Freud's work, precisely because, in Freud's sense, instincts are inborn, unconscious and basically unalterable. The argument in much of the literature seems to concentrate on whether or not "impulse" is a better rendering than "instinct" for the German word *Trieb*. Bettelheim argues that "if Freud had meant instinct, he would have used the specific word *instinkt*. Nowhere has the rendering of *Trieb* as 'instinct' done more harm to the understanding of psychoanalysis than its use in connection with the 'death instinct'" (Bettelheim, 1983, p. 104).

*Klein and primary envy*

At this juncture, it is worth surveying Klein's line of reasoning in what turned out to be her last major original contribution to psychoanalysis. The element that she added in *Envy and Gratitude* (1957) was the idea of primary envy.

> Throughout this section I am speaking of primary envy of the mother's breast, and this should be differentiated from its later forms, inherent in the girl's desire to take her mother's place and

in the boys feminine position in which envy is no longer focused on the breast but on the mother receiving the father's penis, having babies inside her, giving birth to them, and being able to feed them. (1975, p. 183)

Klein had been assuming so far in her theory that the infant's sadistic attacks are triggered by an early onset of the Oedipus complex, and added epistemophilic urges to penetrate, possess, and control the maternal body. Now she ventured the suggestion that one such trigger of early attacks is the infant's primary envy towards the first good object. This universal emotion is present at the beginning of life, and creates a major interference in the infant's struggles to take in fulfilment and goodness from the feeding breast. Furthermore, all this comes about through the tragic circumstance of internal forces. Envy, the tragic flaw of the human species, is an anti-life force that owes its origin to the death instinct. Envy now took the place that sadism occupied in her early thinking, but was also the specific phenomenon that expressed the essence of human destructiveness (Klein, 1957).

Guntrip sets out the Kleinian position when he states that it was Klein's "own clinical work that created the need for theoretical revision". He goes on to explain that:

This was largely because she centred everything on Freud's "death instinct". She did not use her own discoveries about internal object-relations to achieve a more satisfactory structural theory. Thus, her theory remained a mixture of biology and psychology, with (like Freud) no true ego-theory as a foundation for her study of the psychodynamics of ego-object relations. Her internal object-relations discoveries demanded a consistently psychodynamic ego theory, a theory of man as a personal self. (Guntrip, 1968, p. 411)

For Klein, like the biological instinct, the phantasy of its corresponding object "exists from the beginning of life"; that is, the phantasy of the object exists before birth, prior to any experience of an object, so that the infant has an innate phantasy of the breast before he has actual experience of a real breast (Klein, 1957).

This has been disputed by Guntrip (1968), Joffe (1969), and Laing (1965) as an unprovable assumption. Masterson believes that "Klein is often considered the first object-relations theorist, yet in her theory object relations were secondary to and a concomitant of aggression, and were based more on internal phantasy rather than on the actual quali- ties of the external environment" (Masterson, 1999, p. 123).

So the dispute is that if this were in truth an object relations theory, the objects in such theory are internal objects, not real objects. Therefore, in Kleinian theory, instincts are by definition not real-object seeking, but phantasy-object seeking. This distinguishes them from Winnicott's object relations:

> When I speak of the use of an object, however, I take object-relating for granted; and add new features that involve the nature and the behaviour of the object. For instance, the object, if it is to be used, must be real in the sense of being part of a shared reality, not a bun- dle of projections. (Winnicott, 1971, p. 88)

Masterson states that:

> Winnicott took care to explain that what appears as aggression can often be a reaction to impingements from an as yet undifferentiated mother upon the core of an undeveloped self, or a distressed reac- tion to a situation in which the infant feels his mother has failed to hold him. Such "aggressive" responses will, of course, recur in intimate adult relationships. (Masterson, 1999, p. 141)

In Klein's 1957 theory, envy is not regarded as a simple or compound feeling state, nor is it treated as a complex character trait, emerg- ing during the course of, or as a consequence of, development. It is regarded as an innate, primary motivating force in human functioning (Joffe, 1969).

## Counter-arguments to the "death instinct"

The death instinct has been criticised on the grounds that it demands an appropriate set of moral assumptions (Holbrook, 1971). Gallwey rejects the Freudian and Kleinian theories of instinct as being derivatives of a sinful view of human nature incompatible with Darwinian theory (Gallwey, 2008). Klein's views clearly associate her theory of devel- opment with the Pauline doctrine of original sin, suffering, and pen- ance. Barford argues that: "If the organism really aims to terminate its own existence, then the cause of human suffering must be biologically

'hard-wired' into the individual at birth. The death instinct hypothesis, therefore, leads to a species of analysis which places the blame for
human suffering and aggressiveness on the individual, and which dangerously underrates the influence of social and environmental factors"
(Barford, 1999, p. 26). This view is in line with my own disagreement
with the Kleinian concept of envy being innate in an individual. Otto
Fenichel (1954) argues that:

> the death-instinct theory gives many opportunities for unfortu-
> nate misuses. The first such misuse is that whenever the analyst
> comes upon the phenomena of masochism, self-punishment, and
> so forth, he is inclined to fall back on the death-instinct and to
> stop analysing, thinking that he is faced with a primary biological
> fact which cannot be further explained, instead of proceeding to
> search for determining experiences in the patient's life. (Fenichel,
> 1954, p. 370)

For Barford,

> ethical objections to the death instinct arise from the presumption
> that because Freud suggested the death instinct was a biological
> endowment of living matter, this suggests that the individual is
> the source of self-destructive wishes and responsible for his or her
> own pain and suffering. However, as we have seen, Freud insisted
> that the death instinct operated in silence, and outside of what
> he had previously portrayed as the domain of instinct. (Barford,
> 1999, p. 124)

In *Wickedness* (1984), Mary Midgely challenges Freud's concept of a
death instinct as the "central psychological problem" (p. 158). She
questions whether "there can be a motive which is a pure wish for
destruction—not as a means to any good, nor a part of it, but simply
for its own sake?" (p. 87). She develops her argument further by stating that "Freud's suggestion is simple and startling. We have, he said,
a strong wish to die, a wish which is not just one wish among others
but an all-pervasive basic instinct, indeed a natural force" (p. 161). She
points out the oddness of this suggestion as deserving attention:

> On the face of things, it makes far more sense that a wish to injure
> others should sometimes exist, and should sometimes be turned
> inward, than that a wish to die should always exist and should be
> turned outward. Freud's arrangement is obscure, not just because

the idea of a pervasive death-wish is itself puzzling, but because
this death-wish, even if it existed, seems too passive a motive to
generate the lively activity of attack. (pp. 161–162)

Freud's view on aggression was that "the tendency to aggression is an
innate, independent, instinctual disposition in man", one which "constitutes the most powerful obstacle to culture" and is "the derivative
and main representation of the death instinct" (Freud, 1930, cited in
Midgely, 1984, p. 166).

My argument, in line with Masterson (1999), is that the aggression
and destructive intent towards self and significant other is not necessarily derived from an innate drive towards death, but arises out of
experiences of self and other *in relationship*. It is especially important
to begin to disentangle the semantics and supposed motivations of
"death" and "aggression". These have tended to be subsumed under
the notion of an instinct of self-destruction, as clarified by Masterson
(1999), regarding the theory of instincts. Klein (1957) highlighted the
confusion between aggression and the death instinct; she maintained
that the infant suffered extreme anxiety due to its fear of annihilation
from its innate destructiveness. She construed ego-disintegration as a
consequence of this innate destructiveness, rather than resulting from
any lack in external environmental factors, necessary for sustaining the
ego in its tendency towards integration, cohesion, and independence—
which is a very long process.

Klein acknowledged the existence of unconscious communication
between mother and infant. She wrote: "the mother's unconscious attitude strongly affects the infant's unconscious processes" (Klein, 1957,
p. 116). However, she persisted in ascribing all anxieties experienced
by the infant as being due to persecution from its own death instinct,
as opposed to allowing for the effect of possible ambivalent or negative
feelings in the mother.

I agree with Masterson, who writes that:

> The death instinct appears as a useful contrivance on which to
> hang destructiveness, rather than an intrinsically valid notion …
> the wish for death, arising within, is the source of the basic human
> capacity for fear. Its outward expression, in the form of anger, is
> facilitated through encounters with frustrating others. (Masterson,
> 1999, p. 128)

James Gilligan discusses how:

> the person who is overwhelmed by feelings of shame is by defini-
> tion experiencing a psychically threatening lack of love, and any-
> one in that condition does not have any love left for anyone else.
> And when shame so overwhelms these positive feelings, which
> would normally act as inhibitors on rage or violence, aggression
> and destructiveness can ensue. (Gilligan, 2000, p. 113)

Distinguishing between aggression and true destructive hatred is,
according to Midgely, very important:

> Aggression may seem to be different in being a tendency which
> does not just happen to be destructive, but which has destruction
> as its aim—in being in itself a mere wish to destroy. This, however,
> is a misleading idea. It is indeed the way in which Freud conceived
> of aggression. He thought of it as the death wish turned outward,
> as a mere general urge to wreck and kill … later investigations have
> not supported this strange suggestion, either in human life or else-
> where. In other animals, no such vast sweeping motives as either
> the inward or the outward death wish have been found at work.
> What has been found is a far more limited, specific, easily satisfied
> set of tendencies to become irritated by certain sorts of intrusion,
> and to attack intruders to the extent of driving them off. (Midgely,
> 1984, p. 87)

Midgely sees aggression as more in line with the "fight or flight response"
common in most animals: "If we think of aggression, as Freud did, as a
pure wish for destruction, it is hard to see any positive function for it,
and its occurrence, if it did occur, would be a monstrous evolutionary
puzzle" (Midgely, 1984, p. 90). Freud's concept of "a wish for one's own
death is partly based on the fact that he conceives the self as essentially
solitary rather than social. Its deepest wishes must therefore always be
self-directed … not as a natural outgrowth of their interacting facilities"
(Midgely, 1984, p. 176).

My point of divergence from the Kleinian concept of envy, based
on Freud's belief in an inborn form of passivity, which he named the
death drive, is that I do not subscribe to an innate self-destructive
drive as the basic and *primary* problem with which each individual

ego has to contend in its development. I will demonstrate with clinical material, in the following chapters, how survival needs (which depend on environmental provision) are primary, with aggression as a *secondary* phenomenon, a biologically based reaction which is aroused when libidinal or developmental needs are frustrated.

What follows is a brief overview of selected findings that have contributed to my understanding of the development of attachment theory and how this has had a bearing on its evolving relationship with psychoanalysis. As Fairbairn noted:

> My various findings and the conclusions to which they lead involve not only a considerable amount of revision of prevailing ideas regarding the nature and aetiology of envy, but also a considerable revision of ideas regarding the prevalence of primary aggression and a corresponding change in current clinical conceptions of the various ways that traumatic attachments in infant development challenges various classical psychoanalytic concepts. (Fairbairn, 1952, p. 28)

## Attachment theory and psychoanalysis

In Bowlby's work on attachment (1969, 1981), his focus was on human biology, through which social bonds are formed. Bowlby believed that the attachment process enables the development of complex mental functions through complex actions on the part of the mother/carer. The majority of these mental functions are uniquely human. (Fonagy et al., 2002; Hart, 2008). In discussing the human biological capacity for participating in culture, Hart states that:

> we have a biological capacity for taking part in social interactions and communications because we are born with the predisposition for forming attachments and interacting with our caregivers .... It is impossible to determine how much of a child's psychological function is the child's own, and how much is the product of the child's relationships. (Hart, 2008, p. 3)

Given the power of the biological forces driving the human attachment system, it is assumed that almost all human beings become attached. Attachment may be secure or insecure. Secure attachment implies representational systems where the attachment figure is seen as accessible and responsive when needed (Ainsworth et al., 1979). Bowlby was prescient in assuming that caregiver responsiveness was critical in determining the security of the attachment system (Bowlby, 1958, p. 30). Fonagy describes how:

> The most promising area of attachment research from a psycho-analytic point of view is undoubtedly the study of disorganized/ disoriented attachment behaviour (Main and Solomon 1986 and 1990). Main and Hesse's (1990) now classical contribution linked disorganized attachment behaviour to frightened or frightening care-giving: infants who could not find a solution to the paradox of fearing the figures who they wished to approach for comfort in times of distress. (Fonagy, 2001, p. 36)

He points out:

> The majority of studies exploring the effect of maternal depression fail to examine the critical variable, that is, the extent to which the infant is actually exposed to a severely depressed caregiver over a long period of time. In individual studies where chronic exposure to severe depression was independently demonstrated, the association with attachment disorganization appears to be strong. (Fonagy, 2001, p. 370)

Fonagy discusses how:

> Bowlby was deeply influenced by Kleinian thought. His train-ing and experience in the British Psychoanalytic Society was pre-dominantly Kleinian. His focus on the first year of life as a crucial determinant of later developmental outcome is, of course, highly compatible with the Kleinian approach …. Many of Bowlby's ideas, or at least the way he expressed them, were, however, clear reac-tions against the Kleinian influence prevailing at the time. (Fonagy, 2001, p. 84)

He goes on to say: "In a 1981 interview with Ray Holland, Bowlby described Klein as 'inspirational, the antithesis of what I try to be'. He considered Klein to be 'totally unaware of scientific method'" (Holland, 1990, cited in Fonagy, 2001, p. 84).

Attachment theory was criticised as mechanistic, non-dynamic, and explicated according to thorough misunderstandings of psychoanalytic theory. These critiques raise a variety of issues, but at root they boil down to relatively few simple disagreements. Bowlby is seen as having renounced drives, "the Oedipus", unconscious processes, particularly unconscious phantasy, complex internalised motivational and conflict-resolving systems (Fonagy, 2001).

John Bowlby and Silvan Tomkins, noted Nathanson (1992), "stared at the same landscape" but both saw it differently. On the one hand, Tomkins (1962, 1963) studied the facial display of affect and linked it to the very interactions that so intrigued Bowlby. On the other hand, Bowlby, immersed in the new science of attachment theory and behaviour that was derived from the study of fish and birds, two life forms that have no facial affect display, saw everything but the face. Had Bowlby only looked at the face, he might have come to understand the relation between the external display of affect and the internal experience of feeling, and his theory would not have been so dry and devoid of emotional resonance. Bowlby sees attachment as a result of specific, inborn systems built for no other reason than to produce attachment. In this respect, he follows the work of Tinbergen (1952) and Lorenz (1935) with great precision. He chooses to ignore the emotional aspects of attachment, to relegate the affective accompaniment of attachment to a period in life far later than infancy. Therefore, Bowlby and attachment theorists see the human as predisposed by nature to be linked, without considering what the outcome would be if there was a failure in attachment due to environmental circumstances, especially between mother and baby (Nathanson, 1992).

Attachment theorists such as Fonagy, Eagle, and Holmes compare the Freudian unconscious with the unconscious of attachment theory.

Attachment theory is seen as ignoring biological vulnerabilities other than those rooted in the caregiver's behaviour and as reducing aetiological considerations to a single variable: that of physical separation. Bowlby is accused of failing to consider the impact of the developmental state of the ego on the child's ability to make attachments and react to loss. He is also accused of ignoring negative attachment related to the fear of the mother and trauma other than physical separation. Bowlby is seen to be a reductionist in his emphasis on evolutionary considerations at the expense of full recognition of complex symbolic functioning. (Fonagy, 2001, p. 2)

Morris Eagle's 1997 paper examines certain aspects of the relationship between attachment theory and psychoanalytic theories and practice. "Attachment theory constituted a reaction against and corrective to certain aspects of psychoanalytic theory, in particular Freudian and Kleinian theory" (Eagle, 1997, p. 217). He goes on to say:

> There are real differences between attachment theory and at least traditional psychoanalysis with regards to the role of external versus internal factors in development. Bowlby's (1969) reaction to certain aspects of Kleinian (1957) theory was, in particular, its neglect of events in the external world. (Eagle, 1997, p. 218)

Fonagy (2001, pp. 84–85) describes the points of contact between the Kleinian model and attachment theory. As can be seen from his partial list, the Kleinian commentary on infant mental states overlaps with the classification of adult attachment narratives. This may not be surprising since Klein's description was based on work with children and adults, rather than on the observation of infants. It might be argued that Klein explored the sequelae of insecure infantile attachments based on the characteristic narratives of her adult patients. For example, the description of the paranoid schizoid position may well be considered by attachment theorists as a relatively apt portrayal of an adult's insecure state of mind with respect to attachment (Fonagy, 2001, p. 84).

Jeremy Holmes (1993) finds a common evolutionary basis for the attachment theory unconscious and the psychoanalytic unconscious. The attachment behavioural unconscious is rooted in the selective advantage to the vulnerable infant of protection through social relationships. Similarly, the Freudian or psychoanalytic unconscious is rooted in vulnerability, though born of the selective advantage of self-deception rather than protection.

Fonagy describes how "Holmes's contribution to an integration of psychoanalysis and attachment theory has been multifaceted. His central contribution is linking a model of psychological change in all forms of the 'talking cure' to attachment theory ideas via the notion of coherence and biography" (Fonagy, 2001, p. 149). Another thread in Holmes's project is the strengthening of both the attachment and the psychoanalytic approach by creating links to advances in biological psychiatry.

Fonagy discusses how "The third aspect of his work concerns an evolving developmental model that draws on both psychoanalytic and attachment theory ideas. In all these respects, Holmes's contribution stands alone as a thoroughly coherent attempt to build a new school of psychoanalytic psychotherapy based on attachment theory" (Fonagy, 2001, p. 149).

Fonagy also describes how "Daniel Stern (1985) occupies a unique place in psychoanalysis. He has been able to bridge the gulf between developmentalists and psychoanalysis in a very impressive and productive way" (Fonagy, 2001, p. 117). His database is infant research rather than clinical observation, and so in this respect he follows the tradition of the psychoanalytic developmentalists. Stern distinguished three types of relationships of self-with-the-other: self-other complementing, state sharing, and state transforming (Stern, 1985). While these relationships can be characterised by the degree of attachment or separateness they imply, it is their contribution to the structuralisation of the self through the schematisation of experience that was of importance to Stern. "Stern's framework has much to offer attachment theory, particularly in terms of the careful integration of infant observation studies with concepts concerning interpersonal development" (Fonagy, 2001, p. 121).

## Klein's broad influence

Comparing and contrasting the writings of Klein (1957) with Bowlby (1988), Winnicott (1958, 1971), Fairbairn (1952), and Gallwey (1996), it appears that as well as being Klein's critics, they were also as much influenced by her work as her followers.

Bowlby was inspired by Konrad Lorenz's (1935) description of goslings instinctively following their mother, when he developed his biological principles of attachment theory. Although Winnicott and Bowlby were both at variance with the Kleinian concept of envy, it has been claimed by Hinshelwood (1989, p. 176) that there is no published account of their criticism. However, an examination of the literature shows otherwise. Presumably after Hinshelwood's research, Winnicott wrote an in-depth criticism of Klein's 1957 paper *Envy and Gratitude*. This review appeared in *Case Conference* in January 1989, and was published (posthumously) the same year in *Psychoanalytic Explorations*, edited by Claire Winnicott and others, in a chapter entitled "Melanie Klein: On Her Concept of Envy".

Winnicott believed that Klein was to some degree in error in regarding destructive forces—which she considered to be oral-sadistic, as well as anal-sadistic, expressions of destructive impulses—as operating from the beginning of life, with envy existing on a constitutional basis. Winnicott's (1989) argument is that envy implies an attitude, something maintained over a period of time, a perception, he believes, of a property in the object, or an environmental factor. Therefore the word "envy" for Winnicott implies a high degree of sophistication, a degree of ego-organisation in the subject, which cannot possibly be present at the beginning of life. Winnicott believes that Klein's introduction of the idea of innate aggression weakens the main argument of her concept and creates a challenge in the reader to examine other discrepancies that may exist in the total argument. For Winnicott, the personal and environmental factors must be considered in terms of the part they play in inherited aggression. As he put it:

> In my opinion the word "envy" in the term "oral sadistic envy" weakens the concept of oral sadism. Oral sadism is valuable as a concept because it joins up with the biological concept of hunger, a drive to object-relationships that comes from primitive sources, and that holds sway at least from the time of birth.

He goes on to say:

> Klein's argument took her to a point at which she must either deal with the *dependence of the infant on the mother,* or else deliberately ignore the variable external factor of the mother and dig right back in terms of *primitive mechanisms that are personal to the infant.* By choosing the latter course Klein involved herself in an implicit denial of the environmental factor, and consequently she disqualified herself from describing infancy itself, which is a time of dependence. In this way she was forced into a premature arrival at the inherent factor. (Winnicott, 1962, cited in Winnicott et al., 1989, p. 448)

## Self in relation to other

How, some ask, can we say that an infant has a sense of self when it is not yet capable of conscious and internal reflection, when it is unable to meditate on the nature of the self? Donald Nathanson has written about the subject of a sense of self from the beginning of life in his writings on the subject of shame and states that "any action that can be planned, initiated, carried out from beginning to end and remembered as a personally written script will be subsumed under the umbrella of 'me'" (Nathanson, 1992, p. 208).

Infants detect contingencies between what they do and what the environment does immediately following their actions. This has been the basis of the research of Beebe and Lachmann (2002) on infant development. They believe that "This research is entirely consistent with Rapaport's (1960) claim that in early infancy, the 'ego' is already on board, attending to the organization of the environment and learning the organization of the interactive process." In this sense, Beebe and Lachmann argue, "the bedrock of the person is not a chaotic 'id', but an ongoing capacity for self-organization in the context of the interactive field .... Although transformed in various ways, these same capacities continue to operate across the life span and, in the consulting room, usually out of awareness. They may be understood in the form of unconscious memories, enactments or patterns of non-verbal behaviour" (2002, p. 84).

Of crucial importance to our understanding of infant development Beebe and Lachmann describe how:

> Martin and Clark (1982) demonstrated that in the first day of life a neonate recognizes his or her own vocalizations and discriminates between them and those of other infants. When a calm baby hears a tape recording of his or her own cry, the infant vocalizes less, whereas the infant vocalizes more when hearing the cry of another infant. This work has been interpreted as evidence for an auditory specification of a "self" from birth, in the sense that, at a pre-symbolic level, the infant discriminates between his or her own sounds and those of the environment and that there is no original perceptual confusion between organism and environment. (Beebe & Lachmann, 2002, p. 69)

Within classic psychoanalytic theory, *social interaction* cannot be said to exist until self and object are split apart by the forces of libido; the child is presumed to be living in a state of narcissism until this moment. This theory, produced by Freud, links a postulated psychosexual development of the child (this assumed movement of libido from the oral to the anal to the phallic regions of the body), with the hypothesised shift from narcissism to true interpersonal relatedness. I am in agreement with Nathanson (1992, pp. 192–193) that the problem with this scheme is that "it requires us to ignore completely the obvious fact that children, from the earliest days of extra-uterine life, relate to their parents as if they were real people, each quite different from the other, and quite separate from themselves". The focus of attention now being on the affective life of the infant and the interaction between infant and caregiver of affective-related behaviour, the libido theory, and its restrictively sexual notion about the development of self and other, has long ago been discarded (Nathanson, 1992).

In Beebe and Lachmann's and Schore's research on the nature/nurture debate, there is evidence that proves that the development of a me/not me is present shortly after birth.

Beebe and Lachmann's study (2002) brought together proof that an infant is aware of another out there *very* early in infancy. They quote Casper and Fifer (1980): "In the first fifteen hours an infant can distinguish its mother's voice and prefer it to a stranger's voice." Furthermore, they describe the work of De Casper and Spence's 1986 study of pregnant mothers who read aloud to their unborn babies:

> At birth, the babies preferred a tape recording of the mother reading the story heard in utero to hearing her read another story. Infants exposed to their mother's voices over the course of the pregnancy are able at birth to distinguish slight differences in rhythmicity, intonation, frequency variation, and phonic components of speech. (Beebe & Lachmann, 2002, p. 69)

Beebe and Lachmann's analyses sent me back, in particular, to the studies done by De Casper and Fifer (1980) and Butterworth (1990). Indicating that there is a sense of self from the outset, Butterworth reported in "Self Perception in Infancy" (1990) that his work "has been interpreted as evidence for an auditory specification of 'self' from birth in the sense that, at a pre-symbolic level, the infant discriminates between his or her own sounds and those of the environment and that there is no original perceptual confusion between organism and environment".

Winnicott (1971, p. 47) states that "Not me is recognized as *outside*, the repudiated world: what is truly external" and that "to control what is outside, one has to *do* things, not simply to wish or think". He also states that: "As soon as there is the ego organization available, the baby allows the object the quality of being *not me* or separate" (p. 94).

Schore states that "the baby's brain can only develop in the context of the brain of the mother" and he spells out exactly what does happen, or not, and the disastrous consequences for the infant of not having that other brain (Schore, 2003a, pp. 42–43).

Singer and Fagen (1992) point out that "an infant's own emotional state is part of its memory. This work points to an interactive view of the organization of memory, which sees the nature of the organism's state as interacting with the organism's capacity to remember the environment" (cited in Beebe & Lachmann, 2002, p. 72). Thus affect may powerfully influence the nature of early memory development. It is a fact that the brain of the newborn becomes the mind of the adult (Beebe & Lachmann, 2002; Schore, 2003a).

Beebe and Lachmann's research into infants document in detail this two-element relationship, and a number of philosophers have shown remarkable agreement in describing how interactions are organised in pairs, or dyadically (Bruner, 1977; Habermas, 1979; Lashley, 1951; Mead, 1934). We therefore need a theory of the "dyad" as a system within which the relationship of self and object can be conceptualised.

## Object relations theory

Object relations first began to replace instincts as the focal point of Kleinian theory, from the mechanistic to the personal, in the study of mental phenomena. This replaced the earlier concept of psychic life as simply an area of superego and ego control of antisocial instincts. Klein's view on inner psychic reality, on internal objects, and internal object relations created the necessary conceptual framework in which Freud's later emphasis on ego-psychology could be further developed.

For Fairbairn (1951), there is no emotion without the self and no self without emotion. Hinshelwood discusses how:

> Fairbairn was opposed to instinct theory as he was looking for a more humanistic theory. Consequently he spoke only of objects. He quarrelled with the term "oral phase", for instance, saying that it might as well be called the "breast phase", since it is the breast (the object) which is of importance to the child. He regarded the

mouth as expressing a particular *strategy* for relating to the object. In this case the mouth is merely the inborn instrument for the strategy and nothing to do with the instinct. In this way Fairbairn believed he had gone beyond instinct theory and the energy model of the mind which is the cornerstone of classical psychoanalytic theory (Fairbairn 1951). (Hinshelwood, 1989, pp. 302–303)

Winnicott discussed Fairbairn's 1951 work in terms of primary identification with an object and argues that:

> "Now if the object is not differentiated, it cannot operate as an object." What Fairbairn is referring to is an infant with needs but with no "mechanism" or "psychic apparatus" by which to implement them. An infant with needs not "seeking" an object, but seeking de-tension, instinct tension seeking a return to a state of rest, which brings us back to Freud. (Winnicott et al., 1989, p. 419)

Whereas Fairbairn substituted a monolithic and seemingly inflexible system of endopsychic structures (object-relations systems) as an ingenious, object-relations version of the orthodox id/ego/superego structure, Klein, on the other hand, actually went beyond instinct theory in a quite different way. "Klein retained an instinct theory only by redefining the meaning of instinct, and substituted the notion of unconscious phantasy, a flexible and fluid view of internal structure" (Hinshelwood, 1989, p. 303).

Klein reinterpreted the concept of "instinct" to mean the experience of an object "given by" the bodily sensations of the instinctual impulse; while Fairbairn recast instinct as the "energy" to seek out objects (Hinshelwood, 1989).

## A sense of self

Winnicott (1965) contributed most constructively towards providing a developmental description of the origins of the self in the infant–caregiver relationship. This concept has been of great importance in the development of Gallwey's 1996 model, which is explored in detail in the next chapter. Winnicott saw the child as evolving from a unity of mother and infant. Three functions of this unity facilitate healthy development: 1) holding, leading to integration of sensorimotor elements; 2) handling, facilitating personalisation (autonomy); and 3) object relating, resulting in the establishment of a human relationship (cited in Fonagy, 2000, pp. 96–97).

The holding environment provides the setting for the fusion of aggression and love that prepares the way for the toleration of ambivalence and the emergence of concern, both of which contribute to the acceptance of responsibility (Winnicott, 1963). This is Winnicott's version of Melanie Klein's depressive position and an alternative description of a secure pattern of attachment. Winnicott made a further critical point concerning sensitivity in his often misunderstood and somewhat paradoxical assertion that relatedness is born of the experience of being alone in the presence of somebody else (Fonagy, 2001).

Winnicott (1958) postulated an inherent desire to develop a sense of self, a desire that could be hidden or falsified. Masterson's argument is that:

> Whilst recognising Freud's conception of life and death instincts, Winnicott nevertheless held the death instinct theory to be false, because Freud omitted reference to the stage of absolute and unsensed dependence which is prior to instinct. Freud's theory of aggression linked to a death instinct was also deemed false by Winnicott because two aspects of aggression were omitted: that which belongs to the "pre-truth" stage of primitive love, and that which is expressed as a reaction to an impingement. In the infant's experience, "death" is the loss of continuity, a subsequent reaction to an environment which impinges on the sense of self. We are helped to understand the psychological damage caused by early trauma during development through this concept of an insult to experience. (Masterson, 1999, pp. 143–144)

André Green has the view that Winnicott's wish to avoid conflict also influenced his psychoanalytic technique and that Winnicott believed that he should try unconditionally to cure his patients by representing the image of a "good-enough mother" by systematically interpreting the positive function of destructiveness.

> Ruthless love is not enough to explain destruction. The rage to destroy enjoyment by domination of others, and the annihilation of the other's individuality, may be considered as forms of omnipotence enhanced by an impotence produced by the patient's

own narcissistic closure. Trends of this kind are not a form of love, even in its ruthless form: they are a culture of death. We are here beyond ambivalence and beyond any kind of love. We are facing destructive, disintegrative forms of negative narcissism to deny the existence of the other. (Green, 2005, p. 28)

Green (1996) has written about the sense of inner death which can derive from an individual's identification at a critical stage in infancy with a dead internal object in a mother who suffers from depression, following Winnicott who wrote: "Here the infant has to fit in with a *dead* object, or else has to be lively to counteract the mother's unconscious preoccupation with the idea of the child's deadness" (Winnicott, 1965, p. 191).

Winnicott (1965) developed the concept of a "false self", similar to Laing's (1960) "divided self"; a form of existential death as the only way of being-in-the-world for those for whom being alive carries with it feelings of being engulfed, crushed, or overwhelmed by the reality of the aliveness or deadness of another who fails to recognise one's core being. The achievement of a secure sense of identity requires the existence of another by whom one dares to be known (Masterson, 1999, p. 144).

In his paper "Fear of Breakdown" (1974), Winnicott wrote that he believed that in extreme cases the false self commits suicide in an attempt to protect the true self from exploitation and annihilation. Suicide and self-destructive behaviour are frequently understood as manifesting the death instinct. However, from this existential point of view, suicide can be understood as a desperate attempt to escape from being imprisoned in a false existence, where the core of the self is felt to be dead. For Winnicott, suicide as a solution is "sending the body to death which has already happened in the psyche" (Winnicott et al., 1989, p. 93).

Wilfred Bion (1959) would say that the psychotic processes that arise are because of traumatic and painful early relating. This parallel model is that the psychotic processes choose death rather than relating.

The psychic consequences of early and sustained maternal deprivation, particularly in the earliest stages of development, were well documented by Bowlby (1969), who connected anxiety primarily with over-long separation and deprivation. Winnicott (1984) made a substantial difference to understanding object relations theory with his inspired contributions on primary maternal preoccupation, the essential formation of the mother/infant unit and the importance of the good-enough holding mother (Gallwey, 1991).

## Neurobiology

In order to make the exposition of this study as clear as I can, it is relevant to introduce at this juncture the work of a growing body of studies in neurobiology and affect theory which I consider have made a tremendous contribution to attachment theory and psychoanalysis over the past two decades. The opportunity for theoretical integration stems from the latest developments in neuroscience concerning the relationship between brain functions, behaviour, and personality by exploring the way the brain matures in close interaction with the social and physical environment.

A starting place for us to understand neurobiology is to begin with what Badenoch (2008), McGilchrist (2009), Schore (2003a), and Siegel (2007, 2011), among others, describe as "a definition of the mind" (Siegel, 2007). Their stance is that the brain represents the entire nervous system, which generates throughout the entire body, not what is in the skull alone. Mind, brain, and relationships represent a triangle of human experience—three facets of one reality. A working definition of a core aspect of the mind is that it is both an embodied and a relational process regulating the flow of energy and information (Siegel, 2011), a self-organising process that arises from the interaction of elements of a system (neuroplasticity); that is, from the flow of energy within embodied neural activity and relational communication. The social circuits of the brain are also the regulatory circuits of the brain.

Developing the research into the scientific principles of parenting by Ainsworth et al. (1979), Bowlby (1969), and Main and Hesse (1990), Daniel Siegel explores how an interpersonal neurobiology of human development enables us to understand that the structure and function of the mind and brain are shaped by experiences, especially those involving emotional relationships. Discussing "brain basics", Siegel describes how the nervous system begins in the embryo as the ectoderm, the outer layers of cells that will become the skin. Certain clusters of these outer cells then fold inward to form a neural tube, the spinal cord.

> This origin of neurons, the basic cells of the brain, on the "outside" and their journey "inside" the body developmentally reveals

a philosophical point that the brain originates at the interface of the inner and outer worlds of our bodily defined selves. When we think of the mindful brain, it is helpful to keep this inner/outer interface in mind ... the whole nervous system sets up its basic scaffolding, its core architecture, during development in the womb. Genetics are important for determining how neurons will migrate and then connect to each other. In fact, half of our genetic material is either directly or indirectly responsible for neural structure, making genes very important in neural development. As the foetus nears the time to leave the uterus, the connections among neurons are also influenced by experience. (Siegel, 2007, p. 29)

For more information on his "model of the mind", see Siegel's chapter on "Brain Basics", particularly the section on neuroplasticity and left/right brain (Siegel, 2007, pp. 29–50) and also "What do the two hemispheres do?" in McGilchrist (2009, pp. 32–93).

Whenever the term *brain* is used in the writings of neurobiologists, it refers to the brain as an integrated part of the whole body. This reality changes the way we think about the relationship between mind and brain. Because neurobiologists view the mind itself as both embodied *and* relational, they believe that our brains actually can be considered the social organ of the body. "Our minds connect with one another via neural circuitry in our bodies that is hard-wired to take in other's signals" (Siegel, 2007, p. 48).

Moving on to discuss how attunement promotes integration, Siegel believes, in line with Schore (2003a), that:

when relationships between parent and child are attuned, a child is able to feel felt [i.e., contained] by a caregiver and has a sense of stability in the present moment. During that here-and-now interaction, the child feels good, connected, and loved. The child's internal world is seen with clarity by the parent, and the parent comes to resonate with the child's state. This is attunement.

Over time, he goes on to say:

this attuned communication enables the child to develop the regulatory circuits in the brain—including the integrative prefrontal fibers—that give the individual a source of resilience as he or she grows. This resilience takes the forms of the capacity for self-regulation and engagement with others in empathic relationships. Here we see that interpersonal attunement—the fundamental characteristic of a secure attachment—leads to the empirically proven outcome measures we described above. (Siegel, 2007, p. 27)

The work of Damasio (1994), LeDoux (1994), and Schore (1994) offered a thorough introduction to certain aspects of the emotional or feeling brain. Schore's research made the first attempt at integrating and linking these theoretical fields by indicating that traumatic childhood experiences provide the contexts for the roots of adult violence and destructiveness. We now need to look even earlier, indeed to the very beginning of infant development, to help expand our knowledge by hopefully establishing more of an understanding of the essential causal factors. Further neuropsychoanalytic work by Hart (2008), Karr-Morse and Wiley (1997), Schore (2003a), and that of Beebe and Lachmann (2002), to name but a few, shows that environmental influences are of prime importance in infantile development.

This study does not include a full history of neurobiology, but what I consider to be most relevant in reviewing the work of Schore (1994, 2003a, 2003b) and Beebe and Lachmann (2002) in relation to projective identification is that it specifically emphasises the importance of the knowledge that the baby's brain only develops in the context of the mother's brain. The early spurt in the development of the baby's right brain is contingent upon the adaptive attunement of the mother, via her right brain. Schore's (1994) research into brain plasticity, describes how most of the functional capacity of the brain develops after birth. Correspondingly, brain plasticity is at its highest during the developmental stages as infants are most receptive to early life experiences. Therefore, the development of the infant is dependent upon the healthy attachment to the mother, and that disturbed attachments results in anatomical, physiological, and psychological developmental disturbances.

Through the lenses of developmental neuroscience, attachment theory, and infant psychiatry, Schore has traced how severe traumatic attachments result in structural limitations of the early developing right brain, expressed in a number of enduring functional deficits, including a fundamental inability to regulate emotional states under stress (Schore, 2003a, pp. 266–271). Earlier research, including that by Wittling

(1957) and Nakamura et al. (1999) provides useful grounding in this area of neuroscience.

Furthermore, Schore states (2003, p. 288), "Maternal neglect is the most profound behavioural manifestation of maternal deprivation, and so this research on cell death may explicate the psychoneurobiological mechanism by which severe attachment trauma massively alters the trajectory of brain growth."

For the purposes of this study and to support my main argument, the most important affect I would like to focus on from Schore's 2003 research is that of *aggression*. I will discuss how this can become dysregulated by early relational trauma. Schore argues:

> If the intense fear of post traumatic stress disorder (PTSD) represents a dysregulation of the brain's "flight" systems, aggression disorders represents a dysregulation of the brain's "fight" centers .... Each reflects a dysregulation of a pattern of autonomic nervous system (ANS), sympathetic hyperarousal, one associated with intense terror, the other with intense rage. (2003a, p. 267)

In discussing the work of Heim and Nemeroff (1999) in relation to affect dysregulation and aggression, Schore suggests that "these impairments are manifest at early ages in personalities who are high risk for psychiatric disorders" and that "research now indicates that exposure to early life stress is associated with neurobiological changes in children and adults, which underlies the increased risk of psychopathology" (Heim & Nemeroff, 2001, p. 1023, cited in Schore, 2003a, p. 267).

Schore's work in developmental affective neuroscience and developmental neuropsychiatry integrates psychological data of attachment theory and the data of developmental neurobiology.

> This neurobiological perspective focuses on the first two years of life, when the human being grows faster than any other stage of the life cycle ... This interval exactly overlaps the period of attachment so intensely studied by contemporary developmental psychology. A fundamental tenet of Bowlby's (1969) model is that for better or worse, the infant's "capacity to cope with stress" is correlated with certain maternal behaviours. (Schore, 2003a, pp. 270–271)

The central thesis of Schore's work is that: "The attachment relationship can directly shape the maturation of the infant's right brain, which performs essential functions in both the assessment of visual or auditory emotional communicative signals and the human stress responses" (Schore, 2003a, p. 271). According to Schore, "This work bears directly upon the problem of the aetiology of violent personalities. The early traumatic dysregulating transactions with the social environment lead to more than an insecure attachment, they negatively impact the maturation of the brain during its growth spurt from the last trimester of pregnancy through to the middle of the second year" (2003a, p. 271).

## Neuroscience and psychoanalysis

The appearance of a journal entitled *Neuro-Psychoanalysis*, first published in 1991, represented an important step forward towards an active interdisciplinary dialogue between neuroscience and psychoanalysis. The existence of this research indicates that there is now enough common ground between these two perspectives to open an ongoing communication. A consensus has developed that the deeper mechanisms that underlie affective processes, which play an essential role in adaptive functions, "can be elucidated by a neuropsychoanalytic perspective that attends to both psychic structure and function" (Schore, 2003b, p. 205). Shore suggests that "only a developmental perspective can trace that the earliest socioemotional experiences are registered in the deep unconscious, and how they influence the development of the systems that dynamically process unconscious information for the rest of the life span" (2003b, p. 205).

Schore's involvement with such a vast range of subjects relevant to this book began with his earlier work on the phenomenon of shame (1991), which offered a template for the unfolding of his integrative ideas that link psychoanalytic metapsychology and infant development with a vast array of neurobiological and sociobiological research.

## Projective identification

Having discussed certain aspects of the discipline of developmental psychopathology by reviewing what has been published on the subject so far, I turn now to a fundamental clinical and theoretical tool in contemporary British psychoanalysis: the concept of projective identification. Projective identification will become a key point in my questioning of Klein's theory; what follows is a historical overview of the voluminous literature pertaining to its manifold meanings, functions, and uses, to provide the background for later detailed discussion.

Projective identification was introduced by Klein in 1946. *The Dictionary of Psychotherapy* describes it as a term used:

> to describe the *splitting* of the *ego* during early infancy, the *projection* of parts of the self (in contrast to projection of objects) into others, primarily the mother and her breast, and the subsequent *identification* with the split off "bad" parts of the self, now located in "the other". The key idea is that what is projected is simultaneously identified with part of the self and is not (as in the case of projection) seen as part of the other. (Waldron-Skinner, 1986, p. 267)

Klein introduced the term in a paper on schizoid mechanisms (Klein, 1946, p. 8) and she discussed it again when considering the mechanisms of identification. She describes it as originating in the *paranoid schizoid position*, and sees it as part of normal development, although if engaged in persistently it may lead to impoverishment of the ego (if the projected objects are "good") or depersonalisation, a fear of imprisonment (claustrophobia), or to the creation of a hostile, retaliatory, and persecuting external world (if the projected parts are "bad").

Projective identification is a *defence mechanism*, employed by the ego to protect it against the anxieties of being persecuted by and separated from others. As such, it can lead, if excessive, to pathological manifestations and a divorce from reality, but it is also part of normal development, retaining useful functions in adult life (Segal, 1988). Klein (1946) states that projective identification is the basis for the earliest form of symbol formation.

Thomas Ogden has written a comprehensive review of projective identification and discusses in great detail how "it has been to the detriment of (object relations) attachment theory, that psychoanalytic thinking about envy centres on Klein's theory of projective identification, that this concept remains one of the most loosely defined and completely misunderstood of psychoanalytic conceptualizations" (Ogden, 1979, p. 357).

There is a wealth of psychoanalytic literature that discusses the concept of projective identification as being located in relation to other psychoanalytic concepts such as projection, introjection, identification, internalisation, and externalisation. In addition, many other writers attempt to arrive at a more precise understanding of how it differs from projection on the one hand and from identification on the other, and its relation to phantasy. Notable examples include: Gallwey (1996), Grotstein (1981, 1983), Hinshelwood (1989), Joseph (1975, 1982), Kernberg (1975), Meissner (1980), Ogden (1979), Rosenfeld (1987), Schafer (1968), Segal (1957, 1988), Waldron-Skinner (1986), and Weatherill (1999).

The *Dictionary of Psychotherapy* gives Ogden's four suggested ways in which the individual can make use of the mechanism:

> a) as a defence, whereby unwanted or internally endangered parts of the self can be disowned yet kept alive in another; b) as a mode of communication, whereby one exerts pressure on another person to experience feelings similar to one's own; c) as a way of experimenting with object relatedness, the projector perceiving the other as different from self but sufficiently undifferentiated to share feelings; and d) as a pathway to change, by which the projector can identify with and therefore learn from the way in which the recipient of his projections handles them. Projective identification is also manifest in the *scapegoating* process, discussed in the context of the psychodynamics observed in family therapy (Box, 1978), whereby one individual attacks in another, that which has been disowned within the self. (Waldron-Skinner, 1986, p. 268)

Normal projective identification forms the basis of empathy and it is a very good model to describe what goes on between the infant and the attuning mother and what goes wrong in the mother who is not attuned to her infant. It forms the basis of transference and countertransference interactions that are so important in treating severe mental illness. These have been described by Bion (1959), Gallwey (1985, 1992, 1996), Grotstein (1983), Ogden (1979), and Schore (2003a).

However, it must be remembered that, for projective identification to occur, there must be a conception of a container into which the projection can be sent. In other words, there must be an object which has depth so as to be able to contain the projection (Meltzer, 1975). Bion (1959) conceived of the idea of inherent preconceptions (e.g., a breast), which can be thought of as not only at one with nurture, but also as containing one's evacuations.

> There can be no projective identification into a vacuum.
> The translocation of self or aspects of the self into an object always
> presupposes a preconception of an object which is a container.
> An object must be located via primordial scanning, or explora-
> tion and represents a primitive mechanism of normal thinking.
> (Grotstein, 1983, p. 513)

At this juncture, it is important to differentiate between Bion's (1959)
conception of containment and the mirroring mother as denoted by
Winnicott (1956).

> Bion's "containment" is not so much an elastic or flexible impact
> upon a silent maternal object as it is the mother's capacity to inter-
> cept the infant's inchoate communication. Bion's conception is of
> an elaborate primary process that involves feeling, thinking, organ-
> ising, and acting. Silence would be the least part of it. (Grotstein,
> 1983, p. 134)

Projective identification is an object relationship that involves an extension of self into an object rather than a hurling of content into space
(Grotstein, 1983, p. 214). A point that Bion (1959) makes is the idea
that a "projective-identification-blocking mother" can have a severely
destructive impact on a child's development; that is, a mother or parent who cannot allow himself/herself to receive the child's projective
identification. According to Ogden, an essential part of normal development is the child's experience of his parents as people who can safely
and securely be relied upon to act as containers for his projective identification (Ogden, 1979, p. 365). Therefore, projective identification does
not exist where there is no interaction between projector and object.
According to Ogden:

> In terms of communication, projective identification is a means by
> which the infant can feel that he is understood by making his mother
> feel what he is feeling. The infant cannot describe this in words for
> the mother; instead he induces those feelings in her. In addition
> to serving as a mode of interpersonal communication, projective
> identification constitutes a primitive type of object relationship,
> a basic way of being with an object which is only partially separate
> psychologically. It is a transitional form of object relationship that

lies between the stage of the subjective object and that of true object relatedness. (Ogden, 1979, p. 363)

Winnicott rarely used the term projective identification in his writings, but his work revolved around the study of the role of the maternal projective identifications in early development and of the implications of that form of object relatedness, that is, his concepts of impingement and mirroring. The positive element in projective identification is expressed in Winnicott's transitional experiences (1971) and in the origin of play. Winnnicott had earlier described the state of heightened maternal receptivity that is seen in the mother of a newborn which he describes as primary maternal preoccupation:

> I do not believe it is possible to understand the functioning of the mother at the very beginning of the infant's life without seeing that she must be able to reach this state of heightened sensitivity, almost an illness, and then recover from it. Only if a mother is sensitized in the way I am describing can she feel herself into the infant's place, and so meet the infant's needs. (Winnicott, 1956, p. 302)

Hinshelwood discusses how "the critique of the concept of projective identification as too sophisticated is an important one and point to a significant and profound difference between theories of the earliest functions of the ego". It is true, Hinshelwood says, "that the ability to get *into* an object and control the way it feels and responds sounds very sophisticated", but, he questions, "Could such a phantasy exist at birth? The answer to this depends on what sort of object it is that the infant is relating to when he begins functioning" (Hinshelwood, 1989, p. 199).

Meissner (1980, p. 43) argues that Bion's theory of containers is a sloppy extension of the term, that "projective identification becomes a metaphor, translated loosely into the terms of container and contained, which applies to almost any form of relational or cognitional phenomenon in which the common notes of relation, containment or implication can be appealed to" (Meissner, 1980, cited in Hinshelwood, 1989, p. 201). Similarly, Meissner argued, "the significance Segal gives in symbolic equation (Segal, 1957) is equally unwarranted, and he mounts specific arguments to the effect that the concrete use of symbols which

Segal described is not necessarily a result of projective identification" (cited in Hinshelwood, 1989, p. 202).

This aspect of projective identification will be explored in great detail in the clinical examples, in this study, in relation to the underlying psychodynamics of psychopathology.

Ogden makes the important point that:

> The concept of projective identification can be considered entirely on its own merits and bears no essential relationship with Klein's theory. Therefore, the role of projective identification in the child's *positive* relationship with the mother can also be considered, as this involves a process where the projection of a much valued part of the self into another, is part of the process of normal development. (Ogden, 1979, p. 363)

### A psychoneurobiological model of projective identification

Schore suggests: "If Freud was describing (1912–1958) how the unconscious can act as a 'receptive organ', Klein's concept of projective identification attempts to model how an unconscious system acts as a 'transmitter', and how these transmissions will then influence the receptive functions of another unconscious mind." He goes on to say that "This clearly implies that unconscious systems interact with other unconscious systems, and that both receptive and expressive properties determine their communicative capacities" (Schore, 2003b, p. 59).

Schore (2003b) argues that other authors assert that projective identification involves the projection of *affects* associated with self and object representations (citing Adler & Rhine, 1992), and Ogden concluded that "In projective identification, the projector by means of actual interpersonal interactions with the 'recipient' unconsciously induces *feeling states* in the recipient that are congruent with the 'ejected feelings'" (Ogden, 1990, p. 79).

> Klein (1957) originally described projective identification as the projection of unwanted parts of the self into an important other, together with identification of that part with the other. This is usually interpreted to mean the projecting out, in a controlling way, of "bad" *negative* parts that could be dangerous to the self, into another person. (Schore, 2003a, p. 64)

The debate here concerns the specific nature of *what is projected in this primitive communication process*. Schore discusses how:

> It has been commonly accepted that Klein's sole emphasis was on the development of *phantasy* on unconscious cognitions generated within the infant's mind … this seems to be inconsistent with current developmental research revealing that the infant's states are less cognitively complex and more bodily based and sensori-affective. (2003a, p. 59)

A major conclusion of Schore's work from 1991 to 2003, is that "primitive mental states are much more than early appearing 'mental' or 'cognitive' states of mind that mediate psychological processes", and that "they are more precisely characterized as *psychobiological states*' (2003a, p. 59).

So what does this mean?

A developmental psychobiological perspective suggests that affective states are transacted within the mother–infant dyad and that this highly efficient system of somatically driven, fast-acting emotional communication is essentially non-verbal.

The clinical implications for exploring this approach are that this psychoneurobiological model of projective identification enhances our knowledge for clinical practice, about the state in which the therapist receives the projective identification, being identical to maternal receptivity. Therefore both clinical and developmental models of projective identification are now stressing the "critical role of the communication of internal affective states and processes, rather than cognitions and content" (Schore, 2003b, p. 60).

Schore (2003a) proposes that the time is right for a rapprochement between psychoanalysis and neurobiology, and that this integration can lead to a deeper understanding of clinical phenomena. This is especially true of projective identification, which has also been described (Sands, 1997, p. 653) as operating "in some mysterious way that we cannot begin to comprehend scientifically".

"Towards that end", Schore suggests, "current findings from studies of the neurobiology of emotional development are particularly relevant to projective identification, an early appearing process that *requires* a mutually *emotional* response" (Migone, 1995, cited in Schore, 2003b, p. 60; italics added).

An integration of current developmental studies of infant–mother emotional communications (Beebe & Lachmann, 2002), psychophysiological data on affective processing (Beebe, 2000), and neurobiological research (Schore, 1994–2003) on the essential role of the right brain in emotional communication, can offer us a deeper understanding of the mechanism of affective communications within projective identification.

These right-brain-to-right-brain communications embedded within the attachment bond represent what Bion (1959) called "links" and Gallwey (1996) has entitled "primary linking functioning" between mother and infant, and the assertion that "the mother's mind functions as a link describes the link provided by the *mother's right mind*" (Schore, 2003b, p. 61). "This rapidly expanding body of interdisciplinary studies can serve as a source pool for heuristic models of not only normal emotional development, but also of how disorganizing forces in the primary social environment can disturb maturational processes" (Schore, 2003b, p. 61).

Schore states that "the processes associated with projective identification are of vital importance for normal development as well as for abnormal object relations. But it was Bion (1962) who emphasized the central role of this mechanism in all early developmental phenomena" (Schore, 2003b, p. 64). Bion described that when mother and infant are adjusted to each other the infant behaves in such a way that projective identification is a "realistic" rather than a defensive phenomenon, and that "this is its normal condition and function. A conception of mother and infant adjusting to each other's communication describes a model of mutual reciprocal influence" (Schore, 2003b, p. 64).

Schore goes on to say that:

> In a secure attachment the caregiver contingently responds to the child's projective identifications. However, the insecurely attached child is often unable to influence affect-regulating responses because the other is not sufficiently attuned to the child's state and therefore unable to receive the infant's emotional communications. (Schore, 2003b, p. 66)

Psychoanalysis has long been intrigued yet baffled by the mechanisms of inter-subjective unconscious communication. Ogden called this "the analytic third", the "unique dialectic generated by or between the separate subjectivities of an analyst and analysand within the analytic setting" (Ogden, 1994, p. 64).

Bion (1977) suggested that therapeutic "containing" is required because the mother's capacity to contain the child's distressing emotions was insufficient, and they were therefore returned to the child little changed and difficult to integrate. Importantly, the mother herself could not provide a model for the child's containment of its own feelings. Therefore, a deeper apprehension of the developmental and therapeutic changes in the right-brain system that is centrally involved in the regulation of emotional states is therefore relevant to Klein's pioneering explorations in her concept of projective identification that are fundamentally concerned with the "regulation of emotions" (Schore, 2003b, p. 104).

However, as Gallwey discusses, "one of the difficulties with many psychotherapeutic models is that they are far too complex for general use or mask their lack of practical value with esoteric terminology which may, in fact, only restate the problem in another language" (Gallwey, 1985, p. 127). But I am even more convinced that further research on the impact of the environment on brain development will be both groundbreaking and important in integrating attachment theory and psychoanalytic theory and to incorporate neuroaffective knowledge into this integration.

# CHAPTER THREE

# Encapsulated containerlessness

This chapter explores the aetiology of the primitive defences that are used to cope with traumatic and overwhelming experiences when there has been a failure in the establishment of primary linking functioning (Gallwey, 1996). It sets the background against which to approach the clinical application of the Gallwey model. The example case study aims at understanding how destructive behaviour arises in some individuals as a result of their initial violent and unevenly based struggle with the psychological environment into which they were born.

According to Gallwey:

> When the early environment is not only inadequate in its containing functions but frankly retaliatory, so that infantile demands and distress are reacted against with physical abuse, abandonment or collapse, then early projective identification fails both as a defence and a link, and a particular type of malfunction results which differs from both psychotic and neurotic equivalents. The basis of this is not the distortion or fragmentation of containment but *the lack of a container altogether*, with a failure in the functions that spring from it. The result is proliferating turmoil and anxiety without the

capacity to use projective identification effectively as a first line of defence to lessen psychic stress. (Gallwey, 1991, p. 362).

This will be the first extended discussion of Gallwey's theory, and addresses Gallwey's extension of the work of Klein (1946, 1957), Bion (1962), and Winnicott (1984) and his divergence from their thinking.

Although the concept of the death instinct in relation to envy is a theme running throughout the thesis, I will discuss it here in terms of its relevance to what Gallwey describes as "encapsulated containerlessness" (Gallwey, 1991, p. 377).

The advantages of employing the model developed by Gallwey are that it is based on existing theories of attachment which were put forward by the object relations theorists of the British School of Psychoanalysis; it also provides a working model which can be applied to the clinical material I will present throughout this study. One of the aims of the study is developing the work of Gallwey, as his model has not been widely used outside the field of forensic psychiatry and psychotherapy.

## The Gallwey model

From clinical studies, Gallwey identified basic linking functions which are, he suggested, present innately both in the infant and in the nurturing environment as biological real requirements. (The nurturing environment, although it will include paternal functions, are mainly maternal.) The infant's dependency needs are represented by specific serial requirements of attachment to the mother and these specific requirements have to be reflected by parallel ones in the mother herself. Successful reciprocal linking activity will establish a knowledge of an independent self in a safe dependent relationship with a caring object. This is the vital concept. The process by which this state is achieved, or striven for, Gallwey calls primary identification.

## Primary identification

Within Gallwey's model of development, three vital functions have to operate sequentially and reciprocally between the infant and the nurturing environment for the primary identification of the dependent self and dependable other to be conceptualised. He termed these functions prospective linking, holding on, and substantive linking.

## Prospective linking

This first function can be seen behaviourally in early infancy when babies turn their heads searching for the breast and in mothers who become alert and wakeful, even from a deep sleep, at the first stirrings of the child wanting to be held and fed long before it begins crying. Prospective functions on the infant's side are connected with searching for the object of need, and on the nurturing mother's side by alertness to these needs. There is continuity here with Winnicott's "primary maternal preoccupation" (1956, p. 300).

Prospective linking is importantly connected with sight and sound and, when successful, results in a self that is optimistic, explorative, curious, and alert. It provides a sense of trust in existence, a sense of potency, a sense of being in a safe place, and a belief that home can be located. (The ability to conceptualise the absent object is a consequence of having first been able to find it.)

Sight, hearing, and smell are all utilised in prospective functions and when their realisation is faulty, then the conceptualisations that are eventually made will be marked by fear, anger, suspicion, and despair. Trust, optimism, and potency will be absent. The inability to conceptualise the absent object will, at its worst, result in a basic confusion of identity, or if separateness is achieved, then the ability to tolerate absence will be very reduced. A pessimistic voyeurism replaces hopeful searching, and the fear of evil eyes, of spying and being spied upon, dominates a world in which the location of safety is never clear.

## Holding on

In the infant, the second linking function is represented by oral grasping and sucking of the nipple, by the grasp reflex and behaviour such as holding out both arms to be lifted and held. In the mother and father, it is reflected in the need to pick up and hold the baby and, of course, to place the nipple or teat in the mouth.

The instinctual behaviour of infants in grasping with the hands and mouth and the complementary need in mothers to hold and be held by the infant results in a sense of boundary—the psychic as well as physical skin, the importance of which Esther Bick (1968) stressed in her work with psychotic patients. It helps to establish the sense of separateness, which prospective function presages, and confirms the optimism which prospective activity has, by defining the self and its boundaries and confirming the reality of the dependable object.

Good experiences in this domain will result in a sense of being well contained by the object and being well contained in one's own skin. Shape, size, a sense of proportion, and the affirmation of difference are conceptualised. The conditions for the logical connectives of conjunction and disjunction are laid down, as well as the capacity for attention, concentration, and the belief in the existence of a choice.

Clearly, when holding on is faulty, these positive qualities are lost. The body image suffers in direct proportion to the severity of the deprivation. There is a lack of belief in the coherence of the self which either feels fragmented or trapped within another object. A fear of contact and an inability to contain emotions, together with an excessive fear of falling to pieces will occur. Dysmorphophobias, inability to tolerate boundaries, claustrophobic entrapment, and confusion with a cold mechanical cruel object are the most serious outcomes. The rage and fear connected with a poverty in holding on functions can lead to a need to break and enter objects psychologically or actually, with phantasies of violent penetration or their equivalents in such criminal behaviour as rape, burglary, and violent assault.

## Substantive linking

The final linking function in Gallwey's series involves the exchange of warmth, of love, and nourishment, both physical and emotional. It results in a realisation of the self and the object as full of goodness, and dependency as a blissful, healthy exchange of good things. Both the reduction in anxiety and the sense of fulfilment that substantive linking brings to both parties confirm and re-confirm at each experience the most profound sense of goodness in interdependent relating and the uniqueness of oneself and others. Belief in the achievement of reward, of happiness, of creative outcome, and the specificity of cause and effect are achieved and will make possible the logical connectives of material implication and material equivalence when the capacity for abstract thought is acquired.

Disruption in this stage will result in a belief in the badness and valuelessness of the self and others or, at worst, a complete failure in the sense of humanity. The awful feelings of emptiness and impoverishment that lie behind the manic defences of so many forensic patients often mean that they cannot value their own or others' lives. A faulty realisation of the substantive function will result in problems connected with a lack of depth in emotion or an overwhelming sense of being full of hate and fear. More serious defects are self-destructiveness, confusion with an empty object, or an inability to find a sense of meaning other than being in a black hole. The killing and harming of others often reflects the severe failure of substantive experiences. This behavioural expression of destructive envy and the compulsion to destroy anything that represents vitality and life often reflects a severe failure of substantive experiences, and is an explanation of how destructive envy is formulated.

As the word "linking" refers to a link that is made between two people, in this context it refers to a more primitive form of self in relation to other.

The complete failure in the whole series of linking functions will result in a primitive autism. The capacity to think will be *profoundly* affected and show itself through difficulties in learning to talk, to read or to write (Daniels, 1974; Farber, 1976, pp. 43–44; Winnicott, 1974, p. 107). The popular label of dyslexia includes many whose difficulties are due to failure in primary linking. Such thought disorders spring from the failed or faulty achievement of primary separateness and are therefore more intractable than similar ones that are the outcome of the obliteration of separateness due to secondary narcissistic confusion between self and object (Hobson, 2002, pp. 150–181). An envy-induced negativity especially interferes with the capacity to receive and return love. This has a disastrous effect on learning. Berke (1985, pp. 177–178) describes how learning difficulties, whether in children or adults, follow when ridicule, rage, and fear, represented by a blank, impenetrable negativity, replace admiration and emulation.

An autistic child will result if the nurturing environment continues to fail for long enough; more commonly, however, the mother will begin to function better, perhaps after a period of postnatal depression or early difficulties, and then primary linking can begin. However, if the delay has been sufficiently prolonged, then the primary autistic state of mind will be split from the rest of the ego, directly the self has been conceptualised by the arrival of healthier linking functions.

## From primary to secondary phantasy

When the development progresses reasonably well, then at a very early state in neo-natal life, an inchoate concept of the self will be achieved in a safe, dependent relationship with a nurturing object, and this irreducible dual concept (the primary identifications) will form the basis of all ego functioning and later development. Gallwey (1996) describes this as being equivalent to the central ego of Fairbairn (1952), and it represents the sort of early integration that Klein mentioned in her later work (1963). For Gallwey, once this essentially dual object has been successfully conceptualised from what can be described as primary phantasies (*the instinctual preconceptions*), then the way is open for the development of secondary phantasies that will give rise to imagination and thinking and the provision of mental buffers against stress.

Secondary phantasies are the outcome of the separateness to which the self is heir, once the primary identifications of self and other have been achieved. The difference between the self and the dependent object—the psychological and physical gap—will be a primitive perception. It has two aspects: a spatio-temporal one in which absence impinges, and a functional one of differences in need. Secondary phantasy forms the psychological bridge that keeps the self in touch with the object internally, both during its absence and during the alternations of attachment. Secondary phantasies will begin as simple memories and anticipations. Their emotional content will be a reflection of the way the primary identifications were acquired, complicated by the emotional experience of the spatio-temporal and functional gaps. This in turn will determine the extent to which the realities of experience will be altered by secondary phantasies to maintain comfort and ultimately avoid the anxiety of threat to the ego (Gallwey, 1996, pp. 160–170).

Failure to realise the dual primary concept of self and object necessary for the definition of separateness, or primary identifications that are so faulty that secondary phantasy fails, occasionally and habitually, to maintain the dependent link between the self and the dependent objects, will result in insanity or behaviour unmodified by secondary phantasy (Gallwey, 1996, pp. 160–170).

In subsequent chapters—Shame and Envy, Self Envy, Perverse Relationships, and Womb Envy—I have demonstrated how a failure in the achievement of these early stages of personality development can be expressed behaviourally as a symptom, using the Gallwey model of development.

### Autistic entrapment

If there is a profound failure in the realisation of the primary conceptions, then the child self will remain trapped inside an unidentified object and no proper realisation of the self or dependent object can come about. The self is not only lacking in awareness of its own identity but has no capacity to develop secondary phantasies, and cannot therefore use defences to manage fear and frustration; cannot, for instance, split or use projective identification and will remain trapped in an addiction to near-death (Gallwey, 1992; Joseph, 1982), remaining unable to play, explore the world, develop, or properly communicate. Within this autistic domain there will be an increasing despair and helplessness (Gallwey, 1996, pp. 160–170).

However, when the failures are less prolonged and extensive, then autistic elements derived from faulty concepts, which cannot be integrated into the ego, remain as highly anxiety-provoking impenetrable defects in ego structure. Symbol formation is absent, so autistic elements cannot be incorporated into secondary phantasy and are not dreamable or thinkable. If they do appear in dreams or in phantasy they are often experienced as black infestations or a fierce feeling of intense anxiety, resulting in what Bion calls "nameless dread" (Bion, 1962, p. 116). They manifest as night terrors, rather than nightmares. For example, a person will wake up screaming or in a very agitated state (Gallwey, 1996, pp. 160–170).

"Nameless dread" is a term originally employed by Karin Stephen in her paper "Aggression in Early Childhood" (1941) to describe the intense anxiety in children during infancy. Bion elaborated on this term to describe a state of meaningless fear that evolves in the context of an infant with a mother incapable of "reverie", a concept that derives from Bion's theory of "containing" (1962, p. 116).

> Bion describes this as a projective-identification-rejecting-object, who is felt to strip meaning from the experience and the baby: he

> therefore reintrojects, not a fear of dying made tolerable, but a
> nameless dread. With repeated recurrence of this projective failure,
> an internal object is formed through introjection on the same lines;
> this object destroys meaning and leaves the subject in a mysterious
> meaningless world. (Hinshelwood, 1989, p. 349)

An autistic domain and autistic elements need to be distinguished from each other, since the latter derive from the fragmentation of achieved primary objects, whereas the former result from primary failure and are therefore more anterior and more malignant.

Autistic elements will always pose a threat to the ego, but the degree of potential destabilisation will depend upon the quantity and content of the autistic distress and the effectiveness of the ego defences against anxiety.

Gallwey became increasingly interested in the discovery of such areas of encapsulated primitive autism which make an individual vulnerable to catastrophe, both psychologically and behaviourally, in individuals who may otherwise appear normal. The failure of the encapsulation will result in violent catastrophic behaviour if the ego is overwhelmed by the autistic anxiety. If the more healthy ego can preserve secondary phantasy, then a psychotic state of mind with progressive splitting and projective identification, or flights into grandiose manic phantasy, will result. The sudden eruption of homicidal violence in some depressive states, or the escalation of sadism or mutilatory behaviour in previously fairly passive sexual deviants are two examples of the eruption of encapsulated areas of primary autism (Gallwey, 1996, pp. 160–170).

## Anxiety, hatred, and the roots of envy

The fear and violence of states of mind stemming from a lack of established primary linking functions represent the ultimate anxiety that lies at the root of all psychopathology, namely that the self will not come properly alive or, secondary to that, will fail to sustain itself as an independent entity in a safe internal relationship with a life-sustaining object. Gallwey examines the fear of death as the ultimate anxiety, causing both severe psychopathology and violent destructive behaviour, but he does not hold the view that this primitive anxiety is the *basis* for the death drive. He disputes the death drive's clinical relevance as such and believes that the instinct of self-preservation represented by the "fight or flight" response, common to most animals has, in humans, a mental representation that is central to the development of psychopathology of all kinds, including psychosis and violent behaviour (Gallwey, 1996).

There are two sources of "symbolic" death, resulting from the failure in early linking which lead to the primary anxiety of death. The first is failure on the part of the environment, and the second is weakness in the instinct for attachment in the self due to some deficit in dependent functions, which Gallwey (1996) believes is environmentally induced. The re-enactment of these two sources of failure can be expressed in suicidal attempts, which represent a symbolic death, a behavioural expression of how envy can be used as a defence representing a breakdown in symbolic functioning. However, from this existential viewpoint suicide can be understood as a desperate attempt to escape from being imprisoned in a false existence, where the core self is felt to be dead, a view expressed by Winnicott (Winnicott et al., 1989, p. 93). This indicates that a more traumatic effect has taken form, in which the infant develops a sense of "non-existence" as a result of an experience with an emotionally absent mother, that is, when the organism develops a sense of its not being held or contained in the mother's mind.

In such circumstances, envy can be used as a defence not only to enhance and maintain a sense of grievance for what has been lost but also to evade acknowledging the acute pain and sense of loss, sometimes masking a fear of psychic collapse (Morrison, 1989). Spillius discusses how these defences would develop as a result of the individual realising that one wants a good object, but really feels that one does not have or has not had it. "Feeling perpetual grievance and blame, however miserable, is less painful than mourning the loss of the relationship one wishes one had had" (Spillius, 1993, p. 1204). Winnicott described the adult patient's fear of breakdown as representing an original breakdown and failure of defences in infancy, following which new defences were organised constituting the patient's illness pattern or abnormal personality. He regarded adult psychopathy as uncured delinquency that he believed was the result of early childhood deprivation and environmental failure, most importantly inadequate maternal care (Winnicott, 1974).

The effects on secondary phantasy of varying degrees of failure in the reciprocal linking functions result from deficits in primary identification and produce a whole range of aberrations in secondary phantasies. Gallwey describes this further:

> In therapeutic work, both with offenders and non-offenders, it is essential to be on the lookout for phantasies which indicate problems in specific linking functions and to try to unravel them accordingly. Connections between criminal destructive behaviour and historical trauma can then be discovered in the transference in some detail by keeping in mind this process of early linking, of discovery of the self and the good object and the consequences of the failure of these early functions of attachment. (Gallwey, 1995, p. 9)

Developmental psychopathology can certainly be understood in no small measure by the concept of a failure in attachment—that is, failure, whether by trauma or neglect or other environmental influences— deeply rooted in one or another form of a neurobiologically induced disorder of regulation, as described by Schore (1991).

Understanding the effects of partial failure of primary linking also provides useful guidance in the difference between psychosis and delinquently criminal behaviour. Gallwey (1991) defines the psychological factors that help a person to understand the nature of stress and all those behavioural, emotional, and cognitive functions that are driven by the primary attachment instincts as psychopoesis. (Murray Cox writes of *poiesis* (Cox & Theilgaard, 1987, p. 36)—with a different spelling—as a process in which something is called into existence that was not there before, but this bears no relation to Gallwey's term.) Psychopoesis combined with pseudo-genesis (Gallwey's term for the instinctive capacity to create a personal artificial rearrangement of reality) falls along a continuum of human mental activity. As long as pseudo-genesis has a strong link with psychopoesis, then the products of pseudo-genesis are broadly creative. When the link is lost then psychotic-level mental activity takes over (Gallwey, 1991, pp. 370–373).

Psychotic states arise from a failure in the link of pseudo-genesis with psychopoetic realities, resulting in a flight of phantasy into omnipotence and withdrawal from rational interaction with the external world. Criminal delinquent activity, on the other hand, arises *inter alia* from a deficit in pseudo-genesis as a mental activity. Because delinquent individuals cannot alter the impact of experience intra-psychically, including deprivation of substantive experience, they attempt to alter the external world directly in an attempt to assuage their turmoil. Psychotic pseudo-genesis is free floating and excessive, whereas the delinquent has a poverty of pseudo-genesis and an excess of negative attachment experiences. Delinquents are very poorly equipped to manage the impact of the external world, whereas psychotics are overwhelmed with phantasy untethered to safe internal objects of attachment (Gallwey, 1991, pp. 359–381).

This distinction is not true of all criminals and there is a class of individuals who combine omnipotent destructive narcissistic phantasy with internal attachment to ruthless objects and are coldly capable of tyrannical leadership into tyranny (Gallwey, 2008).

If one considers the prolonged and crippling effect of severe post-traumatic stress disorder in adults, then one can begin to understand much more convincingly why the psychopathology connected with early life-threatening experiences is so intractable. Such life-threatening experiences need not be violent or actively abusive, although indeed they may be, but simply threaten the infant's endeavours to establish itself in its own life so that the closeness of death will invade the inchoate self before it has even developed a capacity to buffer such trauma by using its own imagination.

> It is only recently that the effects of life-threatening experiences in adults have been taken seriously and seen as capable of leading to mental disorder. For a long time, post-traumatic stress disorder had been equated with some kind of moral weakness. The fear that universally results from severe life-threatening or cruel experiences can give us some picture of what the early self must be up against when encountering neglect, abuse or outright violence within an environment from which it is entirely unable to escape, and in which its desperate need for caring attachment can be so appallingly denied. (Gallwey, 1995, p. 11)

In behavioural disorders, when an individual has confidence in their omnipotence/grandiosity, as in psychosis, they don't have to do anything to support their delusions by manipulating the environment because they construct the world they want on the basis of delusional systems. In behavioural disorders, when the individual does strange things to the environment, such as in sexually perverse violence, it is more likely than not that their confidence in their hallucinatory world is incomplete, because in order to tell themselves that "such-and-such" is the case, they actually have to make it happen, in the external world, with the act of manipulating the environment, projecting their feelings of self into another person. This is very often the case in sadistic and perverse sexual behaviour. For example, many of the individuals assessed by forensic workers in terms of their suitability to benefit from psychotherapeutic treatment do not have the capacity for secondary phantasies or do not have an internal repertoire of them (Gallwey, 2003).

Leslie Sohn has suggested that some extremely dangerous and violent patients may be understood partially in relation to their experience of loss. He describes how their condition may be the result of a developmental history punctuated by a profound series of losses and a failure in the development in the capacity for symbolisation. For such patients, "loss has been totally and psychotically denied", resulting in a psychological condition "in which total intolerance for any depressive experience leads to a need to act out physically" (Sohn, 1997, cited in Ruszczynski & Morgan, 2007, p. 40).

## Comparing Gallwey with Winnicott and others

### Comparing and contrasting Gallwey and Winnicott

Gallwey describes Winnicott's model of the relationship between neurosis and delinquency as differing from his own model as follows:

> Winnicott's writings on delinquency are an important source for those wanting to develop psychotherapeutic understanding of the "antisocial tendency" as he calls it. However, his theory that delinquent acts imply hope through a delayed testing out of the environment that has failed the individual at the appropriate age because of parental insufficiency (Winnicott 1984), is in a sense too benign. Not only does his theory fail to address fundamental psychic disabilities against learning in persistent delinquents, but it also takes insufficient account of purely destructive, sadistic and revengeful feelings in much criminal behaviour. (Gallwey, 1991, pp. 360–361)

Winnicott had a different perspective from Gallwey in that "Winnicott's optimism has to be set against the fact that much adult bad behaviour derives from severely entrenched psychopathology, which results in poor therapeutic response by offenders; socially harmful, destructive or dangerous behaviour is very resistant to psychotherapy of all kinds" (Gallwey, 1991, p. 361).

Gallwey, working within the prison population, has much more experience as a forensic psychiatrist than Winnicott, with his pediatric background, so there are institutional differences as well as theoretical differences. Gallwey's views are that:

> when individuals have a *persistent* destructive attitude, then a major pre-requisite for engagement in any form of psychotherapy—positive motivation—is simply not present, and in the absence of a thera-peutic alliance, containment is probably all that can be achieved. Furthermore, when individuals have been abused, humiliated and hurt in their formative years, it is understandable that they may live out revengeful feelings against others, particularly those asso-ciated with their bad experiences. Revenge is a powerful and com-monly occurring cause of persistent bad behaviour and can be used as a focus for a therapeutic approach to severe offenders. (Gallwey, 1991, p. 360)

In discussing the implications for psychotherapeutic treatment with offenders, Gallwey says:

> Where individuals suffer from *episodic* bad behaviour, even though, in their better phases, they may be able to engage positively with therapeutic work, the episodes of bad behaviour are usually char-acterized by loss of emotional contact with themselves. As a result anything they may have learned in treatment disappears at the moment when they live out their psychopathology. (1991, p. 361)

Winnicott's 1984 theory of deprivation and delinquency fails to take into account the fact that these early experiences of failure in the mater-nal holding environment can produce severely entrenched psychopa-thology which, when acted out on the environment, are an attempt to restore psychic equilibrium. This is justified by the environment being treated as if it were part of the individual's psychic property and to avoid fragmentation of the self.

This latter phenomenon was first described by Freud (1914c) in his theory on acting out. Gallwey developed Freud's theory further by providing a much sounder understanding as to why an individual resorts to criminality rather than psychoses. His belief is that:

> In order to avoid conscious awareness of conflict, some individuals avoid contact with difficult feelings through unthinking action. Freud saw thought as an experimental form of action, but thinking requires management of the often conflicted and turbulent emotions which underlie it. Management of emotional stress, whether it be from frustration of instinctual needs or the imposition of psychological trauma, has more recently been explored in terms of very primitive defences against such turbulence. (Gallwey, 1991, p. 361)

## Gallwey and Klein and the post-Kleinians

In both the theories of Fairbairn (1940) on functional and structural divisions within the self and of Klein (1946, Chapters 1 and 13), projective mechanisms combined with splitting are held to be a central defence mechanism. Both theories hold that, as a reaction to emotional stress in infancy and early childhood, the integrity of the self is fundamentally altered to maintain psychic equilibrium. Gallwey's stance, as we have seen, is not that the self's integrity is altered or distorted, but that it lacks containment altogether.

Klein's position was more complex for, although she postulates (1957) that the main source of anxiety is a fear of aggression and annihilation of the ego from within, this aggression is essentially linked with frustration, separation anxiety and, crucially, unconscious envy. Separation anxiety must realistically be connected with the fear of death within the individual, since, particularly at early stages of development, the presence of the mother to feed and protect the infant is essential for its survival. The psychic consequence of this reality is peculiarly absent in the writings of psychoanalysts, with the exception of Bowlby (1958), who connected anxiety primarily with over-long separation and deprivation. He failed, however, to develop a satisfactory psychotherapeutic working model. His ideas were based on extensive observations of children's behaviour (Gallwey, 1996).

Gallwey's relation to the post-Kleinian body of work is that he developed his model by incorporating Bion's 1959 views on linking both his concept of containment and his theories on thinking. This was relevant to those individuals Gallwey encountered clinically, in the field of forensic psychiatry and psychotherapy, who were both traumatised and very envious and who appeared to make attacks on their own linking functions as well as those of their object. It was from these observations that Gallwey postulated that, rather than envy being constitutional, as Klein saw it, it emerged when prospective linking failed to establish, resulting in the individual constantly needing to aim his or her attack on both the process and the object.

The linking functions described by Gallwey (1996) are derived in Kleinian (1946, 1957) theory from an introjective identification of the good object. Bion (1959) saw the linking functions of the primitive self as due to a successful introjective identification with the primitive breast or penis. After many years of clinical experience, Gallwey (1995) came to reject this point of view since, for him, it failed to explain how introjective identification, if it is the primary form of linking, can get started in the first place.

Gallwey differs from Winnicott in that he found it unsatisfactory to postulate omnipotent phantasy as a basis for the development of mental health and ego integration. For Gallwey, omnipotent phantasy is a symptom of alienation and the dissociation of phantasy from any contact with the external world (Gallwey, 1996). This is based on the fact that omnipotence and creation are extremely sophisticated concepts to apply to the experience of the infant. This is in line with Guntrip (1968) and Fairbairn (1952), who do not think that they do more than suggest a useful way of thinking about something that we cannot get direct evidence about.

> It is true that there are later clinical facts to the usefulness of these concepts, but they are already contaminated by later and more developed experiences in an ego that has already become split and also oscillates between defensive identifications and growing differentiations with regard to its objects. (Guntrip, 1968, p. 240)

In terms of ego relatedness, Gallwey's 1995 contention seems to be that, owing to the extreme weakness and dependence of the infant at birth, *fear* is bound to develop as the earliest anxiety and remains always the deepest insecurity. This fear is not of a hypothetical death instinct, or destructive instinct working within, but the fear of death coming from the external environment as a result of a crucial lack of the parent's instincts of response to the infant's needs and are the counterpart of the primary instincts which form the basis of the Gallwey model (1996).

Prospective activity—that is, searching for the object of need—is clearly an innate drive which develops into complex learned patterns of behaviour in the initiation of dependent and interdependent activity. It represents a specific form of instinctual linking activity which has a mental representation in primary identification. Primary identification reflects the discovery of the self, and if the mechanism is dependent on itself for its own initial functioning, then it would never become established.

Primary identification from this standpoint reflects Kohut's work (1971, 1977) on the discovery of the self. However, in Gallwey's model, it also establishes a conceptual internal duality of self and other, a representation of a self in a dependent relationship with a dependable separate object. The link between the two is experienced as essential and vital. It forms the basis for love and beauty. When it is threatened, then the most intense anxiety of death from within is the result.

Successfully establishing and incorporating a primary identification of self and object lays the foundation for a capacity to develop a repertoire of symbols that combine as secondary phantasies. These reinforce independence by developing links with the external world but carry, in health, the vital internal dependent link. They lead eventually to the capacity for conscious imagination and for cognitive thinking.

In her views on symbol formation, Hanna Segal (1957) points out that symbols, which form the basis for thinking and imagination, construct a link between the self and the object, so that separation is a *sine qua non* for their formation. She suggests that the obliteration of the difference between self and other caused by projective identification results in a failure in normal symbol formation and produces concrete symbolic equivalents of a kind found in psychotic thinking.

This view is incompatible with Bion's theories on the development of thinking (1957), which rely on a form of projective identification in which the infant utilises the mother's capacity for managing anxiety and for thinking in the absence of its own equivalent capacity. The individual who has not had the experience of maternal "reverie", has not been "contained" by projecting the anxiety in order to have it modified by the mother.

Segal (1993) suggests that destructive narcissism and hostile envy may actually function like two sides of the same coin, where destructive envy is perceived as a secondary phenomenon, operating from within the realm of despair. This is contradicted, however, by way of a tie Segal maintains between this form of envy and the idea of a primary death instinct:

> Using an autobiographical story, *Martin Eden* by Jack London, Segal (1966) also attempts to demonstrate the existence of a death instinct that acts to overpower the will to live. However, this is to take the circumstances out of context, for the complete story makes it clear that the hero's wish to die stems from his inability to bear the loss of a current "object" when his love affair breaks up. (Alexander, 1997, p. 426)

Bion's theories on projective identification (1959, 1962) are a logical extension of Klein's idea (1946) that introjective identification forms the basis for early ego coherence. Both projective and introjective identification are, of course, omnipotent phantasies, and in following Segal (1957), the core of Gallwey's argument is that it is not possible to have a secondary phantasy, omnipotent or otherwise, until the self has been discovered and conceptualised as a separate entity, in the same way that Winnicott has described in his work on the maternal holding environment (1965).

Gallwey holds very similar views to Kernberg on projective identification. For example, Kernberg states that if projective identification implies that the subject has the capacity to differentiate self from non-self, it can be assumed that the subject must have reached a certain level of development before projective identification is operational:

> I assume that there are two conditions that must be fulfilled. Insofar as projective identification implies a phantasy—and in order to phantasize we have to assume the capacity for having one element stand for another and be manipulated in the direction of the desired goal—then the capacity for symbolization must be present. And insofar as the wish is to expel onto another what is felt as undesirable, there must exist a capacity for awareness not only of the difference between the self and the other but also of how one feels, of one's subjective state. Only when we can recognize a particular subjective state as undesirable in *comparison* to other subjective states, does it make sense to attempt to get rid of it by expulsion. (Kernberg, 1992, pp. 161–162)

Gallwey examined the differing and contradictory views on projective identification in detail as it seemed to him that the enormous importance of projective identification as a core pathology in so much mental ill-health has been considerably weakened by its use as an essential mechanism for the development of healthy functions, so that the distinction between pathological and non-pathological states of mind has become very blurred. In fact, because of this, I have found it more satisfactory in practice to adopt Gallwey's 1996 model of mental health, which does not rely on omnipotent phantasy and which does justice to the importance of human interdependency on the one hand, and the features of adaptability and inventiveness on the other.

## Case study: failure in primary linking functions

Perhaps the most salient aspects of Gallwey's work lie in its clinical application, and in order to demonstrate the usefulness of the Gallwey model I will describe my work with Sally. Sally's case history illustrates Gallwey's theoretical model of encapsulated autism, the pathology deriving from two layers: a severe primary pathology which comes from a failure in primary linking functions and a whole string of secondary psychopathologies which derive from the comparative failure in the linking functions. Gallwey's 1995 hypothesis is that *prior* to the very first linking process there is a more primitive state, where not even these primitive linking functions can be employed in order to manage destructiveness.

It is my understanding that the matrix of this woman's psychopathology is in her early background history, and that this is an example of the underlying psychodynamics involved in encapsulated containerlessness. However, it was not until Sally had been in treatment with me for some years that developments led me first to perceive the existence and comprehend something of the nature of an encapsulated area of primary autism.

## Sally

At the time of her treatment, Sally was thirty-five years old and a nursery nurse. Sally's mother was schizophrenic and when she was pregnant with Sally she tried to abort her (this was in the early 1960s, before abortion was legal in the UK). At this time, psychiatrists held the view that schizophrenia was genetically inherited, and clinical decisions would have been based on such theories. However, her Catholic priest assured Sally's mother that she would not necessarily pass on her schizophrenia, and she gave birth to her daughter. Several months later, the mother had a psychotic breakdown. She took a massive dose of Amitriptyline, and then proceeded to breastfeed her baby. She collapsed, was taken to hospital, had her stomach pumped and survived. Baby Sally was cared for by her (also schizophrenic) maternal grandmother, until her mother recovered from her breakdown.

Seven years later, a second child, Tracey, was born into this family. Overall, Tracey was apparently a much-wanted and a loved child, in comparison to Sally. When Sally was twenty-three years old, she had a breast-reduction operation for cosmetic reasons. When she was twenty-six, she had herself sterilised.

I first met Sally many years after these early decisive events in her life when, as nursery teacher in charge of a pre-school kindergarten for children from deprived backgrounds, she asked for a referral for counselling after two of the mothers of the children in her care committed suicide in the same week.

Dr K, the consultant psychiatrist on duty when Sally made her request, was covering for a colleague who was ill. For many years, he had been head of an adolescent unit in a psychiatric hospital which housed young patients who had suffered a psychotic breakdown, some as a result of the use and abuse of drugs. It was here that Sally's mother had had her sectioned when she was 16 years old, after Sally had taken a massive overdose of drugs, and she had become an in-patient on Dr K's ward for 10 months. Sally's maternal grandmother was, by then, an in-patient on the acute ward in the same hospital, and was also a patient of Dr K. The grandmother starved herself to death during the time that Sally was hospitalised in the adolescent unit.

On the day of the referral, Sally saw Dr K but fled the hospital. She later telephoned, insisting she should be assessed by a female worker. I was asked to see her and after the assessment, Dr K told me an extraordinary story about the events leading to her hospitalisation as an adolescent.

When Sally was 13 years old, she was in charge one day of her seven-year-old sister during a family holiday at the seaside. The two daughters were on a pedalo boat, and were quite far out from the shore. The younger sister, who could not swim very well, had fallen off the back of the boat as Sally pedalled it. Instead of pulling her sister out of the water, she pedalled furiously away from her. She then had second thoughts, swam back and managed to put her little sister back into the boat. The younger girl was resuscitated on the beach. The little sister and the grandmother always held the view that Sally pushed her sister off the boat; this remained a preoccupation of the grandmother's, which Dr K remembered very well. It was also the mother's justification for having her daughter sectioned under the Mental Health Act when, at the age of 16, she tried to take her own life. The incident about the alleged attempt to drown her sister was, in fact, eventually disclosed during her psychotherapy.

Sally's ongoing disturbance gradually unfolded during her treatment. Of importance are the psychodynamics underlying the condition of an encapsulated area of autism, and I will describe these in more detail, by giving examples both of certain external events in her life which triggered her encapsulated murderousness, and of the way this evidenced itself during her treatment with me, certainly in terms of the transference and countertransference.

Four major events covered by the therapy identified the external stresses which led to extraordinary reactions by Sally. The process itself highlights the disproportionate nature of those reactions.

### The first event

This occurred during the second year of Sally's treatment, just before Christmas. I had an eye infection, which did not, as far as I can remember, show very much. All that altered was the time of her therapy session, when I asked her if she would mind changing, to which she genially agreed. However, the next day, I had a telephone call from a very worried medical receptionist who knew Sally well, as she often parked her camper van in the hospital grounds for days on end. Sally had left a message for me: whatever I did, I must not use the eye-drops in the cupboard of the staff ladies' toilet, which Sally had broken into. She had put bleach into them. She asked the secretary to put them in the dustbin immediately. I was startled by her acting out, and very concerned that I could well have used the "eye drops", as they were, in fact, my contact lens cleaning solution. I made the interpretation to her that she was feeling very destructive towards me, possibly because there was a Christmas break coming up. In addition, "I had dropped her" to go to the optician; I had failed to notice how distressed she was and would be when she lost my insight into her over the break. She was making an (envious) attack on the means of my perception of her: my eyes.

As Sally rarely made eye contact with me, I did not think she was using, in Kleinian language, projective identification. Nor had her initial reaction to my changing the session time given any indication that such a destructive retaliation would follow. When I discussed this with her, by simply asking her, "I wonder why you felt you had to do that?", there was a peculiar amnesic dissociative reaction to my comment and her response was a dismissive remark. She shrugged and said, "It just *happened*, I don't know why."

This made me realise that she was perhaps not aware of the breakdown of the walls of her encapsulation, at a stressful time such as the imminent family Christmas gathering, and how she was attacking my prospective activity with my own babies/children. Perhaps this was why the violence had erupted, as a result of her only being able to resort to *action*. She did not have the capacity to use projective identification, and she appeared almost to wonder what on earth I was getting upset about.

I believe this was the beginning of my understanding that the patient's extreme reactions were provoked by a fairly ordinary everyday event: a change of appointment. I believe, also, that this was the beginning of my understanding of encapsulated murderousness, and of what the implications are for treating a "delinquent" patient with this area of primary autism, a condition which stemmed from a failure in the early primary linking functions described by Gallwey (1996). Sally was left without a picture, or a symbol of herself, in relation to a life-sustaining object. Separation and frustration were the triggers for action, indicating a disturbance of symbolic functioning.

## The second event

Shortly before an analytical break, I had a message on my answering machine from a woman who claimed to be Sally's housemate, the woman she had been in a long-term relationship with and with whom she fostered children for short-term respite care. The message was as follows: "I am very sorry to leave this news but Sally is no longer with us." My anxiety, of course, escalated, and I was very concerned that she might have killed herself, as she had said many times in the last session before a holiday break, that she "might as well get it over with".

It was only by pure coincidence that I discovered this not to be the case. She was alive and well, as a colleague from work had spotted her chatting away with a friend in a shopping centre. All attempts by me to make sense of this in the next sessions were responded to coldly, as if any responsibility she had had for leaving such a distressing message, or impersonating her housemate, had nothing to do with the person present in the room.

By this time, I had begun slowly to understand when she was likely either to attempt to take her own life or to be threatened by the lure of attachment to what she described as the "black hole": the absence of symbol formation, which was the only image she regularly described during the times I was not available for her, such as holiday breaks. Her inability to conceptualise the absent object was a consequence of not being able to find it in the first place. It was an absence of the development of a psychic primary skin, as described by Bick (1968), therefore the inability to form a "second skin", or Gallwey's "secondary phantasies".

The third event

After a fairly positive phase of her treatment, Sally and her partner took in an adolescent girl, Laura, on a temporary basis. Laura was between foster homes, and her biological mother did not want her back in the house as a result of her previous disruptive behaviour. This stirred up Sally's primary experience of a failure in her own relationship with her mother, of not being able to trust her mother, and fearing that she always wanted to get rid of her. It also evoked the murderous hostility she felt towards her younger sister Tracey, whom she had tried to drown when she was the same age as Laura. She was able to identify with Laura's difficulties, and we were able to make some links and parallels with her own early life, especially her rage towards her younger sister for having mother's love and attention, and how she was expected, as a foster "mother", to provide this for Laura. We confronted the impulse she felt to "drown Laura out", even though a part of her was expected to show Laura an alternative way to the one she was experiencing in her turbulent home life with her own mother. There appeared to be some evidence that Sally was developing a separate sense of self, and there was also some relief, on my part, at her comment that "it all seems to be making sense to me now".

## The fourth event

Sally requested an extra session because of turbulence at home after a repeated attempt by Laura to disrupt the routine by running away. Sally was very well aware that I did not work at the hospital on the day she requested that particular extra session, and in our next session, she became very silent and left halfway through without any explanation. I was also unable to accommodate a further request for a changed time for her next session as she had to attend a training workshop. Most of the attention in her home was geared towards containing the unruly child, Laura, how she was expected to "be there for Laura, unconditionally", as she put it. I had a letter waiting for me the next morning. These letters were never signed by Sally and only addressed to me on the envelope; they are quoted from here with her permission.

> I feel I have lost a part of me. I want to write this letter to you and for you to get it in the first post tomorrow as it all seems so urgent. I walked out of my session without saying goodbye to you as it all seems so final. You have kept me alive for a long time now and I just can't let you keep spending your time and your energy on carrying on doing that for me, when inside me all I see and think about is my own death. I am evil and from the gutter and all I do the whole time is hurt people. I don't deserve to be alive, I am ruining people's lives. And although people can't see, or don't believe me when I say I have tried really hard to be different, well it's not heard and I'm not seen. I am totally useless as a human being, and I am a failure. While I am in therapy I cannot let go and end my life. I don't expect you to understand that because you are on the side of LIFE. My masks have cracked and there is no plaster left to hide the misery. It is time to let you go and you will be rid of me once and for all. I have to stand back and let Em [her partner] get on with life, to help Laura cope rather than drown her out, and without having me hanging around to destroy and spoil it. If only she could understand how difficult it is for me sometimes, as I find having these difficult kids in the house rips me to pieces. I have to get rid of you all.

And she continued:

> I can't pretend I am not scared, I am absolutely terrified. Without
> therapy, I will have nothing to stop me putting an end to my life
> as I am such an evil person. If it is true that my mother tried to get
> rid of me BEFORE I was born, and then tried to do us both in after
> I was born, then I truly wish she had killed me, then I would not
> be wanting to kill myself now. Although you will think this is just
> me wanting to spoil everything I have achieved, and I know I have
> done well since I have been in therapy, I also know this is not me.
> So it has to be the true character underneath all of the pretence. If it
> was not, I would not be in this soup, in this confusion, addicted to
> death, never wanting to be alive, but terrified and frightened I will
> have to give in to this black messenger of death.

I managed to contact Sally, and she agreed to attend her next session. In response to her letter, I had a "nightmare". For the purpose of
expanding on my understanding of the clinical material, and to further
develop the models I am using, especially Bion (1962), Gallwey (1996),
and Segal (1957), I will use this dream to illustrate the complications
that need to be contained and deciphered when working with patients
such as Sally, as there is very little material from them in the form of
their dreams, nightmares or, more usually, night terrors.

> I dreamt that I was in my Regional Secure Unit, RSU, and I was
> sitting with a clinical team. We were trying to get a person out of a
> very large metal container which was filled with soup, and sealed.
> I knew there was a patient inside the container, and I was pointing
> out that it had to be done in stages. The person trying to propose
> ways of releasing the patient from the container, was doing a rather
> awkward job, but trying to find an opening so that the contents,
> the soup, and the person would not pour out. In the first stage, the
> container started to shake violently and topple. In the second stage,
> when the person inside was about to emerge from the container,
> I looked inside and, deep down, I saw a luminous green murderous
> face emerging; it was about to attack the nurse. I leapt at the nurse,
> pushing her to one side, as the image from the container was about
> to erupt, like a flash of lightning. After the eventual safe release of
> the person, which felt like a scene from the film Alien, the atmos-
> phere was fairly genial, then the patient said that after the nurse,
> I would be the next person to "get it". I then left the building, but

the lift was not working, so I had to use the emergency exit. I looked down. On the iron staircase, all the steps were covered with black beetles with exceptionally hard shells. I could not bear to walk on them and crush the shells, so I decided to take a different exit as the thought of crushing the beetles under my shoes was unthinkable, although the other staff using the same exit were happily walking over them to get to the exit.

I tried to process my dream as perhaps a fear on my part that the person in the container, or the murderous image, represented Sally, and the nurse too represented Sally. Which part would she bring to her next session? I was also trying to process, in my dream, both the fact that I was working with an individual, Sally, unable to employ defences such as splitting or projective identification to manage fear and frustration, and how such individuals remain trapped in an autistic prison, in a state of confusion, between self and object, suffering pain, terror, and rage, and fearing ultimate annihilation. The fear and violence of these states of mind, represented by the image inside the metal container in my nightmare, represent the ultimate anxiety that lies at the root of most psychopathology: namely, that the self will not come completely alive, and will fail to sustain itself as an independent entity in a safe internal relationship with a life-sustaining object.

An individual cannot have any form of thought, including phantasy, unless there is a gap between the self and the object of dependency, or some way of experiencing the difference between presence and absence. Without absence, is there phantasy? This follows Segal's work on sym-bol formation. The main core activity between thinking and phantasy is the bridge that links the self with the object. By definition, the autistic self is confused with the object, unable to think because there is no gap to think into. Thus, murderous envy flows into this autistic black hole where there is no sense of a separate self in relation to the other and where there is no gap (Polledri, 2003, p. 200).

In Sally's next session, I decided to say that she was feeling angry and in a rage with me both for not being there or available for the requested session and for changing the time of her usual session. I made an inter-pretation along the lines of her being angry with me for not being avail-able for her, and equally I was seen as a failure, in her opinion, because I had failed to see why she was so silent and upset.

Sally told me that *she* had had a night terror and she had woken up screaming. She then had an hallucination, after waking up, in which two pairs of black leggings on her dressing room table changed into a hooded masked image, a death messenger. She said that one part of her was relieved I had contacted her because she was "shit scared" of her murderousness, in which "she could take her own life", and she therefore needed desperately to attend her therapy. But the other "black mob" part of her (as she called it) was screaming at her in the session, saying "Fail! Fail!" Being back there with her (the therapist) is a fail!

I asked her whether the voice she heard, at that point, in the room, was male or female? She dismissed this by shrugging and saying, "I don't know ... It's just a *thing*!" Sally then became silent, thoughtful, and, after what seemed a very long time, said: "I think it is *my* voice."

She then talked about Laura, the girl she and her partner had temporarily fostered, and the fact that she knew her mother didn't want her. She said she was probably the best person to help Laura, as she had been through the same experiences, but she then said, no she couldn't; it was "too close to home". She couldn't separate herself out from the girl but was muddled in with her. She then said: "Someone has to tell that girl that her mother does not want her. It won't be me, though. I have to know whether she did not want her as a baby and if that is the case, then forget it, we are wasting our time."

I said here that perhaps she could see herself in Laura, as a baby with a mother who did not want her, that she had no picture of two people together, on a dual footing, and that for her, Sally, to be available for Laura, meant involving herself in a two-person relationship. That was also the position she was in with her partner, and with me too, in her therapy.

I added that as she had no picture in her mind of herself in an interaction with a maternal figure, she was attached to her experience of being in a black hole, confused and frightened, fearing the hooded messenger of death. She was finding it very difficult to maintain an intimate relationship, such as the one with her housemate, which required two people. And with Laura, wanting to drown her rather than help her survive, like her did with her own little sister. Tracey suggested that for a very long time she was unable to feel she had a sense of herself as a separate person in her therapy, and that my absence was a threat to her. When I was not available, all she could discern within herself was the "lost" part and the feeling was about death and violence. On the other hand, however, she was able to function, and attend her therapy, and have insight into Laura's problems, recognising the connection between Laura and her sister Tracey, from her own family background.

At this stage, she went into the bathroom, vomited and retched. She went into the waiting room and remained there, sitting on the floor, with her head in her hands, sobbing, like a frightened child. I let her recover, and after she had calmed down somewhat, she came back into the room and she said, with great clarity:

> But if what you have just said, if that is my problem, and I did not have that as a child, it is not fair to my partner, or to Laura, or to you. I cannot hold within that expectation. I can't do my job, it isn't possible. It makes me physically sick to think about myself as caring. So I might as well relieve them of their misery and get rid of myself.

Because she was so frightened of death, she felt attacked by the encapsulated contents. If I started gradually to get her out of that state, in stages, she might become very needy, fearing any dependency, and could act out, pushing everybody out of the way, crushing anybody that got under her feet, including Laura and her partner, Em.

I was reminded here of Rosenfeld (1971) describing the violence of the envy embodied in the wish to destroy the analyst, an impulse that makes its appearance after the analysand begins to emerge from the pathological narcissistic state and is now confronted with the recognition of the existence and significance of a two-party situation. Therefore, it can be understood that the hostility operating here resides within that part of the personality which feels itself to have been cheated of the growth-enhancing, mother–infant, two-person experience and is, due to this secondary envy, opposed to this linking process.

These encapsulated areas do contain a great deal of violence and I think that if the walls break down, and encapsulation fails, out comes the rage, the violence, and the murderousness, as described by the symbolism I was trying to process in my dream. If there are a number of external events and stressors, then encapsulation fails. I think this area, which is autistic in nature, contains a dreadful fear of death. But the more you can interpret that fear, that specific type of pathology, the safer the patient will be (Gallwey, 2003).

*Lessons from the case study*

Sally had a high degree of disturbance in her early maternal environment, with a history of actual threats and attacks on her life, and she did not seem to contain a sense of herself as a separate person in a relationship with a life-sustaining mother. Theoretically, all hope of her surviving as an individual in an adult therapeutic relationship might, to an observer, seem inconceivable. As she said, "I cannot be expected to hold on" as a direct result of not being held in the primary stages of linking and attachment to her own mother.

*However*, if the disturbance in functioning had been complete in its failure, and Sally had never identified herself, never assimilated the vital concept of "mummy and me", she would be completely autistic and would never have been able to attend therapy. So she had achieved some sense of a self. She is a functioning person. One has to be careful, as it is important not to include all of the person's mental life within one process. As she is sitting in the room, talking, she is using symbols and using language. Therefore, she must have conceptualised a self *eventually*, and what we are dealing with is an area of primary confusion. Where this happens, it has a terrible effect and is carried around forever. It is clearly described by Sally in her hallucination about the leggings: the fear of death. But she is not *completely* encapsulated within it.

The autistic bubble is a representation of encapsulated trauma. Such a bubble, frozen in time, can occur through trauma or deprivation in the first hours, days, weeks, or months after life. Depending on when it occurs, it later manifests itself in different forms which are given different diagnostic names, such as Asperger's, psychosis, post-traumatic stress disorder, and so on.

What is very important to understand, as I have learned from this case study, is that it is very rare for anything ever to be complete. One of Sally's preoccupations was to try to lose weight. She had had unreasonable restrictions placed on what she was allowed to eat at meal times, compared with the rest of the family, and had grown up an obese child. What developed was a very severe dysmorphophobia (a fixed distressing belief that one's body is deformed, repulsive, or an excessive fear that it may become so), in which the self had been poorly conceptualised (Gallwey, 1996).

Rosenfeld has interesting insights relevant to this case. In *Impasse and Interpretation* (1987), he writes:

> One has to understand first, that the patient feels helpless and completely unaware of what is going on and therefore there is no point in insisting that the patient is resistant or wants to withhold

information .... On the other hand, interpretations which can make the patient aware that there is a force at work inside him, which is powerfully suggestive and prevents him from thinking and observing what is going on, are experienced as helpful and ego-supportive. This approach gradually mobilizes self-observation .... But most patients need a great deal of help to understand and overcome this silently undermining process because it is very frightening and confusing. What is particularly confusing is the existence of a split-off self or object inside the patient who, by persuasion, and suggestion, exerts a powerful influence over him and assumes the role of an adviser. Any good dependent relationship the patient is gradually developing, such as that to the analyst, is therefore attacked and belittled. (Rosenfeld, 1987, p. 90)

Rosenfeld's model as well as Gallwey's was extremely useful in my work with Sally, and I think it is important to be aware that all the time you are dealing with a whole person, the whole mind, and that you are looking for the most severe pathology. You want to let the patient know that you understand that the fear of dependency is there. Otherwise, there is a danger that you could be annihilating the person altogether. This was expressed by Sally when she said "Well, I might just as well kill myself, so you will all be rid of me." It was necessary for me to add:

That is why you feel inside that you are haunted by death because you feel that the most needy part of you can't actually find yourself. All you can find is death and violence, whereas in other parts of yourself you can be warm and responsive, and you can hold on, as you do with the children in your nursery, and others who need understanding and containment.

It is important to acknowledge that a patient has got *some* sanity, otherwise you could think of them only in terms of psychotic functioning, leaving them feeling stripped of all saneness. It is possible, as this case study shows, to be able to liaise with a rational part of the patient that has developed as a result of the therapeutic relationship. There is a sense of an intact self *somewhere*, which never gives up its efforts to express its will, even if it often does so by destructive means. This has been described by Bion (1957) as the non-psychotic part of the personality.

From my experience, and from the clinical material I have presented on Sally, it is my understanding that infants are born with innate biological attachment impulses. When, for example, Sally wrote: "I also know this is not me", she reflected Gallwey's inference that there is at the very start of life an awareness of a me/not me, a state confirmed by descriptions of mimicking and mirror neurone and other work by neurobiologists such as Beebe and Lachmann (2002) and Schore (1994, 2003a).

Sally's ability to realise a sense of "self" in relation to "other", would have developed from the therapeutic interaction during her treatment with me. To expect her to then move on and see herself in a relationship where there was a self, and other, was near impossible, as the achievement of a two-person relationship was the very basis of her envy.

If there is a failure in the primary linking functions, or bonding processes, autistic states of mind can result. These differ from full-blown autism by manifesting themselves as a lack of a conceptualisation of the self through the growth of a separate relationship with the mother. Biologically, the three vital functions identified by Gallwey (1996) have to operate sequentially and reciprocally between the infant and the early nurturing environment in order for the infant to develop a sense of self in relation to the mother. This is how, in my view, encapsulated containerlessness differs from Frances Tustin's work on autism (1972). Possibly, with autism, I am suggesting, there is always an available mother, ever present, who describes her baby as being "unavailable" to respond to her maternalism. The infant does not frantically try to catch hold of mother, or mother's love. It cannot do so because its separate existence has not been confirmed. The impulse for attachment does not seem to be there in the first place.

To summarise the main focus of the clinical material, Sally exemplifies what can happen when an individual never makes the primary conceptions that enable a full sense of self and of others to develop. This may not be as all-encompassing as full-blown autism, but there remains an inner domain that is "containerless"; it lacks a sense of self and is a seat of despair, confusion, and deep anger.

Envy is a secondary phenomenon, not an instinct, but there may be an absence of instinct for attachment and dependency. The anger, violence, or fear that this engenders is, inevitably, extremely hard to discern as distinct from failures on the part of the environment. And, of course, passivity in the infant will lead to the lack of response in the mother, who is liable to confuse the infant's passivity for contentment.

## Implications for treatment

One advantage in perceiving envy as a secondary phenomenon is that it prevents analysis being used as a vehicle for evading responsibility for the perpetration of strife. However, such an approach also allows the analyst to evade responsibility for failures in their understanding by seeing resistance or worsening in the patient's condition as the result of unresolved envy. All setbacks become negative therapeutic reactions. This refuge has been beautifully challenged by Herbert Rosenfeld's later work. In *Impasse and Interpretation*, he advises that:

> It is important to understand those hidden factors described by Freud in more detail because our therapeutic results in dealing with negative therapeutic reactions may depend on the successful activation of the elusive destructive factors, and this in turn would make the super-ego more accessible to investigation. (Rosenfeld, 1987, p. 97)

And he describes, after Freud (1923b), a *very* valuable differentiation between envy and illness as follows:

> In the end we come to see that we are dealing with what may be called a "moral" factor, a sense of guilt, which is finding its satisfaction in the illness and refuses to give up the punishment or suffering. We shall be right in regarding this disheartening explanation as final. But as far as the patient is concerned his sense of guilt is dumb: it does not tell him he is guilty; he does not feel guilty, he feels ill. This sense of guilt expresses itself only as a resistance to recovery which is extremely difficult to overcome. (Rosenfeld, 1987, pp. 96–97)

Karen Horney makes suggestions about how to handle the negative therapeutic reaction and offers technical suggestions on how to manage this difficult problem. She stresses the patient's fear of improvement through the analyst's help, since such success is always related in the patient's mind to "crushing others and maliciously triumphing over the crushed adversaries" (Horney, 1939, p. 37). Horney sees similarities between Freud's view and her own, although Freud stresses the guilt feelings in this type of patient, while Horney emphasises fear of envious retaliation, a persecutory anxiety situation, which would link up with Klein's observations (1957) on an envious superego.

Joan Riviere (1936) believes that what makes the negative therapeutic reaction so stubborn is the unconscious love and anxiety for the destroyed or dying internal objects, producing an unbearable sense of guilt and pain. The patient needs to sacrifice his own life for others who represent these internal objects, and therefore faces death or suicide.

Klein's observation (1957) of envy being aroused by good interpretations is almost identical to Horney's description (1939) of the competitive patient who devalues the analyst and the interpretation. Horney relates it to the negative therapeutic reaction, however, only in terms of the patient's fear of envy of other people which prevents him from attaining success.

*In conclusion*

Experiences of the infant at the beginning of life have such a powerful influence on everything that follows, and a disruption in positive development at this early stage is of the fundamental problems not only for psychoanalysis but of all interdisciplinary sciences. What emerges most clearly from Sally's case history and the current wealth of infant research is that the individual can only exist in relation to the "other". Not only is this providing us with a more detailed model of human development, it is also being rapidly absorbed into clinical models, where it is radically altering the central concepts of psychoanalysis and psychiatry.

I think that linking up clinical data and concepts and hypotheses is notoriously difficult. It is always doubtful when understanding dangerous behaviour to decipher whether or not the behaviour is an enactment of an experience with a lost and abandoning and dangerous object. But in this study, recognition of the impenetrable autistic areas is a fundamental task in terms of developing any model. It should also be added here that Tustin, in abandoning her earlier idea of normal autism, later formulated the concept of autistic enclaves operating in less disturbed patients, which is pertinent to this investigation (Tustin, 1987). The model has more ramifications than it is appropriate for me to describe in this study, but it has given me a fresh perspective on, and operational renaissance in, the forensic clinical treatment, which is very much a new area and which has to be based on research developed over a long period of time. It has also greatly enhanced my processing of the countertransference. A point made by Gallwey is that "Antisocial behaviour and profound resistance to change go hand in hand, so therapeutic nihilism and the abandonment of patients at the height of their disturbance is common. To retain the ability to think and work out what is going on can keep the treatment and the protagonists alive" (Foreword to Polledri, 1997, p. 476). My contribution aims to demonstrate my own individual attempt to put forward a fresh understanding of envy. My view is that envy is a complex phenomenon requiring much further research and understanding, based on clinical material and experience, rather than being the definitive explanation for attacks on good experience.

Primary identification reflects a discovery of the self, but also establishes a conceptual internal duality of a self, in a dependent relationship with a dependable separate object.

There are many aspects of Sally's case material that I have utilised as a backdrop for furthering our understanding of Gallwey's theory of encapsulated containerlessness. She lacked a containing object altogether, and therefore experienced a failure in the primary linking functions that spring from it. I do not think her primitive anxiety and fear of death was based on Freud's death drive. Her fear of death was based on the actual threats to her life by an uncontaining mother, both before and after she was born. The fear of death was her ultimate anxiety, which caused both severe developmental psychopathology and violent destructive behaviour.

From the case histories I present, I am suggesting that the pathology in autism can be either environmental, when the mother is not able to attune adequately to the baby's needs, or it can be due to a biological deficit in the infant, whereby the infant does not have the impulses that most babies have to try to catch hold of the mother. A significant consequence of this early sense of loss, and one which underpins my main argument regarding Klein's 1957 theory of envy as instinct, is the early development of a destructively envious attitude that becomes directed against the existence of a two-person duality and, in particular, the possibilities that this reality brings forward. The misfortune taking place at this earlier period, described as "affect dysregulation" by Schore (2003a), brings with it a state of fragmentation. The time of life at which this occurs is quite crucial: the mother's inability to function as an adequate receptor to her infant's distress in the first few months of life brings about serious damage to the earliest linking processes and is likely to be more catastrophic than if it occurs in later infancy. This has been investigated by Rosenfeld (1971) in terms of the relationship of its pathological form to envy and vengeance. In these instances, I have no doubt that the mother herself had been unduly affected by a deep sense of deprivation, which evoked, in turn, an expression of hostile envy, and she was thus prevented from experiencing a sense of gratitude in response to giving birth.

As Sally had not established or incorporated a primary identification of self and object duality, she lacked the psychological foundation for a capacity to develop a repertoire of symbols that combine as secondary phantasies. This failure led to her inability to fully develop conscious imagination and cognitive thinking and her loss of what Winnicott describes as "the capacity to relate to objects" causing "autistic states" (Winnicott, 1974, p. 104). Symbols, which form the basis for thinking and imagination and construct a link between the self and the object, rely on separation for their formation. The obliteration of the difference between self and other resulted, for Sally, in a failure in normal symbol formation and produced concrete symbolic equivalents, so very often found in psychotic functioning.

De Zulueta discusses how:

> The complex process of psychobiological attunement between the infant and the caregiver is to be replayed throughout the individual's subsequent relationships and is at the heart of her attachment to others. This implies that any disruption of this essential developmental process leads to serious long-term effects both at a physiological and psychological level. Thus the trauma of loss, deprivation or abuse (whether physical, emotional or sexual), can all have longstanding effects on the individual's capacity to form satisfactory relationships, her sense of self and, in particular, her potential for violent behaviour. (De Zulueta, 1996, p. 179)

Finally, any case history or fragment of a case history is always chosen by the author to support a particular theoretical hypothesis. I believe that Sally's case history was an example of my attempt to bridge psychoanalysis and attachment theory, by introducing and elaborating Gallwey's work on encapsulated containerlessness.

# CHAPTER FOUR

# Shame and envy

Freud had to rely on "instinct" as his explanation for violence, because he had no theory of shame with which to understand and explain it.

(Gilligan, 2000, p. 213)

Reading Joseph Berke it is clear to me that he believes shame includes envy:

Shame is a powerful inner tension experienced as an exquisitely painful sense of inferiority at variance with one's wished for image of personal goodness. The quality and degree of emotional pain is comparable to that of envious tension, so much so that it is likely that shameful tension is a variant of, as well as a contributor to, envy. If this is correct, then we would expect that shame will be followed by murderous rage. This is generally the case. The shamed person either wants to hide further away, to disappear, as the envier does at times, but also wants to destroy the alleged source of shame. So the model is the same, for with shame as with envy, a tormenting tension leads to an angry discharge. But with shame it is

> the former, the tension, that most people recognise as shame. They
> tend to overlook the subsequent response. (Berke, 1987, p. 32)

Within the framework of self psychology the study of narcissism has
made considerable advances since Freud's discoveries, contributing to
a much more sophisticated psychoanalytical model of the personality.
"This has enabled us to understand the complexity and importance of
the experience of shame, rather than seeing it, like guilt, as the guard-
ian of morality" (Pines, 1987, p. 16). Shame is to self psychology what
anxiety is to ego psychology, although it has received much less attention in the literature than anxiety, guilt, and depression. The psychology
of shame in relation to envy has been recognised by Berke (1986),
Feldman and De Paola (1994), Gilligan (2000), Lansky and Morrison
(1997), Nathanson (1992), Nussbaum (2004), and many others, although
the link to envy has not been well understood. There is good reason,
therefore, to explore the early development of how shame becomes a
psychosis, how psychodynamic theories about shame are formed, how
they manifest themselves in institutions, in politics, and, indeed, in psychotherapeutic treatment.

Andrew Morrison suggests that "envy also serves as a *protection*
against the experience of shame, at least with respect to another object".
Envy, he says, "represents yet another means—along with anger, rage,
and contempt—for the self to deal with and banish its shame ... inso-
far as envy undermines the importance of the object, it may also lead
to reduction in shame with regard to the formerly omnipotent other"
(Morrison, 1989, p. 109). In these ways, envy bears a relationship to
shame and is closely intertwined with it clinically.

## Shame as a primary affect

Nowhere in human existence is it as important to understand how
shame figures in the birth of the self. This has been well researched
by Nathanson (1992) in the compass of shame as an "attack self"
system, as:

> it offers a defence against shame in which one bargains with the
> devil. This works fairly well as a perversion, even though one can
> learn many variations on the theme and many ways of attack-
> ing oneself in the name of bonding with others. There are those

who would not consider masochism as a reasonable alternative to unintentional, uncontrolled shame, which they try to prevent by a number of techniques, such as avoidance, withdrawal, attack other, and "attack self". (Nathanson, 1992, p. 334)

Berke believes that, like envy, shame is an interpersonal event that has to do with comparison, malevolent comparison. "The envier scans his environment with a jaundiced eye, and so shame functions in a similar fashion, constantly on the look-out for comparisons, to disparities between how he is and how he should be" (Berke, 1988, p. 43). As the case studies I am presenting highlight, this comparison can take place in the external world, or in the internal world, that is, between a shaming internal figure as a representation of the self. The link between self and object as part of the self has been written about by Kernberg (1992), who calls this an inner part object consisting of self, object, and the affect that binds them. Kernberg would regard this positive complex as an introjected inner object, whereas Fairbairn (1951) would describe the positive experience as part of the nurturing background matrix in which the infant develops.

Janine Chasseguet-Smirgel (1985) explicated the phantasy of narcissistic merger and shame by considering the ego-ideal from the perspective of "malady of the ideal" (cited in Morrison, 1989, p. 59). She suggested that the power of shame and humiliation may be so great as to lead to suicide: "The searing shame that leads to suicide is, then, the true root of *mortification,* and, according to Chasseguet-Smirgel, can lead to phantasies of murdering those in whose presence one has experienced humiliation" (cited in Morrison, 1989, p. 61).

Silvan Tomkins (1962, 1963) described nine primary affects, including shame, which he describes as specific, inborn, biologically determined patterns of physiological response, especially with regard to facial expression:

Tomkins postulated that instead of drives determining affective responses, as suggested by classical psychoanalytic theory, affects serve as necessary *amplifiers* of the drives and hence are the source of motivation, cognition and action. Thus, "they are antecedent to all subsequent human development" (Morrison, 1989, p. 39). These nine innate affects, which can explain every known emotion and emotionally charged situation, are categorized into three types:

two basically pleasant or *positive*, one neutral and six basically unpleasant or *negative*. The positive affects are interest-excitement and enjoyment-joy; the neutral affect is called surprise-startle; and the negative affects are fear-terror, distress-anguish, anger-rage, dissmell, disgust and shame-humiliation, (cited in Nathanson, 1992, p. 59).

Nathanson explores further the nature of shame:

> Shame differs from all other forms of affect in at least one significant feature—it appears to be triggered neither by the detection of specific noxious chemicals as in the case of the attenuators dissmell and disgust nor by variations in the shape and intensity of non-specific internal neural events, as in the case of the six other affects. Shame-humiliation is an inborn script, an attenuator system that can be called into operation whenever there is an impediment to the expression of either positive affect. It depends on the remarkable ability of highly organized, advanced life forms to assemble the data of perception into patterns and to compare those patterns to whatever has been stored as memory. (Nathanson, 1992, p. 135)

Nathanson's whole work and research represents his attempt to shift our language away from adult-orientated emotion vocabulary towards one based firmly on the concept and language of innate affect. The definition of self in the new language of affect theory has been developed by the recent decades of research in infant observation by, among others, Beebe and Lachmann (2002,), Schore (1994, 2003), and Stern (1985). Shame, then, according to Morrison, can be viewed as "an inevitable feeling about the self for its narcissistic imperfection, for failure, for being flawed" (Morrison, 1989, p. 66).

## The eyes of shame

The literature has either overlooked shame as an independent affect, or has only discussed it in terms of emotions such as social anxiety, a sense of inferiority, or narcissistic injury. Despite its natural connection to the psyche, psychological explorations of shame have split from its symbolic and developmental foundations, perhaps because as individuals we are ashamed of experiencing shame.

I wish at this stage to explore more deeply the earlier developmental patterns which manifest themselves in disorders of the self, the role of reflection in the emergence of the child's developing sense of self, and how the mother's eyes and face are internalised by the infant. These all contribute to a healthy psychological sense of self reflected in the responsiveness and empathy of the mother. The lack of this healthy interaction is what I believe to form a psychosis of shame, a pathological narcissism, originating at a pre-verbal stage of development. Charles Rycroft described how "behaviour which is in conflict with the ego-ideal evokes shame" (Rycroft, 1968, p. 40), and Donald Nathanson wrote:

> In the moment of shame we feel isolated, terribly alone, shorn from the herd. Equally shame can make us feel that the eyes of the other, normally the window of a friendly interchange—have become a source or a symbol of oppressive attention. It is then that we wish for the earth to open up and swallow us: Shame makes us long for invisibility. When embarrassed, we feel that we are no longer known to the world by our best attributes, but by our worst. (Nathanson, 1992, p. 220)

Shame is a powerful inner tension, experienced as an acutely painful sense of inferiority that is at variance with one's own wished-for image of personal goodness. What comes to mind here, from the quote from Nathanson above, is the thought of a small child's developing sense of his or her self, as it was very usual for a parent to discipline a child by saying: "Aren't you ashamed of yourself?", only to be met by a blank stare. Eye contact is important:

> Eye contact is one of the core means by which we communicate and build relationships, and is the key mechanism by which we develop attachments. Gaze avoidance or an inability to sustain eye contact is an important signal about the state of the relationship or the emotional state of the individual involved. (Trowell & Etchegoyen, 2002, p. 79)

Shame may also develop through an unreflecting look in the mother's eyes, well before the development of language. This is then internalised, well before verbal shaming comments, depending on the tone of voice, which then reverberates throughout later life. The concept of the "evil eye" is an example of this.

> The child introjects a look in the mother's eyes, a look that lacks a reflective capacity, forcing an awareness of worthlessness onto the child's immature, fragile ego, perhaps due to the mother's own disturbances in attachment to her own mother. The eyes of shame are a concrete, un-symbolised representation of a sensory experience of an uncontaining mother, a mother who leaves the child feeling what Winnicott (1971) described as "not good enough". (Ayers, 2003, pp. 64–65)

"From this it is evident that the eye is the organ of shame par excellence" (Wurmser, 1987, p. 67).

Ayers discussed how:

> Reflection, in relation to the mother and her face, plays a vital mirroring role from the first few weeks after birth, when the presence of the other gives meaning to the self. The infant is in a 'facilitating environment' (Winnicott, 1971), any differentiation between self and other has not yet been experienced and there is no internal differentiation between consciousness and unconsciousness. Although these two states of mind do not exist for the infant, experiences play a vital role because for the baby, the environment *is* the mother. (Ayers, 2003, p. 85)

Children cannot know who they are without reflective mirroring. Parents who are shut down emotionally cannot mirror or affirm their child's emotions. Our identity demands a significant other whose eyes see us pretty much as we see ourselves. Envy uses disguises to cover up the core issue, which is toxic shame. Because of its talent for disguise, envy takes forms that are impossible to recognise (Nathanson, 1992).

It seems to me that the fixed face of the unresponsive mother is experienced by the infant as a reflection—but a *distorting one*—giving a false feedback of deadness. I am suggesting that during the first six months of life, it appears that the subsequent development of a sense of shame is linked to the role the eyes play for the infant in constructing the mother's presence and forming the psychological centre of their relationship (Ayers, 2003; Broucek, 1991).

But how about the eyes, the eyes, the eyes?
Mirrors can kill and talk, they are terrible rooms
In which a torture goes on that one can only watch.
The face that lived in this mirror is the face of a dead man.
Do not worry about the eyes …

Sylvia Plath (1932–1963)

Eyes allow us not only to see, but to see ourselves, to provide a reflection. For Plath (who took her own life the year after she wrote these lines), this disconcerting power is linked to "the paradoxical question: from where might the experience of being dead, while yet alive, arise?" (Masterson, 1999, p. 120).

Daniel Stern imagines what the baby is experiencing from the mother's facial expression:

> I enter the world of her face. Her face and its features are the sky, the clouds, the water. Her vitality and spirit are the air and the light. But this time when I enter, the world is still and dull …. Where is she? Where has she gone? When is she coming back? I am scared. I feel that dullness creeping into me. I search around for a point of life to escape to. (Stern, 1990, p. 58)

Shame must involve more than a self overwhelmed by grandiosity; it must account for disappointment and a failure to establish an internal conceptual duality of a self in relation to other, leading the individual to believe that something has been wrong with them from the very beginning. In the poignant words of a twenty-seven-year-old woman who suffered from a deep sense of shame, "something is broken and it cannot be fixed" (Polledri, 2003). Her psychological history, which is described in the next chapter, illustrates the infant's thwarted intentions as the earliest form of shame phenomenology.

The infant's active use of eye contact and mother's face to engage her and the world and the network of complexes that can develop around the infant's core drive activities of looking and showing are seriously affected if their attempts at attachment and engagement are frustrated. These failures in attachment could be described as resulting in a profound alteration in the early sense of self—the birth of narcissism, which will haunt the individual through every subsequent developmental stage (Ayers, 2003).

The idea of the introjection of the reflection given back to the child via the mother's face is articulated by Winnicott. He says: "What does the baby see when he or she looks at the mother's face? I am suggesting that, ordinarily, what the baby sees is himself or herself …. [But] if the mother's face is unresponsive, then a mirror is a thing to be looked at, not looked into" (Winnicott, 1971, pp. 112–113).

I am suggesting that shame has been neglected historically, and especially the part that is played by the eyes in the psychological development of the child. The lack of attunement and attachment between mother and infant has been minimised and its biological importance scarcely noticed. Despite the fact that psychoanalytical theory has placed so much emphasis on the mouth as an early focal point of body image, because of their salience, the eyes should have more priority, but have been obscured by the Kleinian ideas of "good" and "bad" breast. In terms of instinct, hunger/breast is an obviously vital pairing, but the eyes introduce the idea of psychic, rather than biological life.

Although the literature (for example, Ayers, 2003; Nathanson, 1992; Schore, 2003a) appears to concur that shame precedes guilt, there is some discrepancy as to when shame first appears. "Neuroimaging studies demonstrate that infants as young as two months show right hemispheric activation when exposed to a woman's face" (Tzourio-Mazoyer et al., 2002, p. 454).

> The human maternal response to an infant's cry, a fundamental behaviour of the attachment dynamic, is accompanied by an activation of the mother's right brain …. These moments of imprinting, the very rapid form of learning that irreversibly stamps early visual experiences upon the developing nervous system and mediates attachment bond formation, are described in the current neuroscience literature. (Schore, 2003a, pp. 276–277)

Facial mirroring is one of the interaction patterns that contribute to the pre-symbolic organisation of self and object representations. To the degree that facial mirroring interaction is positively correlated, so that the partners are changing in the same affective direction, the infant represents the expectation of matching and being matched. The infant represents the experience of seeing the mother's face continuously changing to become more similar to his or her own. The infant also represents the experience of his or her own face constantly changing to become more similar to the mother's face. "These 'matching' experiences contribute to feeling known, feeling attuned to, on the same wavelength" (Beebe & Lachmann, 2002, p. 98). The importance of visual contact in relation to shame has also been extensively written about by Broucek (1982), Kaufman (1992), Lansky and Morrison (1997), Morrison (1984), Nathanson (1987, 1992), Pines (1995), Robson (1967), Schore (1994, 2001, 2002, 2003a), Stern (1974), Winnicott (1971), Wurmser (1987), and many others.

Kohut (1971, 1972) has written how "The most significant relevant basic interactions between mother and child usually lie in the visual area; the child's bodily display is responded to by the gleam in the mother's eye." Schore presents multidisciplinary evidence to demonstrate that a particular type of visual information that conveys the primary caregiver's affective response to the infant is critical to the progression of socioemotional development:

> The visual perception of facial expressions has been shown to be the most salient channel of non-verbal communication. And visual modes of communication that precede vocal modes of mutual communication are dominant in the forging of preverbal affective ties in the first year of life. (Schore, 1994, p. 72)

The child's early facial mirroring interaction with the mother is the most powerful way in which emotion is transmitted. For Mollon, "the mother's smile, or lack of it, has a direct effect on the chemistry and development of the infant's brain. A face that is not responsive in the way the baby expects is extremely disturbing to the infant and thus evokes shame" (Mollon, 2002, p. 140).

Shame originates on an interpersonal level but may become internalised or psychically metabolised in such a way that the infant self can activate shame without an externally inducing event (Morrison, 1989; Nathanson, 1987; Tomkins, 1962, 1963). There is, then, no differentiation between inside and outside—a tragic process because what was once outside becomes lodged inside, described unwittingly by some as "a black hole". The symbiotic me/not me with mother is frozen. Just as earlier in infancy, self and object are one and the same, the self is simply what the individual believes he or she sees reflected in the eyes of others. Robson (1967) explains that by the end of the first six months of life, the groundwork has been laid for reading basic human expressive displays, an art that the shamed individual develops with accuracy and precision.

It seems clear that shame occurs long before the acquisition of language, but the debate about when shame appears in development remains a controversial issue. If, as Tomkins (1962) maintains, shame results from any sudden decrement in the affects of interest-excitement and enjoyment-joy, then there is no reason why shame should not appear quite early—as early as the first few months of life. If, on the other hand, one maintains that self-consciousness or objective self-awareness is a pre-condition for shame experience, as Lewis (1979) maintains, then shame experience is not possible before eighteen months. Schore's theoretical model (1994) attempts to place shame at a specific developmental stage by tying the earliest experiences of Mahler's practising subphase of separation-individuation (1979) at twelve to eighteen months and sees the function of shame as an inhibitor of hyper-arousal states. Schore's prototypical shame reaction occurs when a practising toddler, in an expansive, grandiose, hyper-stimulated state of arousal, reunites with the caregiver expecting shared excitement and affective attunement but experiences instead misattunement. Schore (1994) synthesises the views of Mahler (1979), Kohut (1977), and Tomkins (1962) in an attempt to integrate neurobiological, developmental, and psychoanalytic concepts. These controversies about the developmental timing of shame capacity have been explored but not resolved.

*Defences against shame*

A certain number of individuals handle shame by attacking others through the "human sport" of put-down, humiliation, ridicule, contempt, "constructive" criticism, and character assassination. These are the people in our everyday lives whom most of us find extremely dangerous, for no one can really avoid shame successfully and we live at risk of their envy. Those who must attack, rather than withdraw, make our common ground a terrain of danger (Nathanson, 1992, p. 212).

> Freud saw shame, along with morality and disgust, as a *reaction formation* against the scopophilic and exhibitionistic drives and thus as a source of resistance against sexual experiences.

> This aspect of shame in Freud's writing has been little appreciated in the classical assumptions about shame. (Freud, 1905d, cited in Morrison, 1989, p. 130)

Shame's potential relationship to defences, such as anger, rage, and envy, is often the underpinnings of narcissistic rage. The self may attempt to assuage shame through attacks on objects that may momentarily be seen as shame's source. Kohut views shame as a result of self-object failure and that narcissistic rage is then turned upon the self-object for "causing" the shame experience (Kohut, 1972). In fact, each of the emotions of anger/rage, contempt, and envy bear an intimate relationship to shame. These are defensive manoeuvres which demonstrate the frequent intolerability of shame and humiliation and the fact that shame itself is so often hidden and concealed by the individual. Envy serves as a *protection* against the experience of shame, at least with respect to another object.

Envious tension is aroused by the awareness of vitality and, indeed, by life itself. The envier aims to eliminate the torment in himself or herself by forceful, attacking, and murderous behaviour. This discharge, directed against the alleged source of the envy, constitutes a means of self-protection as well as other-destruction.

With regard to fear, Gilligan believes that "when the psyche is in danger, and overwhelmed by the feelings of shame, many antisocial personalities and so-called psychopaths have been described as notably lacking in the capacity to experience fear. Envy is also the most shameful experience and the one, like shame, which is most defended against" (Gilligan, 2000, p. 113). For Gilligan, a central precondition for committing violence, then, is the presence of overwhelming shame in the absence of feelings of either love or guilt; "the shame stimulates rage and violent impulses towards the person in whose eyes one feels shamed. Therefore, the feelings that would normally inhibit the expression of those feelings and the acting out of those impulses, such as love and guilt, are absent" (p. 113). Moreover, envy lingers on, even after a frustration has been overcome, a specific hurt repaid, a rival removed, or an injustice put right. Envy may be associated with real events, but it is more than a reaction to them (Spillius, 1993).

Envy seldom occurs in isolation but is usually an aspect of a more complex set of dynamics operating in an individual. In the words of Diane Barth:

> Traditional explanations of envy pay little attention to the role of self-esteem in the development of the emotion and the defenses against it, despite the fact that most authors who write about it seem to recognize that narcissistic needs and issues of self-esteem frequently arise in connection with envy. (Barth, 1988, p. 198)

Very little attention has been paid to the role of self-esteem in the development of the emotion of shame and the defences against it, despite the fact that most authors who write about envy seem to recognise that narcissistic needs and issues of self-esteem frequently arise in connection with envy.

To object relations theorists, stating that shame is at core a narcissistic defeat truly fails to capture the depth of the disturbance in this affect. Envy is a response to a shame experience and an attempt to deal with it. Although Klein did not use the language of shame, she uses the word envy in a way that is much closer to the concept I am describing as a psychosis of shame: destructive hate that follows shame. She says: "It is clear that deprivation, unsatisfactory feeding, and unfavourable circumstances intensify envy because they disturb full gratification, and a vicious circle is created" (Klein, 1975, p. 187). I am sure these unfavourable circumstances are the outcome of maternal deprivation, which must be what Klein is referring to by using the word "deprivation" in relation to the infant. Although deprivation was the "alternative" that Klein (1957) presented to the death instinct envy of the available breast, it offers a different conclusion, which is a much more forgiving one, about the consequences of early deprivation. How could the baby develop a sense of self and other in such unfavourable circumstances?

Whilst not agreeing with Klein's notion that envy is a manifestation of either the death instinct or primary aggression, based on a reaction to the unavailable breast, I think that envy, like shame, is a self-conscious emotion that develops as a result of seeing oneself as deficient or inferior compared to the other. Envy is the visible companion to unacknowledged or unconscious shame and always follows self-conscious comparison and shame. The ensuing rage and attack comes from shame which has been bypassed and unacknowledged.

Klein may have been well aware of the significance of mortification or humiliation in envy, but that she saw these feelings and the accompanying depression as derivatives of object-instinctual conflicts and would therefore not have seen a need to consider them separately in her theory. However, Klein's theory offers much that is not described in drive terminology and which I believe can be understood without the drive component. As regards her theory of object relations, whether or not what she described is the actual experience of the infant, she has captured the essence of the primitive and often shame-filled feelings of greed and rage that are often part of the experience of extreme envy in adults. This may explain the negative therapeutic reaction Klein encountered in her adult patients, but it does not address the issue of the source of envy.

My case studies in the next chapter demonstrate how envy is too sophisticated a state of mind and pattern of behaviour to exist at birth, and that the cognitive faculties and sensitivity to relationships, such as malicious comparison, only develop in the second year of life (Nathanson, 1992; Schore, 1991). From this point of view, envy would have to be a later derivative, purely because the infant does not have sufficient ego strength to be envious.

## In conclusion

I believe that shame develops during the first six months of life through an unreflecting look in the mother's eyes, internalised by the infant and reverberating throughout its later life. It is at this stage that the infant has not yet experienced him or her self as separate from the mother, as self-awareness has not yet been acquired. Object relations theorists such as Bowlby and Winnicott see the infant's development as being shaped by a human social context. Winnicott's oft-quoted remark "there is no such thing as a baby without a mother" (Winnicott, 1971) also explains how it is that we are biologically wired up to be attached to somebody. Infantile psychological and visual development plays a much greater part in the formation of a sense of self in relation to another than traditional drive-conflict.

Shame is an underestimated emotion. I agree with Morrison's conclusion that "the role of shame is too often ignored therapeutically as a major component in generating envy. Even where shame may not seem a prominent experience of a given patient, it is implicitly involved when envy of another occurs" (Morrison, 1989, p. 110).

Shame denotes an underlying state of self-loathing brought about by the loss of personal integrity. To be ashamed is to feel devoid of goodness, full of badness, and utterly reprehensible. "When envious tension is aroused, the action is then aimed at eliminating the torment by forceful, attacking, murderous behaviour. This discharge is directed at the source of the envy, as a means of self-protection as well as the destruction of the other. The envier feels inferior, rather than empty, and cannot tolerate to see others full of life and goodness" (Berke, 1987, p. 326).

Fonagy describes shame as being experienced as a compelling and concrete annihilation of the self in a much more concrete and absolute way:

> brutalization in the context of attachment relationships generates intense shame. This, if coupled with a history of neglect and a consequent weakness in mentalization, becomes a likely trigger for violence against the self and others, because of the intensity of the humiliation experiences when the trauma cannot be processed and attenuated via mentalization. Unmentalized shame, which remains unmediated by any sense of distance between feelings and objective realities, is then experienced as the destruction of the self. We have called it "ego-destructive shame". (2001, pp. 12–13)

Rage may also paradoxically increase the feelings of shame against which it was originally intended to provide protection. Envy is a reaction to deep-seated feelings of inadequacy, about which the individual is tremendously ashamed. "Reciprocal gaze, in addition to transmitting attunement, can also act to transmit misattunement, as in shame experiences. The misattunement in shame, as in other negative affects, represents a regulatory failure and is phenomenologically experienced as a discontinuity in what Winnicott called the child's need for 'going-on-being'" (Schore, 2003b, p. 11).

Finally, before relinquishing entirely the idea of "instinct" as a theoretical explanation that accounts for violent behaviour, we may have to accept one remaining factor that may be served by instinct theory. It enables some individuals, especially those considered to be violent, to hide their most shameful secret, namely that violence is not an innate authentic part of man's inborn human nature, but serves instead as a "smoke screen", a defence, that hides the unacceptable "unmanly" desire to be taken care of—wishes, which, if gratified, would make many a man feel that he was passive, dependent, infantile, and weak, that is to say, "not a man" (Gilligan, 2000). Gilligan points out that:

violent men would like nothing better than to be thought of as filled with "aggressive instincts"; nothing is more flattering to the shaky self-esteem of a man who fears he is "really a whimp" than to be told, and to believe, that he is actually carrying within himself, very dangerous instincts—instead of regarding it as shameful if men have a need to be helped by each other, and more shameful yet, by a woman. (Gilligan, 2000, p. 213)

As Jacqueline Rose puts it:

Shame is so appalling, it is something which makes us feel so dreadful that, instead of thinking about it, we would rather die, or, to use the colloquial formula for shame ... I wouldn't be caught dead .... Shaming attacks on progress, shameful tension and a feeling of "listen to what I won't be telling you" keeps the psychoanalyst wondering how on earth to give shape and a voice to what the patient would prefer not to experience. (Rose, 2003, p. 7)

# CHAPTER FIVE

# Self envy

. A dog was once crossing a bridge over a river, and in his jaws was
a piece of meat. When he saw his reflection in the water he thought
he saw another dog under the water with an equally large piece of
meat. In his greed he leapt at the other dog, not realizing that he
and it were one and the same, and lost both his meat and the meat
he coveted …

(Aesop, 'The Dog and His Shadow')

At first glance, self envy seems to be a self-contradictory concept.
Envy is generally defined as a reaction toward what the other has
and the self lacks. Under this definition, it would seem impossible
for self envy to exist at all: How can one envy oneself for what one
in fact has?

(Berman, 1999, p. 203)

## What is self envy?

Researchers in the field of mental health have always found it difficult to describe the dynamics of self envy, but I have found that Bion's

model of a psychotic process and a non-psychotic process is very useful in terms of explanation.

Self envy arises as a result of the early traumatic experience in relating. Bion described the breakdown of the earliest interchange between mother and child as a *primitive psychic disaster* (Bion, 1959). The mother's inability to function as an adequate receptor to her infant's distress was communicated, according to Bion, by "normal projective identification" and could bring about serious damage to the earliest linking processes between mother and child. His significant development in the understanding of the psychotic and non-psychotic parts of the mind describes processes whereby certain patients "attack" the links between elements of the mind, such as thoughts, emotions, perceptions, and memories (Bion, 1957). The result is the destruction of meaning and of the capacity for normal thought. In self envy, one part of the self will deal with another aspect of that same self as if they were material from two different worlds. In order to grasp the concept of self envy, it has to be considered that there is the existence of a divided self.

> Although Kleinian thinking currently describes feelings that arise from an envious internal object, they are directed towards *other persons*. In self envy, the same emotions are described but instead of being projected into others in the external world, they are experienced as being directed towards the *internal self* that represents the creative part of the adult self. This is confused with the creative aspects of the parents incorporated and narcissistically identified with as a child. The emphasis is on the relationship between internal parts of the self in comparison with interaction between the self and the external world, originally discovered by Klein. (Polledri, 2003, p. 214)

There have been considerable suggestions in the literature that expand on Klein's thinking. Berman's conceptualisation underscores the interpersonal relations between resources of the self and an aggressive threat to them. The concept assumes that one aspect does not exist without the other. Self envy means there exists a "goodness within" that may arouse envy. Wherever the individual attacks himself and others that are important to him, there also exists a self value that might be threatened by the subject himself and that needs protection (Berman, 1999). In *Impasse and Interpretation*, Rosenfeld writes about this in relation to a

negative therapeutic reaction. He describes how these patients project into the therapist their own envious and shaming selves. They will do anything to defend themselves against the shame of therapy. The major reason for negative therapeutic reactions is when they view the therapist as a dangerous aggressor, masquerading as conveying beneficial insight, but who is really trying to destroy their self-integrity. This is the nature of the intra-psychic conflict in self envy: protective measures to avoid shame parallel defences deployed against envy (Rosenfeld, 1987, pp. 265–285).

Clinically, the overall presenting problem of self envy is depression and negativity, although most envious individuals suffer from an encapsulated murderous aspect of their personalities (Polledri, 2003). They very often describe, whilst explaining their depression, a sense of being accompanied by a "second self", an observer who, not sharing the dementia of his double, is able to watch with dispassionate curiosity as his companion struggles against the oncoming disaster, finally deciding to embrace it, as Styron describes in his writings on depression (1991, p. 64).

While researching the dynamic of self envy in borderline structures within the personality, Lopez-Corvo (1994) describes the condition as resulting from the interaction of different elements forming the Oedipus complex. For example, in the clinical cases on which he reports, a serious increment of envy has taken place during childhood between the child who felt excluded and a parental couple. This, he believes, is an envy usually related to different aspects of parental harmony, control, power, and creativity, which includes the capacity to reproduce.

Lopez-Corvo describes how envious feelings experienced by children towards their parents will remain inside as foreign and active objects, without ever being integrated within the ego. Later on in life, when these children become adults, or have the opportunity to become parents, they will then envy, within themselves, their own capacity to establish harmonious relationships. Because of the severity of the splitting, these feelings are not experienced as one's own, and it is this impression of extraneousness that allows envy to take place.

Self envy is a more common conflict than we have previously thought it to be. Anything that links love, the happy couple, family harmony, and so on, will generate very painful feelings of envy, always creating the scenario that it is unattainable for the excluded part of the envier. A lethal amount of envy, usually concealed, acts as a "secret weapon".

Its main purpose is to undermine the object's goodness as well as any kind of link with it. This encapsulation is what, as we have seen, Bion described as an "attack on linking" (1959).

Segal has directed us to understand that these internal figures contribute to the construction of and are comparable to Freud's *over-severe superego*:

> The projection of envy into the internal object gives rise to an envious superego. The over-severe superego, which Freud describes as the basis of psychical disturbance, often turns out on analysis to be an envious superego. That is, its attacks are directed not only against the individual's aggression, but also, and even predominantly, against the individual's progressive and creative capacities. (Segal, 1979, p. 143)

Berke was perhaps referring to self envy, in his discussion "the internal envier". He believes that "when the envier, beset by self-imposed attacks on his internal world, tries to preserve himself from himself by splitting up and projectively identifying his spite and malice with and into parts of his own mind". He goes on to say: "The result is an envious person who contains a multitude of envious others, all threatening to attack him from within" (Berke, 1985, p. 177).

In relationships, the implications for this seem to be an overwhelming feeling of disappointment (for those in a relationship with the self envier), usually accompanied by a very gradual yet distinctive loss of confidence and self esteem by the other within the relationship. This explains, to some degree, the attack on the conceptualisation of thought, which, during treatment, is transformed into an attack on linking thought between patient and clinician. I will expand on this in the next chapter, when considering perverse relationships in pathological organisations within the personality, but am presenting here two cases that provide insights into the nature and effects of self envy and my observations on its recognition.

## Case study: something is broken and it cannot be fixed

This case study concerns a 28-year-old woman who committed suicide by hanging less than a year after she had completed 18 months of psychotherapy. The circumstances leading to her decision to end her life occurred during the Christmas before her death: she and her partner of seven years had recently moved into a new home, and he had asked her to marry him and to have his children. According to her fiancé, four days after his proposal, she wrote in her notebook that this time she was definitely "going to do it", having already made two unsuccessful attempts by overdosing, and a third in the week preceding her death. She took her life one week after St Valentine's Day and two weeks before Mothering Sunday.

*Rose*

Rose was the younger of two daughters, her sister being three years older. When Rose was a few months old, their mother had a psychotic breakdown, and it was often said by the family to Rose that she was "such a good baby, you never used to cry" and that "mother was all right until you were born". The mother's illness continued throughout Rose's childhood and adolescence into adulthood. Mother had taken overdoses on several occasions, asking not to be saved because she wanted to die. Father was described as a solid, reliable, and hard-working man who devoted his time to caring for his wife and family. Rose would often "baby-sit" their mother when father was working away from home and, on his return, would inform him if their mother needed compulsory admission to hospital under the terms of the Mental Health Act, something of which Rose was very ashamed.

A predictable pattern of events was that, after several weeks in hospital, mother would recover, return home, be well for about six months, and then begin a gradual downward spiral. She frequently hallucinated and barricaded herself in a room in the loft "hiding from the enemy who were coming to invade them". Mother would often talk to her daughters in her depression, saying how wretched she felt because she deserved to die. Growing up under Nazi occupation, she had, in fact, hidden in a loft to escape from the soldiers who had harmed her sisters. (Abraham & Torok's 1994 work regarding transgenerational haunting is relevant here, and I will discuss this in more detail in my theoretical reflections on Rose's case material.)

Underlying all these psychically indigestible experiences, Rose had a deep-rooted fear that she would go mad and end up like her mother. Rose was afraid that there was something wrong with her, that there was a "band of black steel inside her head", which nobody could understand, as she was the only one now in her family suffering from this appalling feeling which was both nameless and indescribable. This is an example of what André Green describes as "blank anxiety" or "blank mourning", all connected to what he calls "the problem of emptiness" and is "the result of one of the components of primary repression: massive decathexis, both radical and temporary, which leaves traces in the unconscious in the form of psychic holes" (Green, 1996, p. 146).

Her attempt to kill herself, a symbolic death, a psychic murder, before she was referred for psychotherapy was, Rose explained, "to break the mould instead of ending up like my mother". She often said in her therapy that she felt guilty about being happy, and therefore did not see how she could get better.

Whenever I made any interpretations in terms of her anxiety about getting better or her guilt about being happy, she would bow her head, then fall silent, frequently remaining like that for most of the session. If I pointed out to her that there was a part of her which she felt nobody could understand, and how difficult she felt it would be to break the mould, she would smile faintly and then stare at the floor.

Shame is about eye contact. We lower our eyes and avert our gaze, which interrupts whatever has been going on between the participants, whereas the envier tries to avoid eye contact for fear of a talion response, known since antiquity as an eye for an eye and a tooth for a tooth (Berke, 1987). Fenichel discusses how: "'I feel ashamed' means 'I do not want to be seen'. Therefore, persons who feel ashamed hide themselves, or at least avert their faces. This is a kind of magical gesture, arising from the magical belief that anyone who does not look cannot be looked at" (Fenichel, 1945, p. 139).

Rose was a young woman who rarely made eye contact and kept her head bowed down during any interaction in her therapy sessions. Perhaps hope was unbearable, which Winnicott describes in "Fear of Breakdown" (Winnicott, 1974, pp. 103–106). He also sees a positive element in a wish for non-existence: "only out of non-existence can existence start" (p. 107). When I enquired about how her fiancé would have felt if she had killed herself, Rose replied: "Perhaps I would mean more to him in my death than I would in my life."

During her therapy, Rose would often say:

> I have to rely on myself. I cannot expect you or anyone else to be there for me. I cannot depend on you, it has to come from me. In that sense, I am my own worst enemy. I know I sound like a

broken record, but there is nothing there. I do not have a picture of a lively mum and a dad inside my mind.

When I asked her to describe in more detail what the absence of that picture in her mind of two people represented, she said, rather dismissively:

> Badness in me ... and deadness in her .... A crazy mother who disappears, and a dad who is a closed book. You really cannot help me with this. I would only repeat this appalling experience if I had a baby. To have his babies would only be repeating with my baby what I have been through. How ghastly!

All my attempts to interpret what I considered to be the negative therapeutic reaction, which regularly emerged after some very faint improvements, were met with blankness. The characteristics of the transference were either a withdrawal into silence, or an indifference that felt more like despair than anger whenever the idea of any hope or acknowledgement of Rose's negativity entered into the therapeutic alliance. Rose would say very quietly that I did not have a clue about how depressed she was, how trapped she was in "that black hole of hopelessness" and how she must have been depressed "even as a baby". I wondered whether for Rose to "get better" would perhaps be betraying her internal mother, fearing she would "let her down" if she did not end up like her actual mother. Most of these interpretations were experienced by Rose as if I had been talking to someone else who was not in the room and I would experience in the countertransference an overwhelming sense of emptiness.

Slowly there seemed to be a very slight improvement. Rose said she felt "much better". When the company she worked for moved to a different area, Rose moved too and terminated her therapy on that basis. About a year later I heard from her GP that she had taken a second overdose. Her sister had subsequently taken her back to see the family doctor, even though she had moved out of the catchment area. Her GP said he thought she should get back in touch with her therapist (myself), to which Rose replied, "She can't help me any more ... she did her best." When her doctor asked her why she had tried to kill herself the previous day, she looked him straight in the eye and said: "Because, when I woke up, I felt better ... and I couldn't stand it."

It is important to think about Rose's comment to her doctor, which is relevant to our understanding of the eyes of shame. Unless the underlying shame sensitivity is worked through as such in psycho-therapeutic treatment, with individuals such as Rose the affects of self-disgust and self-dissmell (Tomkins, 1962) are fused with shame, and these individuals feel they should not get better, that their ill-ness is richly deserved. Similar to masochists, they seem to oper-ate within a bizarre frame of reference, where it is *good* to feel bad (Nathanson, 1992).

With Rose, I wondered whether this had been an example of envy as the externalisation of the death instinct directed towards the external good object, that is, her image of herself as a healthy person (Klein, 1957). Good and bad impulses and good and bad objects appeared to be confused.

About ten days after her second overdose, she took a third. The GP refused to prescribe any further medication and referred her to the psychiatric day hospital. She was aware she could restart her psycho-therapy but was reluctant to do so. She had promised her sister and her parents that she would not take another overdose, so she hanged her-self instead. According to her fiancé, her suicide note said: "Something is broken and it cannot be fixed."

What she wrote powerfully illustrates the intractability of these troubles of the mind. I find it poignant and humbling in its real-ism, whether mistaken or not, in that it opens a window into her agony. It is also very strongly reminiscent of Winnicott's "Fear of Breakdown" (1974), when he describes how the infant, "at the time of absolute dependence" is dependent on the mother supplying "an auxiliary ego-function" (p. 104). This results in a "loss of the capacity to relate to objects" (p. 104). Winnicott's account does not describe the active internal destruction of emotion and relationship, in iden-tification with that originally experienced from the mother, which is found in what Modell describes as "psychic murder syndrome" (2001, pp. 53–76).

## Implications for treatment

As was my experience with Rose, psychotherapeutic treatment of this phenomenon seems to mobilise, in the transference, the past trauma of encapsulated containerlessness (Gallwey, 1991). The *presence* of the good object (i.e., the therapist) reminds the patient of the object who was *absent* from the early nurturing environment. This reinforces the self-loathing and the belief that she contained something bad inside her of which she felt deeply ashamed. To use her words, *something is broken and it cannot be fixed*. It seems impossible for any healthy internalisation to occur during treatment as the patient is attached, internally, to a duality that represents a black hole, a lack of the life force, and a lack of the drive for attachment. Rose's description—"there is a band of black steel inside my head"—is an effective one. From the point of view of containment, psychotherapeutic treatment is, in a sense, offering the patient the very thing they have never had, so they do not know what to do with it or how to internalise the experience of the therapeutic attachment. In that context, the historical past is repeated in the transference. The presence of an encapsulated autistic area (Gallwey, 1996) is suggested, when persistent severe anxiety or destructive acting out accompanies an apparently successful psychotherapeutic working alliance.

Referring back to Rose's case history, what needs to be emphasised is the importance of recognising the relationship between internal parts of the self in comparison with the interaction between the self and the external world. This has been described by Colman as follows:

> Since the destructive narcissistic organization is an *internal* structure, it operates not only against others, devaluing the object, but also operates against the *self*, attacking and destroying any good experiences which *are* taken in, thus making it extremely difficult to develop sufficient internalized good objects to form a strong and containing ego … this maintains a sense of a lack of the other within the compass of the self, which is the source of the envious person's feeling of having something missing at the core of their being. (Colman, 1991, p. 365)

In her treatment, Rose often generated an attitude comparable with a negative therapeutic reaction. When the intricacies of the internal relationships of self envy are taken into account, "intra-psychic interpretation" of the interaction between each of them is absolutely necessary (Rosenfeld, 1987).

Implications for psychotherapeutic treatment are discussed by Rosenfeld who, challenging the Kleinian concept of envy, claims that in his experience interpretations relating to the patient's envy, particularly if these are frequent, cause more pain than insight. The patient is likely to feel inferior and humiliated by the fact that the therapist understands him so much better than he does himself. In clinical practice, this evokes in the analysis an overwhelming sense of latent shame that is almost never expressed, least of all articulated, during the therapeutic alliance. This is particularly true of those individuals who may have felt humiliated and inferior in their past, particularly in relation to shame as I have described in the previous section. Frequent interpretations transferentially may increase the sense of shame and pain. The aim of the treatment is to create an atmosphere of acceptance and containment (Rosenfeld, 1987).

Self envy, the turning of destructiveness against the self, is a very important clinical phenomenon which has been previously described by Rosenfeld (1987) as *negative narcissism*. This was developed out of Rosenfeld's application of Kleinian thought to an understanding of a personality structure in which an internal destructive part attacks the good parts of the ego that have made some progress in psychoanalytical treatment. Clinically, any progress seems to be experienced as a negative therapeutic reaction that, in turn, mobilises the destructive aspects, seen as envious, turning against the analyst, who represents the object who is the source of life and goodness. Rosenfeld describes this as:

> the narcissistic patient wanting to believe he has given life to himself and is able to feed and look after himself ... faced with the reality of being dependent on the analyst ... who stands for the parents, particularly the mother. He would rather die, to be non-existent, deny the fact of his birth, destroy his analytic progress and insight representing the child in himself which he feels the analyst has created. (Rosenfeld, 1987, pp. 106–107)

Rosenfeld wonders whether this represents Freud's description of "pure" death instinct or the death instinct in complete diffusion. He goes on to describe this as being caused by the activity of destructive envious parts of the self which become severely split off and encapsulated. The whole self becomes identified with the destructive self. In this way, Rosenfeld writes, these patients give the impression that they have dealt with their struggle between the loving caring side by identifying almost entirely with the destructive narcissistic part of the self, providing them with a sense of superiority and self-admiration. A part of the self which is felt to be bad has a perverse hold over the good part. One part of a person can envy the aspirations as well as the achievements of another part and sabotage their future fruition and continuity in growth (Rosenfeld, 1987).

## The dead mother syndrome

Crucial in the development of my understanding of Rose's case history was André Green's "dead mother syndrome". As Modell (2001) explains, Green believes that the phenomenology of the dead mother remains one of the most intractable therapeutic problems that any clinician can encounter, and I consider it to be very apposite when thinking about the further development of self envy, not only from a clinical, but also from a theoretical understanding of how we can expand our knowledge to work with individuals who lack a sense of self in relation to the other and the implications of this for treatment in the clinical setting.

Green employs the term "dead mother" to describe the intensely malignant clinical syndrome when there is a primary identification with an emotionally dead mother. In formulating his concept, Green clarifies his theory by discussing the difference between the *actual* death of a mother and that of an image that has been constituted in the child's mind, following post-natal clinical depression. "This brutally transforms a live object, which should be the source of vitality for the child, into a distant figure: toneless, inanimate, deeply impregnating the emotional life of certain individuals, and weighing on the destiny of their object relationships and narcissistic future" (Green, 1996, p. 142).

Green elaborates further by describing how the "dead" mother remains alive while psychically dead in the eyes of the young child in her care. The main characteristic (for the purposes of developing this painful realisation) is that in the treatment setting, the adult patient experiences a conflict with any object that is close, rather than displaying symptoms of a depressive nature.

Modell describes a mother's affective withdrawal from her infant and young child as a relatively common occurrence, whereas the dead mother syndrome, which bespeaks psychopathology, is quite rare. The individual's response to an emotionally absent mother, in Modell's view, illustrates the importance of a "selective process" within the individual as a response to the traumatic disruption of maternal relatedness. Modell uses the term "selection" in a Darwinian sense, stating that it does not represent a "conscious voluntary choice" (Modell, 2001, p. 76).

This has important implications for treatment, as otherwise patients may continue to believe that their mother blocked their communication because of their intrinsic defectiveness or badness. The consequences of this have been described by Beebe and Lachmann (2002), Kaufman (1992), Nathanson (1987), Tomkins, (1962, 1963), and Schore (2003a) as one of the essential causal factors of shame. Their research indicates that "exposure to early life stress is associated with neurobiological changes in children and adults which may underlie the increased risk of psychopathology" (Heim & Nemeroff, 2001, p. 1023). The question as to whether it is possible for us to make definitive statements about the early roots of violence can only be considered if we examine this in the context of early roots of human life, the *process* of development itself. How can we possibly assume that experience that takes place in infancy, the very earliest events of human life, are so critical to every-thing that follows? Schore argues that: "We know enough about the structural biological development of the brain, that we must go beyond purely functional psychological theories of a pre-disposition to violence and disorders of the self" (1994, p. 268). In other words, traumatic dis-ruption of maternal relatedness warrants a deeper understanding of the genesis of psychopathology and must integrate both the psychological and the biological realms. The concept of trauma, which is by defini-tion psychobiological, is a bridge between the domains of both mind and body.

Rose's case history is intended to give a more in-depth study of the implications for treatment, and an example of the clinical application of some of these theoretical models, in order to test out their effectiveness in understanding self envy.

The main themes of Rose's case study exemplify Green's hypothetical questions when formulating the dead mother syndrome. They are:

> What is the relation that one can establish between object-loss and the depressive position, as general given facts, and the singularity of the characteristics of this depressive configuration, which is cen-tral, but often submerged among other symptoms? (Green, 1996, pp. 143–144)

For Green, it is surprising that the general model of mourning that underlies the concept makes no mention of the bereavement of the mother nor the loss of a sense of self in relation to her. The black hole of depression, blankness, is only a secondary product, the consequence rather than the cause of a blank anxiety that expresses a loss that has been experienced on a narcissistic level. The problem of emptiness and deadness is the result of one of the components of primary repression that leave traces in the unconscious in the form of "psychical holes". Green describes how:

> this depression only breaks into the open in the transference. As for the classic neurotic symptoms, they are present but of secondary value. Impotence to withdraw from a conflictual situation, impotence to love, to make the most of one's talents, to multiply one's assets, or, when this does take place, a profound dissatisfaction with the results. (1996, p. 148)

> They become dead and lifeless in the clinical setting. They maintain a corpse-like posture, and speak in a dead-seeming voice drained of all affective valences. (Modell, 2001, p. 80)

What we are dealing with is *transference depression*, a term which Green has coined to oppose it to transference neurosis. This transference depression is an indication of the repetition of an infantile depression, the characteristics of which may usefully be specified (Green, 1996, p. 149).

As individuals we build our character through introjection—taking into ourselves our experiences of our early relationship to our carers and others close to us in infancy and childhood. If, for whatever reason, envy prevents us from building loving, warm, trusting relationships, our whole inner world will be influenced and we are likely to remain correspondingly insecure. According to Joseph (1986), this insecurity or sense of inadequacy in forming attachments will increase hatred of others who can do so, who are more comfortable, more confident, and more stable, by self comparison. In other words, this insecurity increases the envy, creating a vicious circle.

Both attachment theory and psychoanalytic theory, says Fonagy, assume that early relationships provide the context within which certain critical psychological functions are acquired and developed.

Key findings from attachment research exploring the effect of maternal depression as a cause of disorganised attachment fail to examine the critical variable, that is, the extent to which the infant is actually exposed to a severely depressed caregiver over a prolonged period. In individual studies where chronic exposure to a caregiver with severe depression was independently verified, there appears to be a strong association with attachment disorganization. (Fonagy, 2001, p. 37)

Bowlby was unequivocal in his conviction that differences in the security of infant–mother attachment would have long-term implications for later intimate relationships, self-understanding, and psychological disturbance. (Fonagy, 2001, p. 28)

Survival instincts and the desire for attachment impulses vary between infants. In some cases, this is lacking from birth and such infants therefore tend to get neglected. They don't cry out and are very often "good babies". They don't prospect and they don't hold on, and their carers treat them as contented infants. Despite the fact that they are not demanding it, they actually need a great deal of active attachment. This deficiency leads to a self-generated neglect. Although described as "good babies" (Rose, for example, was often "such a good baby"), they are, in fact, *passive* babies.

In therapy, Rose's individuality was completely lost as she became submerged within the mother she had constructed. In the transference, those who suffer from the dead mother syndrome evidence great difficulties "in being with the other". In addition, and perhaps more specifically in relation to the dead mother syndrome regarding self envy, there is an inability to experience pleasure. Pleasure itself, the pleasure of simply being alive, is absent and cannot be taken for granted (Green, 1996; Modell, 2001).

Rosenfeld describes how envy obscures input from the environment, suggesting that, in the transference, the patient reconstructs the impasse they experienced as a child. If, he adds, the therapist ascribes this solely to envy, resulting in a negative therapeutic reaction, due to the patient's resistance to improve, the subtleties are missed. So-called innate envy is a secondary characteristic, especially if there is a lack of a positive drive for attachment or a lack of vitality—not present as something bad, but as a lack of the drive for attachment (Rosenfeld, 1987, pp. 85–104).

Stern, who was influenced by Green's concept of the dead mother syndrome, observed the infant's "micro-depression" resulting from its failed attempts at attachment and to bring the mother "back to life":

> Compared to the infant's expectations and wishes, the depressed mother's face is flat and expressionless. She breaks eye contact and does not seek to re-establish it. There is less contingent responsiveness. There is a disappearance of her animation, tonicity, and so on. Along with these invariants coming from the mother, there are resonant invariants invoked in the infant: the flight of animation, a deflation of posture, a fall in positive affect and facial expressivity, a decrease of activation, etc. In sum, the experience is descriptively one of a "micro-depression" (Stern, 1994, pp. 12–13).

Rose would at times display all these symptoms in her sessions with me, and I was reminded of her comment: "I am told that I was even depressed as a baby."

According to Kenneth Robson, "if the bond through eye contact is not established, or if it is characterised by disruption, distress or depression, the infant's ability to form relationships will be damaged" (Robson, 1967, pp. 17–18). When visual behaviour does not exist in the relationship between human beings, something deviant or pathological is present. In shame, one stays merged with the eyes of mother (hence the daughter's deepest psychic disturbance). The looking of mother is a looking at, not a looking after, or into.

'The dead mother is a ghost which pervades the entire analytic process' (Green & Kohon, 2005, p. 80). This is in line with Abraham and Torok's theory of the transgenerational phantom, in which "the phantom which returns to haunt bears witness to the existence of the dead, buried within the other" (1994, p. 175).

## The transgenerational phantom

Re-reading Abraham and Torok's *The Shell and the Kernel* (1994) for the purposes of this case history proved fruitful, especially the chapter by Nicolas Abraham entitled "The Theory of the Transgenerational Phantom". Abraham's theory of the transgenerational phantom is relevant to Rose's case history, as he suggests that "the unsettling disruptions in the psychic life of one person can adversely and unconsciously affect someone else". Abraham likens the foreign presence to ventriloquism, and calls it a "phantom" or a "phantomatic haunting". The concept of the phantom redraws the boundaries of psychopathology and extends the realm of possibilities for its cure by suggesting the existence within an individual of a collective psychology comprised of several generations, "so that the analyst must listen for the voices of one generation in the unconscious of another" (1994, p. 166).

"The psychoanalytic idea of the phantom concurs, on the level of description, with Roman, Old Norse, Germanic, and other lore, according to which only certain categories of the dead return to torment the living: those who were denied the rite of burial, or died an unnatural, abnormal death, or suffered injustice in their lifetime." In Abraham's view, "the dead do not return, but their lives' unfinished business is unconsciously handed down to their descendants" (1994, p. 167).

In one of Rose's sessions with me, she had been silent as usual, eyes downcast, when suddenly she started to laugh in an embarrassed, nervous way, saying: "Oh my God, have I been speaking to you in German just now?" When I replied that no, she hadn't, she looked extremely uncomfortable and said: "Why would it ['a voice'] be speaking to me in German?"

The following may explain Rose's torment in relation to the torment her mother vicariously experienced through her two younger sisters, who, as young girls, were raped and tortured by Russian soldiers invading Germany. Abraham describes this as follows:

> But in the psychoanalytic realm laying the dead to rest and cultivating our ancestors implies uncovering their shameful secrets, understanding their nameless and undisclosed suffering ... We should engage in this unveiling and understanding of the former existence of the dead, not because we may want to appease them, but because, unsuspected, the dead continue to lead a devastating psychic half-life in us. (Abraham & Torok, 1994, p. 167)

This may well explain some of Rose's torture when she describes her disturbance as feeling like "a band of black steel inside my head".

The concept of the phantom may also give one a basis for positing the unwitting transmission of a shameful family history as the hidden motivating force that blindly drives some individuals into behaviour which is inexplicable, as Rose (unlike her mother) had no *direct* contact with wartime Nazi reality.

In relation to Rose's case history, the concept of the "phantom" moves the focus of psychoanalytic enquiry beyond the individual being analysed because it postulates that some people unwittingly inherit the secret psychic substance of their ancestors' lives—in Rose's case, her mother's experience of the Holocaust, in which she survived, unlike her two sisters. The "phantom" represents a radical reorientation of Freudian and post-Freudian theories of psychopathology, since here symptoms do not spring from the individual's own life experiences, but from someone else's psychic conflicts, traumas, or secrets (Freud, 1934b).

The idea of the phantom has implications far beyond the understanding of Rose's case history and must be extremely valuable in any further research. "Aspects of this concept may account for the process of transmission which assures the survival of the memory traces derived from the experience of earlier generations" (Abraham & Torok, 1994, p. 166).

This has also been acknowledged by Schore discussing the work of Karr-Morse and Wiley (1997) as being "ghosts from the nursery" which "negatively impact not only on individual lives, but whole communities ... they are, in essence, the enduring right brain imprints of the non-conscious inter-generational transmission of relational trauma" (Schore, 2003a, p. 306).

## Reflections on Rose's case

Envy, often accompanied by rage and violence, is a defence against shame. Self envy is *always* associated with self-destructiveness. For Rose, self-destruction must have seemed her only possible response to her self envy, which stemmed from a shame not of her own making. It was probably also the only way she saw of projecting her inner self.

To summarise my understanding of Rose's suicide; from Gallwey's standpoint, perhaps she intended that, by finding her hanging, her fiancé, a solid, reliable man, should experience what she could not project into him. Perhaps she was always looking for a live object but could only find a dead object. This must have been such a dreadful experience for her, in terms of preverbal memory as a baby, that she could not get rid of it by projective identification. So, in the end, she had to alter the external environment, as she could not alter her internal environment by omnipotently managing it in any other way (Gallwey,

1996). Perhaps she engineered it so that her partner would actually have the experience that she could never articulate, and could not project.

Rose did not seem to have had the initial experience of a life-sustaining object; therefore, a particular type of malfunctioning resulted, differing from both psychotic and neurotic equivalents. The basis of this was not the distortion or fragmentation of containment as we see in psychosis, where the mental illness affects the whole personality, where defences are achieved without altering reality or the external environment. It is the *total lack of a container altogether* with a failure in the functions that spring from it. The result was proliferating turmoil and anxiety without the capacity to use projective identification effectively as a first line of defence to lessen psychic stress. This is in contrast to Green's dead mother complex, in which a mother provides at first a vital source for the child, and only later becomes an unresponsive object lacking in warmth and colour due to depression or other distancing trauma.

Maybe Rose did have some capacity for phantasy and imagination, but not enough, and because of her early dislocations in her development, she had to live it out. In her death, Rose may have been actively trying to use projective identification, but she was, like the majority of forensic patients, unable to use projective identification as an omnipotent phantasy and was forced into acting out the conflict behaviourally by attempting suicide, as an expression of a breakdown in symbol functioning.

In terms of the application of the Gallwey model to Rose's clinical material, the vital concept, once established between mother and infant, becomes the mainstay of sanity and the reference against which comprehension and imagination can be explored. Without the realisation of the vital concept, no strategies in phantasy, omnipotent or otherwise, can develop to protect the ego from unmanageable stress. Splitting and projective identification is not an option. Interference with the realisation of the vital concept results in varying degrees of psychopathology, depending on which specific linking function is most affected, the most severe and extensive causing an anguished autistic confusion between self and other. If this state is not superseded by a late but inevitably flawed realisation of the vital concept, then an individual with an autistic spectrum disorder will result (Gallwey, 1996). When it is overcome it will nevertheless persist as an impenetrable black hole in the ego— Rose's "band of black steel" inside her head.

These autistic lacunae produce states of mind that have the characteristic of envy of good experience, but these states need exploration of their origins. They may be a reaction of revenge at being cheated of the beatific promise of the vital concept and thrust instead into a near-annihilation, or they may be a reaction to a deep awareness of a defect in identity. This latter state of affairs is particularly so when life experience calls on the individual for a creative response when they are unable to respond because the vital area of their own identity has not been conceptualised. The subsequent profound despair and dread, because of the absence of defensive secondary phantasies, results in a spoiling attack on the initiating experience. To mistake this for envy *per se* is ultimately unhelpful (Gallwey, 1996).

I am suggesting that Rose possibly had an identity which was primarily flawed in the way I have described, so she could not find the concept of motherhood when it was apparently natural that she should. She would then have been overwhelmed by despair and, without any intra-psychic protection, escaped into death in a way designed to confront her partner's prospecting efforts with an horrific dead dependent object. Rose's case history is not an example of projective identification, which was not available to her, but its enacted equivalent. At the moment her fiancé found her hanging, he would have experienced something of the undreamable nightmare that had been her mother's legacy to her when she was an infant.

In his later work, Rosenfeld challenges the Kleinian concept of innate envy when he expresses the view that early dislocations in nurturing, in which the dependent self has been unable to thrive, were recreated in the illness and within the transference (1987, p. 80). He attempts to distinguish between reactions arising from mistaken interpretations and defective technique from those arising from an envious backlash. When treating patients with Rose's type of history, he suggests, these early impasses to development needed to be understood by closely examining the countertransference. According to Rosenfeld, there are many obstacles in treating these disturbed patients, particularly the analyst's sense of hopelessness and frustration. These are potentially very fruitful areas of research into the study of the mother/child duality, since they derive from early dislocations in development. He places less emphasis on envy as being innate as the central variant which causes grave pathology than can be found in the work of contemporary post-Kleinian authors.

Rozsika Parker (1993), writing about maternal ambivalence and unconscious phantasy in mothers, describes how disowned aspects in the mother are often carried by her child.

> If a mother cannot allow consciousness of her ambivalent feelings, experienced both in her own childhood and again re-lived in relation to her children, this unconscious generational baggage, with its destructive phantasies leading to unhealthy denial or enactment of destructive impulses, will profoundly and adversely affect the child's identification with her, especially a daughter's. (cited in Masterson, 1999, p. 144)

Perelberg writes about habitual violence towards either the self or another and she states that it "may reflect a failure to meet the fundamental need of every infant to find his mind, his intentional state, in the mind of the object. For the infant, internalization of this image performs the function of 'containment' (Bion, 1962), which Winnicot has written of as 'giving back to the baby the baby's own self' (Winnicott, 1967, p. 33)" (Perelberg, 1999, p. 62).

## Origins of despair

In relation to external environmental influences, the clinical material from both Rose's and Sally's case histories extends my theoretical argument that a disturbing traumatic effect had taken form, in which, as infants, they developed a sense of "non-existence" (Alexander, 1997). This was probably as a result of experiences with a murderous mother, in Sally's case, and an emotionally absent, depressed, and suicidal mother in Rose's case, where the organism develops a sense of its not being held or contained in the mother's mind during the phase of "unsensed dependency" on the object for its survival. In his work on the origins of despair, Richard Alexander writes of:

> gradual development of a destructive envious attitude that eventually gets directed against the existence of a two-party presence, and in particular, the possibility that this brings forward as being one of the serious implications for treatment. The ego is, indeed, in a state of existence, but lacking in cohesion and thus, is quite vulnerable. The failure at this stage of development brings with it a state of ego

fragmentation, but, I consider that this type of disruption does not take place directly, but secondarily. (Alexander, 1997, p. 425)

This supports the view I hold and which constitutes a major thrust of this book. After Alexander: "Disruption of the ego would thus take place when the forces of reality finally break through this defensive structure and, in an extreme case, may give rise to the formation of a psychogenic autistic state" (Alexander, 1997, p. 419).

Understanding suicide and suicidal behaviour in females, as demonstrated in the clinical material of Sally and Rose, involves understanding that the ego has "given up" on the primary object, leading to a belief that no good object, or hope, or reality, ever existed for them in the first place. These women were operating from an aggrieved and vengeful position: "A sense of uncertainty was originally overwhelming to the point that the fear of dying had deteriorated, in its state of despair, into a wish to die" (Alexander, 1997). My broader clinical experience, as well as these two case histories, has suggested that the failure of the actual birth of the child to inspire hope in an otherwise depressed and self-destructive mother may have come about when the mother herself had been unduly affected by a deep sense of deprivation. This evoked, in turn, an expression of hostile envy and the mother was prevented from experiencing a sense of gratitude in response to giving birth—"This produces hostile envy which operates from within an inner atmosphere of hopelessness" (Alexander, 1997, p. 421). These descriptions are consistent with the outgrowth of an infantile despairing type of depression. The characteristics are developmental arrest, manifestations of which includes a marked disturbance in the capacity for intimacy with self and object, and an inhibition of a two-person, heterosexual desire (Berke, 1997).

Although Berke wrote about women having a sense of biological and social insecurity heightened by envious and jealous rivalries with mothers and sisters (1987, p. 452) (as did both Sally and Rose), and this also has serious implication for treatment countertransferentially, women are innately closer to the figures whom they wish to harm as well as emulate. Therefore, the pattern of violence is different; it is more likely to be directed inwards rather than outwards. As a young woman, Sally had herself sterilised and had a breast-reduction operation, leading to the negation of function. The external circumstances surrounding Rose's suicide was that her partner proposed to her, because he wanted her to have his babies. She said: "I would rather die than have his babies", and "Perhaps I will mean more to him in my death than in my life". Seemingly an attack on the self, it inevitably embraces a vicious onslaught on the "internalised other" (Berke, 1987).

Underlying the above, which stems from a defensive manoeuvre to survive rather than a death instinct, and from the effects of the psychic withdrawal, lurks the development of a most dangerous configuration. This has the potential for malignant growth, a development that can take hold when the uncontained excessive distress and anger turn into a rage of murderously irrational proportions. Destructive envy of this kind emanates not from love of the object, but from the loss of that love, and in response to the unbearable disappointment that is part and parcel of this loss. Inadequate containment of the primitive fear of dying and needs, gives rise to an overwhelming survival anxiety, hostility, and ultimately to despair (Alexander, 1997).

Cases in which self envy is the underlying cause, however, are not necessarily so bleak and unforgiving. Gallwey describes a certain clinical type as showing virtually normal development with some patches of anxiety—possibly a phobia, perhaps a history of night terrors or bad dreams, perhaps an occasional depressive state or an eating disorder. He says:

> In treatment, such patients are very often very intuitive and take interpretations very well. You feel you have understood the clinical material but then there is a curious "negative therapeutic reaction". Often it is not very startling, more a low-grade kind of pessimism. The patient will describe a general feeling of being "much better" but somehow this improvement is not maintained. Then you begin to wonder, perhaps, about envy. In some cases there is no evidence of that and what evolves in treatment is the feeling that the patient is walking into a black hole, a coal mine. It is not so much symbolism, but contact with an area of dangerousness, confusion and impenetrability. (Gallwey, 2003)

The next case study describes this and is also an example of Green's dead mother complex, where the mother is *initially* experienced as the source of vitality and is *afterwards* brutally transformed by depression into a toneless, inanimate, and depressed object.

*Case study: why should anyone attack their own capacities?*

This briefer clinical example highlights the psychic phenomenon of the internalised envier attacking the psychic representation of the good object. In self envy, one part of a person can envy the aspirations as well as the achievements of another part, and sabotage their future fruition or continuity of growth (Khan, 1974).

> In the intra-psychic situation, the infant in relinquishing its expecta-
> tions of gain from the primal object, acquires the unconscious belief
> that help in the real world does not exist and, thereby, becomes a
> player in a pathological narcissistic defence system. Destructive self
> envy develops as an incipient outgrowth of the ensuing survival
> mentality that takes form, the basic aim of which is to undermine
> hope. (Alexander, 1997, p. 417)

*Caroline*

Caroline, now twenty-six years old and a highly talented theatre costume designer, first contacted me when she was having difficulty
deciding which fashion design college to attend. She had previously
benefited from some short-term psychotherapy when, as a very attrac-
tive adolescent, she constantly picked and attacked her face, due, she
insisted, to "too many blackheads". Her peers were vicious and nick-
named her "crater face", of which she was so ashamed that she would
not leave the house, attacking her beauty even more violently. She sab-
otaged her chances of an interview with a top fashion design college
by failing to keep her appointment. Several months of treatment left
her feeling she had understood her problems, and she said that she felt
"much better".

When Caroline was three years old, her parents divorced. She
claimed that the divorce "did not affect her in any way", although
her mother became severely depressed and "lost the will to live". Her
mother remarried and was "much better". Caroline and her seven-
year-old brother saw their father at weekends, although she felt very
betrayed by him throughout her childhood. She was ashamed of the
fact that her father, in her eyes, did not think she was very pretty, especially as the woman he left home for had two beautiful daughters who
were "drop-dead gorgeous". She turned the anger she felt towards her
parents, especially her father, onto herself: her skin, her creativity, and,

in a defensive way, by attacking her own capacities. She could then "rubbish" and denigrate anybody or anything she perceived as being of value in her orbit, for example, the spoiling of any pleasure in her sexual relationship for herself and her fiancé.

After a recent attack on further progress, when she had spent many months designing the costumes for her finals, only later to destroy most of them by cutting them up, she came back to see me. In her first session, she described two dreams.

In the first dream, she was in a stately home designing corsets. There was an old friend there who had once hurt her. Caroline had made a beautiful white silk corset. It was the best one in the whole class and she was going to be nominated for an award for designing this garment. She then tried it on the friend who had hurt her and it looked stunning. Then a man in the dream, who was also a designer, murdered the girl in the corset. The white corset was now completely stained with red blood and had been shredded to pieces with a knife. She then decided to go and tell her mother, who was quite dismissive and told her to go and take a bath. When she went to the bathroom, there was the ghost of a friend, in the bath, haunting her, and then she woke up.

After this dream, she started to feel very depressed. She thought her designs were rubbish and actually not good enough, and that she would not get through her finals. Those doubts eventually passed. Then, after three or four days, she began to believe that she did not have any friends. She thought she looked ugly and started "on the blackheads again" by "digging them out of her skin". She also started quarrelling with her fiancé, James. She eventually snapped out of it, but only when James seriously questioned their relationship, complaining that he was sick of "banging his head against a brick wall by trying to constantly reassure her that she was lovely and very talented". In their sexual relationship, she was convinced she was "not very good", so James was not really enjoying it and sooner or later he would have an affair with someone behind her back. Then, with the nastiest look on her face she said: "To be honest, I actually spoil it for him every single time."

The most important aspect of Caroline's therapy was to explore her feelings of envy and how this masked, in a defensive, cruel way, a deep sense of shame that "she would rather die than admit to or reveal". Shame was located in the obsessional devaluation of her own achievements and the attack on her own beauty. The patient attacks his own conceptualisation of thought, what Bion (1959) described as "attacks on linking".

In the second dream, she was in a car park in Sainsbury's. Her fiancé, James, had had a promotion in his professional life and had bought a new Volkswagen car. In her dream, every time she stopped and reversed her car into a space, it shot backwards out of control and damaged all the other Volkswagens in the car park. There were about five or six of them. All the owners came out, and she was worried they would know it was she who had caused all the damage, so she quickly drove out of the car park. She then drove back and the very same thing happened again. She parked and as she was about to put her car into neutral it shot backwards again, hit a Volkswagen, and was completely out of control, no matter how hard she tried to keep the handbrake in its locked position.

After she had the dreams, she started to feel very depressed because she knew she would have to have more psychotherapeutic treatment, and the dream work was where she would need to focus primarily. The thought made her even more depressed because she thought she had "sorted herself out" by having therapy before, especially, "as it had made her feel so much better"… and having to go back to this "horrible business of envy again" was something she did not want to accept as necessary. The only person, she added resentfully, who would benefit from further treatment, would be her therapist.

## Lessons from the case study

In presenting this vignette from Caroline's clinical material, I demonstrate how devaluation of the other may be seen as a defence against shame which works its way through the internal world and becomes processed as envious tension. Shame has also been described by Phil Mollon as "the result of a broken connection between one human being and others, a breach in the understanding, expectation, and acceptance that is fundamentally necessary for establishing a sense of being a valued member of a human family. The solution to shame is the empathy provided by another" (Mollon, 2002, p. 107).

Self envy appears as an excluded self-object part's desperate need for destruction, directed against inner states of goodness, friendship, creativity, harmony, and, above all, against any kind of idealised relationship such as self-object representations of incorporated images of a parental couple. The envious attack on the harmonious internal parental couple, by an excluded child part-self, is enacted in the transference as an attack on the harmony of the good working alliance, interfering with the relationship between the reasonable and helpful part of the self and the therapist (Lopez-Corvo, 1992). The patient cannot bear any favourable connection between them or benefit for very long from the insight gained. At times, the effect of the therapy is indifference and a retreat into inaccessibility, rather than the sense of an envious attack.

The implications for treatment are that, although the patient's internal relationships are externalised in the transference, they can be understood and discerned by the patient's dreams, associations, and phantasy life. With self envy, it is more akin to the murder of thought, creativity, and imagination. These often help the therapist to understand what is going on and to avoid acting out with the patient in the transference (Steiner, 1981).

This is in line with Rosenfeld's view (1987) that there should be less emphasis on envy being the central variant causing such grave pathology and more thoughtful reflection, this being a very fruitful area of study in developing our knowledge of shame in relation to envious tension.

To think in terms of a negative therapeutic reaction is to underestimate the impact of the patient's destructiveness towards the therapeutic process and the influence of the enviable internal objects on the therapist's capacity for thinking and symbolic functioning—or, in Gallwey's model, on prospective activity. These processes are more difficult to recognise than other forms of envy because self envy inhibits any enjoyment of the patient's own good qualities in himself if he is threatened by any external recognition of their worth.

Like Caroline, a patient may appear to be stronger but unable to act as though there has been any improvement, because a part of the self is envious of the improved part and, in order to avoid envy, will not let the improved part function.

Klein (1957) describes feelings that arise from an envious inner object and are directed towards others. In self envy, the same emotions are described, but instead of being aimed at others in the outside world, they are an attack on an introjected part of the self, representing the creative part of the adult self. The emphasis is on the importance of the relationship between internal parts of the self in comparison with the interaction between the self and the outside world.

To grasp the concept of self envy, it is necessary to keep in mind how a failure in primary linking functioning—that is, a failure in the infant's biological expectation for attachment to a dependable and consistent experience in the primary phase of development—is at the root of this split within the self. This mechanism has been observed clinically by various researchers, including Berke (1985), Bion (1967), Gallwey (1985), Kernberg (1975, 1992), Lopez-Corvo (1994), Rosenfeld (1971), and Segal (1979).

In mental health, self envy is generally described within the umbrella of borderline personality disorder, or the aggressive aspects of narcissism, especially in failed therapeutic transactions by individuals who have experienced difficulties in establishing and sustaining interpersonal relationships throughout their lives. This is hardly surprising because, in essence, the therapeutic transaction itself, as a process, is offering the patient the very thing the person has never had, so it is inevitable that it will be extremely difficult to grasp the concept of a mutual attachment in the first place.

It would be comforting to assume that one could turn to the literature on self envy to discover some help in this direction. Unfortunately, the situation regarding the existence of an envious enclave has become increasingly confused and, although much of the Kleinian-based literature on the subject is interesting, informative, and sometimes helpful, there is also an enormous muddle that has grown around definitions of the use of the term. Bion's description of a psychotic and a non-psychotic part of the personality (1957) is the most helpful model to apply to self envy: he describes the psychotic process as being composed of superego fragments, and the process has as its task the job of destroying any relationship with the other—the psychotic process cannot bear to allow the healthy self to have any meaningful relating or dependency on the another. The psychotic process arises as a result of the very early disruptions in communication, as described by Gallwey (1996).

This case history characterises the psychotic process in self envy Bion (1959) describes, in terms of severing links with anything creative and positive within the psyche: that is, Caroline's artistic talent for costume designing, and, externally, her relationship with her fiancé James.

I will end this chapter with William Blake's apposite metaphor of shame and envy:

'The Sick Rose'

O Rose, thou are sick!
The invisible worm
That flies in the night,
In the howling storm:

Has found out thy bed
Of crimson joy:
And his dark secret love
Does thy life destroy.

William Blake (1757–1827)

# CHAPTER SIX

# Perverse relationships in pathological organisations

... Fantasy ... that vehicle of hope, healer of trauma, protector from
reality, concealer of truth, fixer of identity, restorer of tranquillity,
enemy of fear and sadness, cleanser of the soul .... And creator of
perversion.

(Stoller, 1975, p. 55)

Most psychoanalytic thinkers and clinicians, following Freud's
own description and understanding of perversion in the first
of the "Three Essays on the Theory of Sexuality" (1905a),
have drawn a distinction between perverse elements of behaviour or
phantasy that may occur in any subject alongside more "normal" or
socially acceptable sexual behaviour, and a perverse *structure*, implying
a fixed, sclerotic rigidity of psychical organisation. Authors of canoni-
cal studies of perversion—Chasseguet-Smirgel (1985), Glasser (1998),
Kernberg (2006), Khan (1974), Limentani (1989), Nobus and Downing
(2006), Steiner (1993), Stoller (1975), and Welldon (1988)—argue that elements of hatred, aggression, and intimacy-inhibiting alienation underlie
the perverse structure, leaving the pervert inevitably to find difficulty
in many relationships and areas of social functioning, not only those
immediately related to their sexuality.

Turning away from the traditional psychoanalytical theory of drive-conflict and object-instinctual explanations of the destructiveness of human dynamics has led to the exploration of alternative ways of thinking about perverse behaviour as previously understood from these perspectives. Envy is one of the emotions in need of a re-examination, as very little attention has been paid to the concept of perversion and its link with envy and the part shame plays within that structure (Polledri, 2003).

The glue that binds together elements of a pathological organisation is perversion. Because of the instant gratification this provides to both victim and perpetrator, it is very difficult to give up. John Steiner (1993) believes that "we are not just dealing with a split between good and bad but with the consequences of a breakdown in splitting and a reassembling of the fragments into a highly pernicious mixture, under the dominance of a narcissistic structure" (Steiner, 1993). *This organisation, in my view, represents and replaces the failed attachment in early infancy to the primary maternal object.*

I am suggesting that perversion is a component of envy and represents a breakdown in symbol formation. The psychopathology connected with perverse activity is complicated and derived from many levels, although most forensic clinicians would agree that the contribution from psychotic areas is very great (Polledri, 1995). In this chapter, I want to explore symbol formation as it reflects the nature of the infantile link between primitive ego and the primary object.

Segal describes symbols as a three-term relation in which the symbol acts as a link between the thing symbolised and a person; in analytic terms, these are the ego, the symbol, and the object. Segal maintains that human symbolic functioning springs from the experience of the gap in time and space between self and object and is a reflection, therefore, of the capacity to bear frustration, loss, and depressive guilt. She connects symbol functioning with the potential for meaningful thought and communication within the context of dependent relationships. She contrasts this development of healthy symbols with what she calls symbolic equations, which give rise to concrete thinking and are due to excessive projective identification of the self with the early objects so that separation experiences are obliterated (Gallwey, 1996; Segal, 1957).

However, it is very rare for a perverse patient to present with an open thought disorder, and very often there seems to be a particular development of various modes of symbolic expression. It is definitive of perverse activity that there exists an intense link with an object, albeit a very peculiar one. Gallwey suggests that within the perverse psychopathology, the primitive link between self and object is not completely obliterated by projective identification. The confusion of selective parts of the self and the early objects, and the calling into play of very specific splits and omnipotent phantasies, results in a rearrangement of the dependent relationship in such a way that there is some kind of inversion of the real situation producing a largely delusional separateness (Gallwey, 1978b, 1994, 2003).

The partial confusion of the self with the object and the artificial conditions upon which separateness emerges results in varying degrees of concretism, on the one hand, concealed behind an apparently freer but ambiguous symbolic functioning, on the other, the ambiguous symbols having a developmental potential, although a limited one, in their own terms. The result of this for analytic work is that one is likely to be doubly misled, as I will describe in my clinical examples of womb envy in the next chapter.

In describing perverse relationships between parts of the self, Steiner states that:

> in treatment, in order to liberate the healthy sane part of the patient, we have to understand the *whole* picture. We have to appreciate the sense of hopelessness and despair, but also those occasions when a collusion develops and the individual gets a perverse gratification from the dominance of the narcissistic organization. (Steiner, 1993, p. 115)

Steiner believes that destructive narcissism and early unresolved trauma in relation to attachment figures are usually the basis for the formulation of a pathological organisation within the personality (Steiner, 1993). When destructiveness is part of an individual's character structure, any loving, caring, or interdependent expectations in a relationship are devalued, attacked, and destroyed with pleasure, as I will demonstrate in my clinical material on womb envy.

Self envy is the sophistication of the primitive, destructive part attacking the dependent parts of the personality which have never been integrated and combined, nor learned to live together in harmony. My argument here is that non-containment, or the lack of an "internal duality", which is based on the lack of a solid, reliable attachment figure, is why self envy takes such a hold. It is the bedrock of why the cruel part attacks the primitive part of the self. Whilst the strength of the destructive part and libidinal parts of the self is an important factor in determining the outcome, the so-called normal individual has been fortunate enough to base that on a self that has developed in relation to another or as a reflection of self and other, and is evidence that this duality has been established.

## Perversion: which version?

To reflect briefly on the theory, at this juncture, in order to understand the processes involved: Steiner uses the word *perverse* to refer primarily to a twisting or perversion of the truth, and the relationship between this and actual sexual perversion is not always apparent (Steiner, 1981, p. 243). The link to sexual perversions undoubtedly exists in that the defensive function of perversions and the important role of eroticisation of object relations form the core complex in perversions, whereas the "solid" self can be thought of or identified by contrast with the failure of perversion.

Steiner does not seem to link shame with these very powerful defences, except in the clinical example he provides, in which his patient describes the only source of comfort being masturbation, which left him feeling ashamed and inadequate. But in a very apposite clinical example, he describes the following reference to shame:

> very occasionally he did let me see a needy dependent part of himself … for example when as a small boy he forgot to get off the bus near his home, he had to walk up a very steep hill alone and miserable and too ashamed to admit it … he had very painful memories of being reprimanded by his father and of being smacked by his mother for wetting the bed … but most of all for being called a fool and being laughed at. (Steiner, 1981, p. 224)

Steiner acknowledges that the two parts of this man's personality were complex, each containing some good and some bad parts of the self. He goes on to describe that "this fact disguised the essentially destructive nature of the narcissistic organization on the one hand, and on the other, enabled perverse elements to be associated with the libidinal self which maintained a corrupt collusion". He points out that "What is of significance here is just how much of an individual's life and energy is spent maintaining this corrupt collusion, its main function and aim being that it acts as a healer of this early trauma" (Steiner, 1981, p. 245). Of crucial importance to this thesis are Steiner's observations regarding the difference between perversion and negative acting out of other sorts, in that the sadistic element is more prominent and has become addictive, first as a phantasy and then as an action (Steiner, 1981).

Rosenfeld (1987) again challenges the Kleinian concept of envy as the cause of a negative therapeutic reaction following a positive phase in the analysis. He believed that "this impasse in treatment brought about a severe deterioration in the individual". Rosenfeld's study suggests that envy is not the sole factor that can cause this impasse. His suggestion is that we recognize the presence of a hypnotic figure internally, influencing the destructive figure posing as a benevolent one. If this is interpreted, the patient becomes more aware of what is operating within his internal world, which lessens the paralysing influence this has on the progress of the treatment. This enables the patient to distinguish between "the threat of the murderous inner attack and his own angry, murderous feelings against external objects". (Rosenfeld, 1987, p. 267). It does not, solve the problem of interpretation *preventing* impasse, but, according to Rosenfeld, "much more analytic work can then be done to reduce the potential that the internal destructive figure has to paralyse the individual's progress" (Rosenfeld, 1987, p. 88).

Reading the literature on the implications for treatment with envious individuals, it has been suggested that making conscious either the hostile destructive wishes or the feelings of inadequacy and inferiority before the patient has built a stronger sense of self is often impossible and, when possible, may be more destructive than helpful to the patient. Barth (1988), Gedo (1979), Epstein (1978), and Rosenfeld (1987) all suggest that the patient will hear any interpretations as further evidence of the analyst's superiority and their own inferiority. In these cases, the interpretation will increase, rather than decrease, the intensity of the envy and the defences against it. These recommendations for more flexibility in the analytic work echo Horney's earlier ideas about "the importance of learning the historical meaning of the material for each individual patient". Horney paid active attention to the significance of self-esteem in the development of envy. It will usually be found, among other dynamics, that the existence of a damaged self-esteem and shame lie beneath the aggressive, greedy, and hostile envious feelings.

Recognising these dynamics, when they exist, assists in determining appropriate and inappropriate interventions and enriches the therapeutic work (Horney, 1939, 1948).

Although these and many other analysts, including Hyatt-Williams (1998), have always recognised that narcissistic injury may trigger off envious feelings, the significance of shame and low self-esteem as both motivator and respondent to envious feelings have not been sufficiently explored. It is my view that the focus on drives and repetitions of early patterns of object relations does not always take into account the significance of the sequence in which a disturbed sense of self from the failure in attachment leads on to envy and the urgent need this generates, albeit in an obsessional defensive fashion, to keep such painful feelings out of conscious awareness. Perversion puts shame in its place, by putting it into the other, using projective identification to achieve this.

This sequence has been described by Rose (2003) and Gilligan (2000) as depending on how one defines perversion: "If there is a link between shame and celebrity, there is also a link between perversion and shame. Shaming might be seen as a form of perversion in itself" (Rose, 2003, pp. 202–203).

## History, ideology, and ethics

> The notion of perversion is becoming an increasingly controversial one, is not considered "politically correct" and is both *normative* and *punitive*. (Nobus & Downing, 2006, p. 149)

In *Perversion: Psychoanalytic Perspectives* (2006), Nobus and Downing have developed a very impressive study on issues of history, ideology, and ethics in perversion. The authors review the literature on perversion in order to explore the ways in which "articulations of knowledge about the other's desires" inevitably carry political implications. It is problematic to think the diagnosis of "perversion" without thinking about the historical conditions of this term's production, the networks of ideology that produced it, and the type of power that may be shored up whenever it is employed.

Nobus and Downing provide an overview of some ways of thinking about perversion between psychoanalysis and politics; between liberal and radical ideologies; and in ethical terms. They bring together both psychoanalytic essays on perversion and critical accounts of the concept, and encourage reflection upon what happens when we think about the term "perversion" self-consciously, in full awareness of its cultural as well as its clinical implications. They believe that within the various psychoanalytic models and clinical methods, and according to the value systems and attitudes of individual clinical practitioners, the status accorded to perversion varies considerably.

Louise Kaplan (1993) argues that there is the shortage of psycho-analytic theorisation of perversion in the feminine, stating that such constructed perverse scenarios as fetishism and sadism, which over-emphasise masculine techniques of objectification to compensate for the threat of loss (castration), are probably "male" perversions. For Kaplan, "perversion is a distorted exaggeration of the socially pre-scribed gender characteristics thought proper to each sex". Kaplan follows Stoller in insisting on the immensely limiting rigidity of the perverse solution, rather than on its transgressive or utopian quali-ties. "What distinguishes perversion is its quality of desperation and fixity. A perversion is performed by a person who would otherwise be overwhelmed by anxieties and depression, or psychosis" (Kaplan, 1993, pp. 9–10).

Kaplan claims that, "although perversion does not mean the same thing for men and women, in both cases it is a reaction to, and against, sexual difference and gender division". Emily Apter (2006), on the other hand, takes psychoanalysis's denial of female perverse capacity and its purported tendency to negate the female body as two symptoms of the same underlying problem: the gynophobia of psychoanalysis. This is in opposition to Kaplan's claim that "fetishism would be nonsensical as a female perversion" (Kaplan, 1993, pp. 9–10).

Both erotic life and psychoanalysis are fields fraught with ethical chal-lenges. "These underlie, and are stimulated by, both sets of 'practices', the analytic and the sexual. And both are characterised by the sheer range of their expression and the differences between them." Exam-ining many theoretical concepts from Reichian bodywork, through a Lacanian conception of the subject as constituted by and in language, to the Kleinian emphasis on infantile aggression and primary narcissism, Nobus and Downing discuss how psychoanalysis has developed many faces. "Types of psychoanalysis and types of sexual pleasure may differ to such an extent that one may be forgiven for the observation that they appear not to belong to the same category of phenomenon as each other at all" (Downing, in Nobus & Downing, 2006, pp. 160–161).

## Furthering understanding of perverse relationships

Envy causes pain, discomfort, and shame because it inhibits the capacity to love. It creates what Rosenfeld has described as "thin-skinned narcissistic patients" who were severely traumatised repeatedly as children in their sense of self in relation to other. They seem to have felt persistently and excessively inferior, ashamed, and vulnerable. If, in their treatment, this is interpreted as anything to do with envy, but *not in a containing way*, the patient feels it as a severe narcissistic blow and feels humiliated. As Rosenfeld discusses, "the destructive aspects of narcissism are mobilised by the interpretation as something bad within the person, something once again to be ashamed of possessing and of feeling inferior about" (1987, pp. 98–99).

Humiliation, states of being humbled or depressed, were issues of which Klein was well aware in relation to envy, but she viewed these feelings and the accompanying depression as derivatives of object-instinctual conflicts and may not have needed to have considered them separately in the development of her theory. She captured the essence of the primitive and shame-filled feelings of greed and rage that are often part of the experience of extreme envy in adults. Many of the clinical examples she describes in *Envy and Gratitude* (1957) can be understood as early trauma in infancy being repeated in the transference; but in Klein's discussions of the clinical vignettes, she seems to place more emphasis on the *mechanisms* which, to her, are inherent in envy, more so than object attachment. Two examples follow:

> I shall enumerate some of the defences against envy that I have encountered in the course of my work. Some of the earliest defences often described as I have described before, are omnipotence, denial, and splitting, and are reinforced by envy. (1957, p. 216)

> The fact that envy spoils the capacity for enjoyment explains to some extent why envy is so persistent. It is clear that deprivation, unsatisfactory feeding, and unfavourable circumstances intensify envy because they disturb full gratification, and a vicious circle is created. (1957, pp. 186–187)

Exposure of the self as envious gives rise to shame, especially in the context of an interpretation during treatment. This reaction to the exposure of envy evokes narcissistic wounding to an already fragile sense of self and mobilises a reaction that, in turn, is aimed at restoring the narcissistic equilibrium. A sense of injustice and rage stirs up the need for revenge, oblivious to the consequences the destructive attack has on the self. Envy hides shame, which is, itself, already well concealed. That is why I am placing so much emphasis on the development of our understanding of shame and envy, which leads to containment, rather than an interpretation of envy, which has previously been suggested by Steiner (1981) and Rosenfeld (1987) in their guidelines for treatment.

To understand the attack on the self by the other part of the self is to develop an understanding of the destructive and murderous nature of self envy, originating from the narcissistic omnipotent organisation, which is perverse in its aim to destroy the infantile dependent part of the self by turning against it. This is not always useful, nor is it necessarily accessible, by way of interpretation during treatment. It is a mistake for the therapist to write it off as "just the patient's envy" in the context of an interpretation. The relevance of an *intra-psychic interpretation* is that it avoids transference collusion in some individuals who harbour a perverse psychopathology, and provides the ego with a proper perspective when dealing with conflict and interpreting self envy mechanisms (Lopez-Corvo, 1992).

If we are fully to understand perverse relationships and the existence of a pathological organisation that governs the perversions within a relationship, then we need to tease out and examine all the traumatic variables that are, developmentally, at the basis of this peculiarly perplexing organisation.

The sadism of one part of the self and the masochism of the other part of the self, as Freud (1937c) described it, do complement one another. Freud attempted to link this resistance to the silent experience he encountered during his clinical experience as being the influence of the death instinct and a sense of guilt that thwarts recovery. It was actually Karl Abraham, in 1919, whose work brought hidden envy to the surface. He linked narcissism and envy, explaining them in relation to a negative therapeutic reaction. More attention is now placed, of course, on the patient's inner world of object relations and on looking much deeper for any depressive elements as being the underlying facets of narcissism.

Self envy in destructive narcissistic people always shows itself by the individuals displaying behaviour patterns throughout their lives that are a rejection of and a harming of the worlds of those they come across, and with whom they form loving relationships. They put all their energy into being sadistically strong, by withholding their affection, thus disappointing their loved ones' attempts to enjoy any mutual loving and sexual interactions. They also regard any love in themselves as a sign of weakness. This was the bedrock of Robert Stoller's studies of perversion (1975) as "the erotic order of hatred". Stoller later concluded that:

> pornography as the perverse subject's key daydream, is psychodynamically about the same as his perversion. It is the highly condensed story of his perversion; its historical origins in reality, its elaboration in phantasy, its manifest content that disguises and reveals the latent content. (Stoller, 1981, p. 83)

These observations has also been well documented in the work of Gallwey (1992, 1996), Hopper (1995), Hyatt-Williams (1998), Joseph (1975), Lopez-Corvo (1994), McDougall (1995), Rosenfeld (1987), and Steiner (1981), who all give examples of their work to illustrate how such patients express a prolonged resistance to treatment and very often have a history of failed attempts at a two-person relationship. All describe these therapeutic encounters as very often ending in a pathological impasse.

Envy in relation to pathological organisations within the personality is a very complex set of dynamics arising out of narcissistic injury, self envy, and shame. None of these ever occurs in isolation but is always an aspect of a more complex set of dynamics, operating within an encapsulated enclave within an individual.

These are all significant aspects that have not been fully understood, nor examined, in perversion. My intention so far has been to provide a clearer understanding of the phenomenology of self envy in relation to perverse behaviour, originating from an alliance with an "internal saboteur" (Fairbairn, 1952) which makes a takeover bid for the healthier, dependent part of the primitive self.

Fairbairn's work is extremely relevant to the subject of attacks on the self, and he differentiates between different types of these attacks: "The attack on the tantalizing mother by the internal saboteur and the attacks on the frustrating and rejecting mother by the internal saboteur" (1952, p. 108). Fairbairn's model is very useful in describing the attacks on the self, envious or otherwise, and is comparable to Bion's model (1957) of psychotic and non-psychotic processes where the attack is on any attempt at linking, dependency on, or loving the other.

McDougall writes in *The Many Faces of Eros* (1995) about "erotic destruction in which deviant desires are a way of regaining control over a body and a self which was experienced as in the power of another" (p. 263). She describes how, in the early pre-conditions of perverse scenarios, "the child is denied autonomy by a mother who opposes psychic separation by using him/her as a transitional or counter-phobic object for herself" (p. 263).

The next chapter attempts to make some connection regarding the issue of sexuality in perversion, in line with Abraham (1927), Berke (1997), Kernberg (2006), McDougall (1995), and Polledri (2003), by focusing on a particular and little-understood form of controlling perversion fuelled by shame and envy.

# CHAPTER SEVEN

# Womb envy

In traditional psychoanalytic theory, women have been described as wanting the penis/phallus and the "power" it symbolizes. However, much less has been said about men's desire for women's "power" of pregnancy and childbirth and its effects on the psychic economy of men and women and society at large.

(Silver, 2007, p. 411)

## Which version of perversion is womb envy?

Using the word "perversion" puts one in jeopardy. As Stoller (1985) describes, there is little to the word but insult: hostility that aims to humiliate and subjugate others. According to Stoller, perversion as a label has been a power tool used by society to transform those who are different into those who are bad. The criteria for the judgement have been in the hands of the authorities, such as psychiatrists or the courts, and these judgements have been made not on the basis of what an individual did—what the act meant to the person—but on the basis of the anatomic parts used by the culture's customs (Stoller, 1975). But here, I will use the term to highlight much of the underlying psychopathology of envy; that is, "the desire to harm, to hurt, to be cruel to, to degrade, and, in the case of womb envy, destroy the creativity of one's sexual partner" (Stoller, 1975, p. 97).

In other words, womb envy is a version of "a perverse hostility in which one wishes to harm an object in a way that differentiates it from *aggression*, which often implies only forcefulness" (Stoller, 1975, p. 4). In line with Stoller's theory, "the hostility in perversion takes form in a phantasy of revenge hidden in the actions that make up the perversion and converts childhood trauma into adult revenge" (Stoller, 1975, p. 4). Therefore, we can expect to find phantasies of revenge against the traumatiser, primarily the mother. As Stoller points out, the more one equates one's immediate object with the object who originally forced one to create the perverse dynamics, the more dangerous the perversion. From this perspective, placing hostility at the forefront, the perversion in womb envy lies in the meaning of the act, wherein it is hatred and a need to damage, not love, one's partner. To understand the perversity of womb envy requires a deeper exploration of the paradoxical nature of destructivity and creativity in life, sexuality, and perversion (Long, 2008).

## The nature of womb envy

Hatred and fear of the feminine has not really been explored in the literature to discover why it is that a certain *category* of male partners has a deeply disturbing reaction to pregnant women, Eva Kittay being the exception (1995, p. 144). I would suggest that it is necessary to explore the concept of womb envy as a component of a pathological organisation to explain hatred of women, as well as violence towards female partners during pregnancy. From my clinical experience, working in the forensic field of psychotherapy, I argue that the violence is a symptom that is enacted in a behavioural way as a defence against what is being denied. According to Jukes's research into domestic violence (1993), fifty per cent of abuse towards women occurs during pregnancy and stays long after the children are born.

Furthering my understanding of womb envy, I re-read Karl Abraham (1927) on sadism, in which he says:

> the sadistic element, in which a normal man's emotional life
> is of great importance once it has undergone appropriate

transformations through sublimation, appears with particular strength in the obsessional character, but becomes more or less crippled in consequence of the ambivalence in the instinctual life of some persons. It also contains destructive tendencies hostile to the object, and on account of this cannot become sublimated to a real capacity for devotion to a love-object. (p. 380)

Envy stands out clearly as the main character trait for Abraham, the connection to womb envy being that the "envious person shows not only a desire for the possessions of others, but connects with that desire spiteful impulses against the privileged proprietor" (p. 371).

I recall a young woman I once had to assess in order for her general practitioner to justify a request for a termination of pregnancy on psychological grounds. She had recently married, and it emerged that, for her husband, her role was to provide sexual excitement and to serve food for him. When she became pregnant, which she said they had both discussed, planned, and indeed had looked forward to, he insisted that she have a termination shortly before the period when it was illegal for her to do so in the UK. The husband's rationale for hoping that the GP and I would agree to this was that he had made a terrible mistake in marrying her and that she should return to her country of origin. I, unfortunately, did not know enough at the time about womb envy or about the husband's history, and it only later became apparent that he was destructively enacting an underlying trauma: his encapsulated childhood anger and hatred towards his mother for abandoning him when she became severely depressed after he and his two younger siblings were born. His envy manifested itself in his intent to destroy the happiness of his young wife. It was painful and confusing for her to come to terms with his "disappointment in her"—so much so that he had convinced her that she was not "good enough" to have his baby. Nor would he allow her to mix socially with his friends and family, completely isolating her from any interaction with them. His rationale for this was that they were "disappointed by the fact that he married a foreign girl". Much later on, I learned, by pure chance, that he had repeatedly made her pregnant and then changed his mind, insisting that she have a termination on two other occasions (Polledri, 2003).

I did ask to see this couple to discuss the possible relevance of his unresolved childhood experiences. He attended the appointment on his own. As I began to describe to him how I thought he was repeating his sibling rivalry towards his unborn baby, he replied angrily: "Sibling bloody warfare you mean!". When I asked him to consider whether the unresolved conflict within the relationship he had with his mother might also be one of the reasons he was reluctant for his wife to become a mother, his response was: "I can't remember what you just said as I was too preoccupied with looking at your breasts." Was this a longing for the lost nurturing breast from his childhood ... or an attack on my mind?

Long discusses that "Whereas hate may wish to destroy the other, [womb] envy wishes to spoil and destroy the very quality that is envied" (Long, 2008, p. 93).

## Symbolic wounds

Bruno Bettelheim first suggested the concept of womb envy in 1954. He turned to ego psychology to help him detect womb envy, but he did not integrate mothering into his view of male envy's destructiveness, as a cause of envy of women's procreative power, and subordination of women in attempts to master womb envy (Bettelheim, 1962; Kittay, 1995). He was met by stony silence or occasional criticisms by anthropologists and psychoanalysts. The limitations of Bettelheim's view contributed to neglect of male envy by Freudian psychology. How could a theoretician as astute as Freud have ignored or missed the significance of such a concept as womb envy?

Kittay (1995, p. 127) argues that Freudian perspectives on female sexuality, which define it in terms of men's desires and needs, are shown to be responsible for this omission, along with the biological determinism of Freudian psychology. Bettelheim could see the importance of men's envy of women, the theme that pervades *Symbolic Wounds* (1962). In a series of clinical observations of young boys who were resident in an institution for disturbed children where Bettelheim was based, he describes ambivalence in boys:

> Each boy stated repeatedly, independently of the other, and to different persons, that he felt it was "a cheat" and "a gyp" that he did not have a vagina. They made remarks such as "She thinks she's something special because she has a vagina", or "Why can't I have a vagina?". Referring to another boy's unhappiness, one of them said, "I know why he's crying, it's because he wants a vagina".

More persistent than the desire for female organs however, was the obsessional wish to possess *both* male and female genitalia. They said "Why can't I have both?". Disappointed in this desire, and envious of women because women, they felt, had the superior sex organs. Both boys frequently expressed a wish to tear or cut out the vaginas of girls and women. More benign, but often just as pervasive in boys is the desire to be able to bear children and the feeling of being cheated because it cannot be done. (Bettelheim, 1962, pp. 32–33)

Gregory Zilboorg speaks of the "woman envy on the part of man, that is psychologically older and therefore more fundamental than penis envy" (1944, p. 290). Zilboorg felt that the true bio- and psycho-social role of woman has not been fully understood by psychoanalysis; that Freud was aware of the problem in most of his studies, but was hampered by his masculine bias; and:

When it is resolved not to overlook how much feminine there is in the masculine attributes, and when the fundamental envy with which man treats woman is borne in mind, then I am certain that clinical observations will become enriched with new material which heretofore was obscured by androcentric bias. (1944, p. 294)

In Freud's case histories, in particular the Wolf Man (1918, p. 274), men who expressed desires to give birth were interpreted as expressing anal, autoerotic, or homosexual desires, *not* envy of woman's capacity to give birth. This was Freud's blind spot, and it needs to be understood how Freud's skewed conception of femininity is central to his blindness to men's envy of women's procreative powers. Yet Bettelheim (1962) assigns to these a more obvious and, as I have argued, a more accurate reading.

Despite its merit, Bettelheim's *Symbolic Wounds* has remained undervalued and has too often been ignored. The efforts to master envy have themselves perpetuated the domination of women by men. "Ultimately, we need to build on Bettelheim's insights to find healing solutions for envy that are not at once destructive to women" (Kittay, 1995, p. 127).

Before presenting the following case history, I was reminded of denied envy previously being discussed by Klein (1957). She does not refer to womb envy as such, but touches on this when she writes about *"the devaluation of the object"*. In the text, Klein states that: "I have suggested that spoiling and devaluing are inherent in envy. The object which has been devalued need not be envied any more." She elaborates further: "This soon applies to the idealized object, which is [by being] devalued and therefore no longer idealized." In some people, Klein concludes, "this remains characteristic of their object relationships" (1957, p. 217).

## Case history: denied envy

In a more recent case, I was able to decipher the psychodynamics of womb envy, eventually, as the denied envy was diffused with associated destructiveness. Denied envy is one of the most dangerous aspects of envy, for it cannot be modified by loving, grateful, and reparative wishes. Denial is quite often an important defence: some people deny the denial so they can honestly say that they are who they are not (Berke, 1985). The envier is likely to use the mechanisms of envy, in the form of powerful projective processes, in order to dissociate himself from a major part of himself (i.e., his own destructiveness). The individual may not only project a part of his own badness to attack the envied object, but do so in order to rid the anguished and envied part of himself. "The result is a loss of self, experienced as an increasing inner impoverishment. This loss stimulates murderous rage, because the more impoverished the envier feels, the angrier he gets with others and the angrier he gets with himself for hating and feeling so empty" (Berke, 1985, p. 175). Moreover, the world of inner or outer reality becomes suffused with dissociated destructiveness and readily becomes a bad and threatening place. Hence, envy may have a paranoid flavour (Berke, 1985).

## Nicola

Nicola was a recently divorced young mother of two children whose ex-husband, Paul, was determined to gain residency and total custody of their children (two daughters, aged three years and eleven months respectively). Nicola was described by her GP, and then by the psychiatrist who assessed her suitability for psychotherapy, as a very calm, loving, and good mother to her children. She and her family tried to allow for the fact that Paul was the children's father, and they did not want to deprive them of a relationship with their father because of the breakdown of their marriage.

Having originally instigated divorce proceedings, Paul then took his case for total custody to the Royal Courts of Justice, claiming that his ex-wife was an abusive, violent woman. He was concerned that, if she were given custody of the children, she might harm them.

Nicola asked for help. Her husband, she said, was attempting also to get her struck off her professional register, which would have ruined her career. He was accusing her of being a child abuser, and attempted to have her sectioned under the Mental Health Act as a mother unfit to be in charge of her children. Nicola went as far as to suggest to social services that their staff should spend time observing her with the children in case she *was* a bad mother. She had been referred to two psychiatrists for a further assessment at her ex-husband's insistence, for the purposes of a court report.

Nicola's GP was puzzled by Paul's "gentlemanly" behaviour, which appeared contradictory, since he had treated Nicola for severe cuts and abdominal bruising during her second pregnancy that the doctor had no doubt were caused by her ex-husband. This contrasted with Paul's claims about his wife. He would, in fact, self-harm and go to the same GP saying: "Look what my wife did to me, doctor." Prior to her referral to me for psychotherapy, Nicola had been arrested by the police, detained in a cell overnight, and charged with actual bodily harm, when, in fact, the husband had harmed *himself*, and then accused his wife of inflicting the injuries. (On closer medical examination, there is, of course, a major difference between self-inflicted bruising and injuries caused as a result as being struck by another.)

After Paul had spent ten months preparing for the court hearing, having subpoenaed the psychiatrists and the doctor to appear in court, the judge made it clear in his summing-up that he saw through the father's manipulation, and he awarded custody and residency to the mother with supervised access to the father. Two weeks after this "unexpected" verdict, Paul admitted himself to hospital, complaining of a rash, chest pains, and anxiety. Following a period of observation, he was eventually transferred to a psychiatric unit, where, twenty-four hours later, he suddenly died.

During the build-up to the court case, the medical professionals involved in the assessment of the family all expressed concern for the father, and the police and social services were as determined as he was to remove the children from Nicola's care. Her male health visitor and the probation officer diagnosed postnatal depression, which they claimed the GP had failed to recognise, although there was no evidence of such depression from the two recent psychiatric assessments prior to her referral for therapy. Paul's rather chilling comment shortly before the hearing was: "Come what may, if it is the last thing I do when I leave this house, I'm taking those two children with me."

Nicola's psychological well-being deteriorated considerably during the run-up to the court hearing, although the more she tried to be fair, thinking about how this was affecting the children, the more sadistic Paul became, and she began to doubt her own personal and professional judgement. She began to lose her confidence and her vitality but, despite her overwhelming concern for her children, she never lost faith in the judicial system and was determined to fight back. Paul had employed very expensive defence lawyers to build up a profile of Nicola as an "hysterical psychopath" (among other gender-specific expletives) in the hope of having her discredited as a mother and in her professional capacity, to deprive her of everything that was precious to her, namely her children, her family, her career, and her psychological well-being. Perhaps if he stripped her of all of these attributes, she would be less enviable.

Chronic doubts of one's judgement can be the result of an envious attack, the envy being designed to destroy the very qualities the envious person might otherwise value and benefit from. Nicola's judgement and her maternalism were under siege and, like Shakespeare's Othello, she was up against the threat of an attack "that judgement cannot cure" (Kermode, 2001). The attack was also experienced by proxy in the countertransference from Paul during Nicola's therapy. For example, Paul came to the conclusion that both Nicola and her therapist "were into penis envy". Here, the denial of envy was to dissociate himself from his own envious destructiveness.

Like a victim of racial and sexual prejudice, the envied person feels that their essential self is under attack, rather than some fault or virtue that can be changed or detached from one's central self. Instead, one's very hold on life, one's connection to the good, is the problem (Polledri, 2003; Ulanov & Ulanov, 1983, p. 21). I did not know anything about Paul's early family history, but it struck me that he was spoiling and attacking the initial source of goodness, which leads in turn to destroying and attacking the babies that his wife was producing, and the body producing them. In other words, this is an example of the underlying psychopathology of womb envy. Nicola often commented that this was "an attack on her femininity". Paul was fairly genial and supportive during the first eighteen months of their marriage, changing dramatically when their first baby was born. He behaved like a "sulky brooding boy"; he was even more physically aggressive when Nicola was pregnant and did not even visit her in hospital when their second baby was born. He subsequently deprived her of all physical and sexual contact, accusing her of being the reason for "his decline in libido". Nicola only discovered much later that he was heavily reliant on pornography and regularly downloaded pornographic images from the internet.

This case history is a clinical example of womb envy, an envy of the creative capacity of women. The decline of Nicola's self-confidence and her inability to believe in herself could have been the result of her husband's envy and self-hatred, negated and reversed and put into her by his defensive projective identification. Contemporary psychiatric literature, such as Jaffe (1968), Jukes (1993), Kittay (1995), and Knight (1971), includes much material on crises men suffer, not uncommonly when their wives or lovers are pregnant, including depressive and suicidal tendencies, or an extreme aggressivity and hostility which can be used to cover a sense of inferiority.

## Penis envy and womb envy

In womb envy, the target of attack is not one's doing but one's *being*, so why has the notion of an envy parallel to women's penis envy not penetrated the heart of psychoanalysis?

Maria Torok writes about the significance of penis envy in women as "the exacerbated wish to possess that which women believe they are deprived of by fate—or by the mother—expresses a basic dissatisfaction some people have ascribed to the fact of being a woman" (Torok, 1994, p. 41). She goes on to say: "Yet, it is remarkable that, of men and women, only women should trace this state of lack to their very own sex", and "How is so radical a depreciation of one's own sex conceivable? Is it perhaps rooted in real biological inferiority?" That is why, Torok suggests, both "penis envy and the attempt to make women relinquish it are doomed to come to an impasse in Freud's psychoanalytic perspective" (p. 42). She summarises her hypothesis as:

> The woman, envious and guilty, can thus become man's unacknowledged "feminine part" which the man must then master

and control. That is why man will be driven to prefer a mutilated, dependent, and envious woman to a partner, successful in her creative fullness. (p. 170)

It was Horney, a follower of Freud, who first took issue with his theory and proposed the idea of womb envy. She produced the first full-blown critique of Freud's theories in the late 1920s and 1930s. Horney argues in her paper "The Dread of Woman" (1932) that men are deeply envious of women's capacity for motherhood and are subject to womb envy. In this paper, she argues that "male envy of women is as powerful as their desire for them and that this is evident in the widespread existence of myths and legends, folk-tales, fairy stories, poems, and religious stories which contain warnings and cautionary tales of what happens in relations between men and women" (p. 348).

Regarding gender, in the context of both history and contemporary culture, the concept of unconscious male womb envy or envy of women seems very suggestive. Broader cultural issues such as gender and sexual politics in relation to womb envy and penis envy have been discussed in great detail in the writings of Ellman (1970), Kittay (1984), Minsky (1999), Silver (2007), and Torok (1994). Minsky discusses how, in contemporary culture, "the idea seems to be widely recognised by psychotherapists and analysts, but has not been taken up very much in universities in areas such as literary, film and women's studies where there has been a considerable interest in gender and psychoanalytic ideas" (Minsky, 1999, p. 391).

Minsky describes how male envy of women has had such dramatic cultural repercussions on the way men and women live, both historically and in the present day:

> In terms of contemporary culture, the very idea of unconscious womb envy may reflect the resentment that is felt by the improvement in the social position of women who have, over the last twenty years, moved into areas traditionally associated with cultural "masculinity", generally experiencing an increase in status. (Minsky, 1999, p. 391)

Conversely, when men have entered areas traditionally associated with women, such as child care and domesticity, and have been equally as emotionally open to nurturing, they run the risk of losing status, in their own and others' eyes, due to the fact that femininity continues to be of low cultural status. This may be due to women no longer relating to their traditional feminine roles of passivity, vulnerability, and lack, set alongside social and economical changes in which women no longer need to be in men's care and protection as much as they used to be. This may well be the emotional scale of the problem. Minsky believes that "an eclectic reading of psychoanalytic theory suggests that for many men, because of very early unconscious experiences of womb envy, which remain emotionally unresolved, the subordination of women and the denial of their particular forms of physical and emotional creativity has traditionally been a crucial means of psychical survival" (1999, p. 392). A woman who thinks for herself and speaks her mind, who does not see herself as "lacking" (a penis or anything else), effectively throws the lack back on to men, which may then threaten some of them with psychical death (Irigaray, 1987).

Winnicott's "transitional space" provides the basis for modern feminist object-relations-based theory, though it largely ignores the importance of the father as such, as a psychological space in which the child negotiates its way from phantasy to liveable reality. Winnicott (1971) describes this "transitional space" as a space which the "good-enough" mother develops between herself and her child out of the special kind of relatedness she has allowed to come into being between them. In Winnicott's theory, however, Minsky argues, "the transitional space is associated exclusively with the mother. The mother and baby exist together in a self-sufficient unit which eventually enables separation to take place without the divisive intervention of the father as a third term" (Minsky, 1995, p. 339). In general, eclectic analytical psychotherapists recognise that the transitional space must also involve the father as well as the mother. The quality of the relatedness with him also determines the child's ability to make the transition from phantasy to reality. Minsky states that: "It becomes a space in which the child may, through creative play, involving phantasies about being in love with the father as well as the mother, negotiate its way into the external world beyond the mother's body, partly in response to its recognition of difference" (1995, p. 339).

Considering that both penis envy and womb envy have a biological and social component, if penis envy is to be taken as envy of the physiological difference, then womb envy comes to be seen as the envy of women's physiological difference. If penis envy is understood not only to be envy of the biological organ *per se*, but also of the power and privilege that the organ signifies, then womb envy must also be envy of some power that is not only physiological but social. Only if we look back at the pre-Oedipal mother–child relationship does the social nature of womb envy emerge. In the case of penis envy, the biological organ seems only incidental to the social power it symbolises, yet in the case of womb envy, the biological capacities seem central to the power of the mother. Womb envy may or may not be at the origin of male domination, but it is a powerful motor driving male domination (Kittay, 1995; Minsky, 1995).

Berke explores the intense hostility that female potency and the womb generate for men (as well as other women). He argues that it may be more prevalent than penis envy, tracing the history of hatred of the womb and focusing on other significant hatred of womb function such as pregnancy and childbirth. His view is that "what most women want is to be women. He explores the parameters of such hatred in order to redress the balance of analytic thinking: he considers that what has been inappropriately termed '*penis envy* may be more appropriately recognised and acknowledged as *womb envy*'" (Berke, 1997, p. 444).

In the literature, male envy of female sex characteristics and reproductive capacity is a widespread and conspicuously ignored dynamic. Kernberg (1972) finds that envy and hatred are defensively dealt with by depreciating and devaluing women. The question arises as to whether envy and devaluation of women is confined to those individuals with severe psychopathology, or whether it is a more pervasive if not widespread dynamic in the male population. This subject is a pervasive one, expressed in the institutionalised values regarding gender and cultures universally. In this culture, I believe that the envy-devaluation constellation is reflected in the selection of which traits, qualities, behaviour, and roles are deemed appropriate for each sex.

Horney (1923, 1932) relates both the idealisation and depreciation to the violently aggressive desires for revenge that stem from the mother's dominance and power and the small child's related feelings of weakness, impotence, and humiliation. Chasseguet-Smirgel (1974) suggests that another determinant in the need to reverse the infantile situation is the fear and terror of women that a man may feel.

Steiner (1993) discusses gender envy and what Freud referred to as a "repudiation of femininity". More recently, he has beautifully encapsulated what he considers Freud was referring to as an "intolerance" of a receptive dependence on good objects, which seems to present similar problems for both men and women and is, in fact, the position infants of both sexes have to adopt to the relationship with the mother and her breast: "It is not simply then seen as feminine, but also as infantile, and the relationship with a good object can lead not to growth, pleasure, development, and gratitude, but to embarrassment and humiliation" (Steiner, 2008, p. 140). A marked preference for giving over receiving is what Steiner considers to underlie both penis envy and masculine protest, and what he considers Freud correctly identified as an important source of resistance to change.

Envy is never out in the open, nor is womb envy. It is secretive, scheming, Machiavellian, behind the scenes. Envy is especially malignant because, as we have seen in Chapter Three, the destruction it engenders is directed at what is seen as desirable, not bad. It is this feature of envy that is at risk of being neglected when envy is subsumed simply as an aspect of aggressive conflict (Berke, 1997). For womb envy to qualify as such, it has to have an undercurrent of malevolence.

Berke describes how "The womb is the core of female potency. It is a part of the body that is perfectly placed to be idealized and envied for feeding and breeding, for loving and being made love to" (Berke, 1997, p. 433). It also stirs up the most uncontrollable rage in a certain category of men who feel that they had no control whatsoever over the mother, or the womb, and in turn subject the female partner to the most violent abuse during pregnancy and continue to punish her for the loss of the most treasured of all experiences, the loving tenderness the infant is entitled to receive from its mother, of which he felt severely deprived, setting up the cycle of injustice, brooding, envy, and destructive murderousness. Envy is a very potent element in men's hatred of women (Jukes, 1993).

Horney (1923, 1926, 1932) confronted the Freudian view of women as seen through men's eyes. Male depreciation of women, and Freud's normal contempt, arose from male envy of the capacities of women's reproductive organs, and so female masochism is actually enforced passivity. However, while Freud's understanding of masculinity has stood the test of time, his theory of femininity is severely limited by his failure to take into account male violence and power, although throughout his work he stresses the enigma of femininity too. Nevertheless, he was attempting to understand how gender differentiation came about. But Freud's paper "On Narcissism" (1914) is a thinly disguised denigration of women. Female sexuality is defined entirely by referring to women's relation to the absent penis.

Adrienne Rich argues that:

> Freud represented female castration as a metaphor but precisely because he did not pursue the psychic meaning of this social mutilation of women, which would have forced him to explore male psychology in more depth, his work, on both sexes, lacks a basic truth, and is presented as political, poetic and scientific as well. (1977, p. 202)

The situation in which the pregnant young wife, whose husband repeatedly insisted on her terminating her pregnancies, found herself reminded me of Freud's paper "On the Universal Tendency to Debasement in the Sphere of Love". Freud describes the whole sphere of love as being divided:

> whereby the individual loves but does not desire and desires but cannot love, in order to keep his sensuality away from the objects he loves. The need is for a debased sexual object, or a woman who is perceived to be ethically inferior, to whom he need attribute no aesthetic scruples, who does not know him in his other social relations and cannot judge him in them. (Freud, 1912d, p. 83)

As the womb has been referred to as "the dark continent", the underlying politics and psychology of male power and violence towards women is more commonplace than it is deviant. This fully expresses, behaviourally, men's uses and oppression of women. It represents the visible and unacceptable face of male power over women. Violence is so much more behaviourally expressive than a defensive reaction to feelings of impotence and helplessness, as well as a defensive reaction against the unbearable experience of envy, supposedly evoked by a woman's refusal to live up to "womanly" behaviour or expectations (Berke, 1997; Jukes, 1993).

Stoller has explored the sexual fantasies in sadomasochistic behaviour, and his concept of the phantasy as a means of making triumph out of disaster could not be more clearly illustrated and confirmed than in the clinical observations he made in the USA. The denial of the rage and the pain of abandonment and loss are more clearly expressed in

real life, not in sexual masturbation and phantasy, when relationships
are formed and attacked in this destructive way. Violence exposes the
phantasy structuring the real relationship (Stoller, 1975, 1991). This does
not explain why the need and fear of dependency that arises from the
male child's experience of the loss of his basic unity with his mother
can create such existential anxieties about falling apart or dying that
become a primary encapsulated psychosis, as I have described in the
cases of the two husbands outlined in this chapter.

Dorothy Lloyd-Owen explains it in terms of containerlessness, when
she states:

> Where there is an incapacity of the maternal object to contain the
> baby's projections, there will be consequently *a core of despair*. This
> may be hidden, but is responsible for powerful perverse projec-
> tive identifications, and all forms of violent control of the object.
> (Lloyd-Owen, 2003, p. 285)

We see again how in perverse enactment, the aggression aroused
by early anxieties is sexualised and becomes a matter of sadistic
pleasure—the individual is now in the "superior, vengeful, triumphant
position" (p. 285).

She describes further:

> The source of perversion lies in a disturbed infant–mother
> relationship. A feature of the perverse individual is a longing for
> closeness, yet profound anxiety about engulfment and annihila-
> tion, leading to hostile pulling away from the apparently desired
> object, usually an object that stands for the mother or the infant.
> (p. 285)

## A path of destructive envy

Returning to the question at the beginning of this chapter: which version of perversion is womb envy? Both Nicola's case study and the fate
of the young wife whose story I described briefly at the beginning of
this chapter are examples within my clinical experience. They demonstrate that perversion is at its very basis linked to destructivity and
domination in womb envy. "The 'other' is experienced instrumentally,
becoming a subject to be *used* rather than *known*" (Long, 2008)—hence,

the inherent subjectivity of the other is actively attacked in the perverse relationship. Long discusses how it is not just the other who is attacked, "the subjectivity of self is also in danger of being destroyed. Perverse pleasure is gained *through* but not *with* the other" (Long, 2008, p. 90), as was the case with the two mothers presented here.

A feature of the perverse aspects of womb envy is that it could be thought of as an evacuation of a communication, or a repetition of early, unprocessed traumatic experiences that have become encapsulated and are no longer available to conscious thought. This is acted out in a behavioural way and, unlike sexual perversion, in expression it destroys self as well as other. The perverse relationship is both destructive and creative, for it must keep alive that which it wishes to destroy (the mother). Therefore, to understand the perversity of womb envy requires a deeper exploration of the paradoxical nature of destructivity and creativity in life, sexuality, and perversion. The dynamic in womb envy is to have power over the other, to take out from the other all that is desirable to them, and destroy it. This aspect of envy, the desire to destroy what is good in the other, is ultimately an attack on goodness.

In July 2008, the press reported a case in which a man had fed his young pregnant wife a cocktail of drugs designed to cause an abortion, by hiding them in her food. Eleven weeks into the pregnancy, the father of the baby (a chef by profession) had crushed an abortion pill into a sandwich he had prepared for her breakfast. Within an hour, his wife was experiencing stomach cramps and bleeding, fearing she was having a miscarriage. After he called an ambulance, and "caringly" tried to reassure her on the way to hospital that she would be all right, it was eventually confirmed that she had not miscarried. Fearing the baby would be "deformed" by the pill, the next morning the husband laced a yoghurt with another abortion-inducing tablet, which he bought over the internet. The same reaction occurred again—hospitalisation with immense stomach cramps and bleeding. His wife left him after he confessed his actions to a psychologist, but he spent days camping out on her doorstep, begging her to have a termination in case the baby was "deformed". He was sent to prison, and eventually the wife gave birth to a healthy baby.

Behind the envy of the object, and the need to destroy and spoil anything good that might come from contact with it, lies unconscious identification with the originally hated and needed object. Womb envy may be considered as both a source of a primitive form of hatred and a complication of the hatred that derives from the fixation of trauma. Kernberg puts this very succinctly:

> Primitive hatred takes the form of an effort to destroy the potential for a gratifying human relationship and for learning something of value in that human reaction. Underlying the need to destroy reality and communication in intimate relationships is unconscious and conscious envy of the object, particularly of an object not dominated from within by similar hatred. (Kernberg, 1992, p. 25)

In forensic clinical practice, it is relatively common to come across a level of destructiveness and murderousness that is of such intensity that it could be readily interpreted as resembling an anti-life force in whose powerful grip someone will systematically destroy any hopes, aspirations, good feelings, and so on, in himself and others. Rather than resorting to the idea of a death instinct, one could take it a step further and relate it to a universal urge to return to the safety and security of the womb, to a period in man's life when passivity reigned, when no response was required, no demands were made. I am suggesting that this "paradise lost" evokes such rage and murderousness as to engender the wish to destroy anything that represents its absence—life, consciousness, and reality itself. This would imply that violence and destructiveness are a fundamental hostility to otherness and separateness.

# SUMMARY AND CONCLUSIONS

I have always considered Klein's 1957 definition of envy as the ultimate pathology to be its greatest weakness. To look beyond the brick wall of a doctrine that is at once a universal explanation for human ills and at the same time obscures the part played by adverse life experience has led me to formulate a different account of early mental processes.

The tenets of this account are that:

- The nature of instinct is to enhance the chances of survival, therefore the notion of a death instinct is an absurdity. Envy cannot be a straightforward manifestation of instinct.
- The infant has, by birth, a pre-realisation of its self as an independent entity, including an expectation of continuing care from the womb to the world where it expects to be nurtured. Babies are born sane and with a desire for life.
- From birth, the full realisation of the self, its identity and potential, depends upon the operation of complementary instinctual linking functions between the infant and the nurturing parents, hopefully in the main a breastfeeding mother.
- Two of these linking functions, prospecting and holding, can be observed to occur naturally in the behavioural interaction between

154

mother and infant, and have, in themselves, important consequences for the development of specific mental attributes.

- If the linking functions are able to progress, the infant will quickly develop a dual concept of itself in a dependent relationship with a caring other. This is the *vital concept*. It replaces the more unitary and magical Kleinian concept of the introjected "good breast" and, once established, becomes the mainstay of sanity and reference against which comprehension and imagination can be explored.
- Creative and defensive phantasies develop to bridge the spatio-temporal and functional gaps between the self and the dependent other. Without the realisation of the vital concept, no strategies in phantasy, omnipotent or otherwise, to protect the ego from unmanageable stress can develop. Splitting and projective identification are not options.
- Interference without the realisation of the vital concept results in varying degrees of psychopathology, depending on which specific linking functions are most affected, the most severe and extensive causing an anguished autistic confusion between self and other. If this state is not superseded by a late, but inevitably flawed, realisation of the vital concept, then an individual with an autistic spectrum disorder will result. When it is overcome, it will nevertheless persist as an impenetrable black hole in the ego.
- These autistic lacunae cannot be expressed in thought or phantasy. They impinge as nameless dread and in children's sleep give night terrors rather than nightmares. Later in dreams, they are often represented as fearful black objects. They frequently give rise to somatic symptoms and dysmorphophobia and, in this respect, the criminal acting out and dissocial behaviour has developed as opposed to the development of psychoses.
- Moreover, autistic lacunae produce states of mind that have envy of good experience, and these states need exploration of their origins. They may be a reaction formation of revenge at being cheated of the beatific promise of the vital concept and thrust instead into a state of near annihilation, or they may be a reaction to a deep awareness of a deficit in identity. This latter state of affairs is particularly apparent when life experience calls on the individual for a creative response and they are unable to respond because the vital area of their own identity has not been conceptualized. The subsequent profound despair and dread, because of the absence of defensive secondary

phantasies, results in a spoiling attack on any two-person relationship. To mistake this for envy *per se* is ultimately unhelpful.

Recognition of the impenetrable autistic areas is a fundamental task in developing any model. Gallwey's model has more ramifications than is appropriate for me to describe in this study, but it has given me a fresh perspective and operational renaissance in forensic clinical treatment, and has greatly enhanced my processing of the countertransference. Antisocial behaviour and profound resistance to change go hand in hand, so therapeutic nihilism and the abandonment of patients at the height of their disturbance is common. To retain the ability to think and work out what is going on can keep the treatment and the protagonists alive. My contribution is an attempt to demonstrate a fresh understanding of envy.

Envy is a complex phenomenon requiring further understanding, rather than a definitive explanation for attacks on good experiences. Primary identification reflects a discovery of the self, but also establishes a conceptual internal duality of a self, in a dependent relationship with a dependable separate object. This dual conceptualisation, and the link between the two, is vital because it forms the basis of sanity and a platform for the development of the self. When primary linking functions are faulty, various types of psychopathology result. If primary linking functioning *fails*, there can be no resulting secondary processes, so that the self not only lacks awareness of its own identity, but has no capacity to develop secondary phantasies. Unable to employ defences such as splitting and projective identification to manage fear and frustration, the individual will remain trapped in an autistic prison in a state of confusion between self and other. Because the central pathology represents an autistic state of mind, it actually cannot be expressed. So in its purest form, it is simply indigestible. It is unknowable, unmetabolised, psychic detritus.

Working at the coalface over a period of fifteen years, as a display of my eclecticism, I have applied theories that have mainly derived from Freud, Klein, Bion, Fairbairn, Winnicott, Segal, Bowlby, Gilligan, Fonagy, Gallwey, Rosenfeld, Hyatt-Williams, Welldon, Green, Schore, Beebe and Lachmann, Ogden, Berke, and many other pioneers in object relations theory. When I reflect on my clinical experience, and consider the knowledge built on both theory and practice, what I have gradually come to understand is that:

1. Encapsulation and autism are like two lenses, the one sliding over the other, if not actually the same thing. The underlying pathology of this part of an individual derives from two layers: a severe primary pathology that stems from a failure in primary linking functioning, and a whole string of secondary psychopathologies that derive from the comparative failure in the linking functions (Polledri, 1999).

2. I agree with Gallwey's hypothesis that *prior* to any possibility of linking, there is a more primitive state where not even primitive omnipotent mechanisms can be employed in order to manage destructiveness and envy, borne out of this failure in attachment. Thus, I would argue, certain individuals can be thought of as in possession of an autistic ego, which persists due to internal and external failures connected to the early nurturing environment and can be associated with encapsulated containerlessness (Polledri, 1995, 2003).

3. Infant research bears out the fact that an infant is born with a preconception of itself as separate from the mother. If that is confirmed and realised, then the primary linking functions operate quickly and quite successfully in the first few weeks of life. The infant is then able to bridge that gap between itself and the mother and make separation through the production of secondary phantasies. The child's primary phantasy is of itself, in a separate relationship with the mother, the primary instinctual knowledge. It is confirmed by the successful operation of primary linking functions. What follows is a relationship between two people. This is vital. However, the failure of the child to achieve this conceptualisation of mother/child duality results in confusion. In this state, the infant self frantically tries to catch hold of the object, but it cannot do so because its separate existence has not been confirmed. Eventually, the confusion that results is primary in its degree. It is at the core of psychopathology, which develops during the maturational years.

I am in agreement with Gilligan (1996, 1997, 2000), who concludes, in his research into violent behaviour: "Over the past century the most popular theories have suggested that impulses toward violent and aggressive behaviour are part of our instinctual endowment, inherited from our animal ancestors" (2000, p. 209). He questions Freud's theory of the death instinct when he states: "One version or another of the idea have postulated that violence is determined by inborn instinctual or biologically determined drives. There are so many problems with this explanation of violence and aggression that it is valueless, and dangerously unhelpful as a theory" (2000, p. 211). If, by definition, we cannot eradicate instincts because they are inherited, then what is the point in ever thinking that we can do anything substantial towards preventing violence? In line with Gallwey (1996) and Midgely (1984), Gilligan concludes:

> The reason this concept is dangerous is because it leads us to believe that violent impulses need to be discharged periodically or they will build up to the point where they explode spontaneously and uncontrollably. Perhaps if we can see more clearly how misleading this concept is, we may be able to retire it as an explanation of violence5, and turn to human emotions such as love, hate, shame, guilt, envy and so on, emotions which act as motives or causes for aggressive behaviour. (Gilligan, 2000, p. 211)

The emphasis Rosenfeld (1987) placed on identifying the normal healthy dependent part of the self as the sane element within the personality offers another way of understanding the basis for mental health in terms of a primitive part of the self which is not dominated by omnipotence. As Gallwey states: "The development of psychopathology can then be understood as any interference with this essential healthy development function and not as a simple persistence of the primitive or a regression to omnipotent levels of development" (Gallwey, 1996, p. 159).

The study of envy in relation to the development of psychopathology and its ramifications is a huge enterprise, far beyond the reach of a single study, and one that continues to develop and evolve. What I have aimed at here is to capture my re-examination of both the concept and the affect of envy, and to offer an innovative way of examining envy and confronting the concept of it as instinct. I trust that both the exploration of alternative theories and the supporting clinical material will have some meaning and usefulness from both a theoretical and clinical point of view.

# REFERENCES

Abraham, K. (1919). A peculiar form of resistance against the psychoanalytic method. In: *Selected Papers of Karl Abraham*. London: Hogarth.

Abraham, K. (1927). *Selected Papers of Karl Abraham*. New York: Brunner-Mazel.

Abraham, N. & Torok, M. (1994). *The Shell and the Kernel*. Chicago, IL: University of Chicago Press.

Abrahamsen, D. (1973). *The Murdering Mind*. London: Hogarth.

Adler, G. & Rhine, M. W. (1992). The self-object function of projective identification. In: N. G. Hamilton (Ed.), *From Inner Sources: New Directions in Object-Relations Psychotherapy*. Northvale, NJ: Jason Aronson.

Ainsworth, M. D. S., Blehar, M. C., Waters, E. & Wall, S. (1979). *Patterns of Attachment: Assessed in the Strange Situation and at Home*. Hillsdale, NJ: Lawrence Erlbaum.

Alexander, R. P. (1997). Some notes on the origin of despair and its relationship to destructive envy. *Journal of Melanie Klein and Object Relations*, 15(3): 417–429.

Andrews, I. & Murra, L. (2000). *The Social Baby*. London: CP. Publishing.

Apter, E. (2006). Maternal fetishism. In: D. Nobus & L. Downing (Eds.), *Perversion: Psychoanalytic Perspectives*. London: Karnac.

Aulagnier, P. (2001). *The Violence of Interpretation: From Pictogram to Statement*. A. Sheridan (Trans.). Hove, East Sussex: Brunner-Routledge/ Philadelphia, PA: Taylor & Francis.

Ayers, M. (2003). *Mother–Infant Attachment and Psychoanalysis*. London: Brunner-Routledge.

Badenock, B. (2008). *Being a Brain-Wise Therapist*. New York: W. W. Norton.

Barford, D. (1999). In defence of death. In: R. Weatherill (Ed.), *The Death Drive: New Life for a Dead Subject?* (*Encyclopaedia of Psychoanalysis, Vol. 3*). London: Rebus.

Barth, F. D. (1988). The role of self-esteem in the experience of envy. *The American Journal of Psychoanalysis, 48(3)*: 198.

Bateson, G. (1979). *Mind and Nature*. New York: Dutton.

Beebe, B. (2000). Co-constructing mother–infant distress: the microsynchrony of maternal impingement and infant avoidance in the face-to-face encounter. *Psychoanalytic Inquiry, 20*: 412–440.

Beebe, B. & Lachmann, F. M. (2002). *Infant Research and Adult Treatment*. Hillsdale, NJ: The Analytic Press.

Benedek, T. (1953). Dynamics of the countertransference. *Bulletin of the Menninger Clinic, 17(6)*: 201–208.

Benjamin, J. (1988). *The Bonds of Love*. New York: Pantheon.

Benvenuto, S. (2006). Perversion and charity. In: D. Nobus & L. Downing (Eds.), *Perversion: Psychoanalytic Perspectives*. London: Karnac.

Berger, J. (1972). *Ways of Seeing*. London: BBC/Penguin.

Berke, J. (1985). Envy loveth not: a study of the origin, influence and confluence of envy and narcissism. *British Journal of Psychotherapy, 1(3)*: 171–186.

Berke, J. (1986). Shame and envy. *British Journal of Psychotherapy, 2(4)*: 262–270.

Berke, J. (1987). Shame and envy. In: D. L. Nathanson (Ed.), *The Many Faces of Shame*. London: Guilford.

Berke, J. (1988). *The Tyranny of Malice*. London: Summit.

Berke, J. (1997). Womb envy. *Journal of Melanie Klein and Object Relations, 15(3)*: 443–466.

Berman, E. (1999, July). Psychoanalytic supervision: the intersubjective turn. Paper presented at 41st International Psychoanalytical Congress, Santiago, Chile.

Bettelheim, B. (1962). *Symbolic Wounds*. New York: Collier.

Bettelheim, B. (1983). *Freud and Man's Soul*. London: Chatto & Windus.

Bick, E. (1968). The experience of the skin in early object-relations. *International Journal of Psychoanalysis, 49*: 484–486.

Bion, W. (1957). Differentiation of the psychotic from the non-psychotic personalities. *International Journal of Psychoanalysis, 38*: 266–275.

Bion, W. (1959). Attacks on linking. *International Journal of Psychoanalysis*, *40*: 308–315.

Bion, W. (1961). A theory of thinking. *International Journal of Psychoanalysis*, *43*: 306–310.

Bion, W. (1962). *Learning from Experience*. London: Heinemann [reissued New York: Jason Aronson, 1977].

Bion, W. (1967). *Second Thoughts*. New York: Jason Aronson.

Bion, W. (1992). *Cogitations*. London: Karnac.

Blackburn, R. (1993). *The Psychology of Criminal Conduct: Theory, Research and Practice*. New York: Wiley.

Bollas, C. (1987). *The Shadow of the Object: Psychoanalysis of the Unthought Known*. New York: Columbia University Press.

Bollas, C. (1995). *Cracking Up: The Work of Unconscious Experience*. London: Routledge.

Bowlby, J. (1958). The nature of the child's tie to his mother. *International Journal of Psychoanalysis*, *38(9)*: 350–372.

Bowlby, J. (1969). *Attachment and Loss, Vol. 1: Attachment*. New York: Basic.

Bowlby, J. (1973). *Attachment and Loss, Vol. II: Separation: Anxiety and Anger*. New York: Basic.

Bowlby, J. (1982). *Attachment and Loss*. New York: Basic.

Bowlby, J. (1988). *A Secure Base: Clinical Applications of Attachment Theory*. London: Routledge.

Box, S. (1978). An analytic approach to work with families. *Journal of Adolescence*, *1*: 119–133.

Britton, R. (1998). *Belief and Imagination*. London: Routledge.

Broucek, F. J. (1982). Shame and its relation to early narcissistic developments. *International Journal of Psychoanalysis*, *63*: 369–378.

Broucek, F. J. (1991). *Shame and the Self*. New York: Guilford.

Bruner, J. (1977). Early social interaction and language acquisition. In: H. Schaffer (Ed.), *Studies in Mother–Infant Interaction*. New York: W. W. Norton.

Bruner, J. (1986). *Actual Minds, Possible Worlds*. Cambridge, MA: Harvard University Press.

Bushman, B. J. & Baumeister, R. F. (1999). Threatened egotism, narcissism, self-esteem, and direct and displaced aggression: does self-love lead to violence? *Journal of Personality and Social Psychology*, *75*: 219–229.

Butterworth, G. (1990). Self-perception in infancy. In: D. Cicchetti & M. Beeghley (Eds.), *The Self in Transition—From Infancy to Childhood*. Chicago, IL: University of Chicago Press.

Chasseguet-Smirgel, J. (1970). Female guilt and the Oedipus complex. In: *Female Sexuality: New Psychoanalytic Views*. Ann Arbor, MI: University of Michigan Press. [Reprinted, London: Karnac, 1985].

Chasseguet-Smirgel, J. (1974). Perversion, idealization, and sublimation. *International Journal of Psychoanalysis, 55*: 349–357.

Chasseguet-Smirgel, J. (1985). *Creativity and Perversion*. London: Free Association.

Chodorow, N. (1978). *The Reproduction of Mothering: Psychoanalysis and the Sociology of Gender*. Berkeley, CA: University of California Press.

Clavreul, J. (1980). The perverse couple. S. Schneiderman (Trans.). In S. Schneiderman (Ed.), *Returning to Freud: Clinical Psychoanalysis in the School of Lacan*. New Haven, CT: Yale University Press.

Cohen, D. (1998). Culture, social organization, and patterns of violence. *Journal of Personality and Social Psychology, 75*: 408–419.

Coles, J. (Ed.) (1984). *Shakespeare: Othello*. Cambridge: Cambridge University Press.

Colman, W. (1991). Envy, self-esteem and the fear of separateness. *British Journal of Psychotherapy, 7(4)*: 356–367.

Copjec, J. (2002). Sour justice or liberalist envy? In: *Imagine There's No Woman: Ethics and Sublimation*. Cambridge, MA: MIT Press.

Cordess, C. (1992). Pioneers in forensic psychiatry: Edward Glover (1888–1972): psychoanalysis and crime—a fragile legacy. *Journal of Forensic Psychiatry and Psychology, 3(3)*: 509–530.

Cordess, C. & Cox, M. (Eds.) (1996). *Forensic Psychotherapy*. London: Jessica Kingsley.

Cornell, D. (1995). *The Imaginary Domain: Abortion, Pornography, and Sexual Harassment*. New York: Routledge.

Cox, M. (1982). The psychotherapist as assessor of dangerousness. In: J. R. Hamilton & H. Freeman (Eds.), *Dangerousness: Psychiatric Assessment and Management.* London: Alden.

Cox, M. & Theilgaard, A. (1987). *Mutative Metaphors in Psychotherapy: The Aeolian Mode*. London: Tavistock.

Damasio, A. R. (1994). *Descartes' Error: Emotion, Reason and the Human Brain*. New York: Grosset/Putman.

Damasio, A. R. (1999). *The Feeling of What Happens: Body, Emotion and the Making of Consciousness*. London: Heinemann.

Daniels, M. (1974). The dynamics of morbid envy in the etiology and treatment of chronic learning disability. *Psychoanalytic Review, 51*: 585–596.

Darwin, C. B. (1872). *The Expression of Emotion in Man and Animals*. London: Fontana, 1999.

De Casper, A. & Fifer, W. (1980). Of human bonding: newborns prefer their mother's voice. *Science, 208*: 1174.

De Casper, A. & Spence, M. (1986). Prenatal maternal speech influences newborns' perception of speech sounds. *Infant Behavior and Development, 9*: 133–150.

Dell, P. F. (1982). In search of truth: on the way to clinical epistemology. *Family Process, 21*: 407–414.

De Paola, H. (2001). Panel Reports: envy, jealousy and shame. *International Journal of Psychoanalysis, 82*: 381–384.

De Shazer, S. (1982). *Patterns of Brief Family Therapy: An Ecosystemic Approach.* New York: Guilford.

Downing, L. (2006). Perversion, historicity, ethics. In: D. Nobus & L. Downing (Eds.), *Perversion: Psychoanalytic Perspectives.* London: Karnac.

Duke, J. E., Astbury, J., Atkinson, J., Easteal, P. L., Kurrle, S. E., Tait, P. R. & Turner, J. (2000). The impact of domestic violence on individuals. *Medical Journal of Australia, 173*: 427–431.

Dunn, J. (1996). Children's relationships: bridging the divide between cognitive and social development (The Emanuel Miller Memorial Lecture 1995). *Journal of Child Psychology and Psychiatry, 37*: 507–518.

Dworkin, A. (1981). *Pornography: Men Possessing Women.* London: The Women's Press.

Eagle, M. N. (1990). The concepts of need and wish in self psychology. *Psychoanalytic Psychology, 7* (supplement): 71–88.

Eagle, M. N. (1997). Attachment and psychoanalysis. *British Journal of Medical Psychology, 70*: 217–229.

Eichenbaum, L. & Orbach, S. (1983). Presentation on competition among women (unpublished).

Eissler, M. J. (1921). Pleasure in sleep and the disturbed capacity for sleep. *International Journal of Psychoanalysis, 3*: 30–42.

Eissler, M. J. (1967). Notes on the problems of technique in the psychoanalytic treatment of adolescents with some remarks on perversions. *Psychoanalytic Study of the Child, 13*: 223–254.

Elliott, D., Hamburg, B. & Williams, K. (1998). *Violence in American Schools.* Cambridge: Cambridge University Press.

Ellman, C. (1970). An experimental study of the female castration complex (PhD dissertation, New York University).

Epstein, L. (1978). The therapeutic use of countertransference data with borderline patients. *Contemporary Psychoanalysis, 15(2)*: 248–275.

Etchegoyen, H. (2008). Foreword to P. Roth & A. Lemma (Eds.), *Envy and Gratitude Revisited.* London: Karnac.

Ewins, D. (1976). The Butler Report. *British Journal of Law and Society, 3(1)*: 101–109.

Fairbairn, R. (1940). Schizoid factors in the personality. In R. Fairbairn, *Psychoanalytic Studies of the Personality.* London: Routledge & Kegan Paul, 1952.

Fairbairn, R. (1951). A synopsis of the development of the author's views regarding the structure of the personality. In: R. Fairbairn, *Psychoanalytic Studies of the Personality.* London: Routledge & Kegan Paul, 1952.

Fairbairn, R. (1952). *Psychoanalytic Studies of the Personality*. London: Routledge & Kegan Paul.

Fairbairn, R. (1954). Observations on the nature of hysterical states. *British Journal of Medical Psychology, 27*: 105–125.

Fairbairn, R. (1955). Observations in defence of the object-relations theory of the personality. *British Journal of Medical Psychology, 28*: parts 2–3.

Farber, L. (1976). The faces of envy. In: *Lying, Despair, Jealousy, Envy, Sex, Suicide, Drugs, and the Good Life*. New York: Basic.

Farrington, D. P. (1989). Early predictors of adolescent aggression and adult violence. *Violence and Victims, 4*: 79–100.

Feldman, E. & De Paola, H. (1994). An investigation into the psychoanalytic concept of envy. *International Journal of Psychoanalysis, 75*: 217–234.

Fenichel, O. (1945). *Psychoanalytic Theory of Neurosis*. New York: W. W. Norton.

Fenichel, O. (1954). Brief psychotherapy. In: H. Fenichel & D. Rapaport (Eds.), *Collected Papers: Second Series*. New York: W. W. Norton.

Ferenczi, S. (1919). On the technique of psycho-analysis. In: S. Ferenczi, *Further Contributions to the Theory and Technique of Psycho-Analysis*. London: Hogarth, 1950.

Ferenczi, S. (1923). Review of group psychology and the analysis of the ego. *International Journal of Psychoanalysis, 4*: 183–187.

Ferenczi, S. (1926). *Further Contributions to the Theory and Technique of Psycho-Analysis*. London: Hogarth, 1955.

Ferenczi, S. (1933). Confusion of tongues between adults and the child. In: *Further Contributions to the Theory and Technique of Psycho-Analysis*. London: Hogarth, 1955.

Ferenczi, S. (1952). *First Contributions to Psycho-Analysis*. London: Hogarth, 1955.

Ferenczi, S. (1955). *Final Contributions to the Problems and Methods of Psycho-Analysis*. London: Hogarth.

Ferenczi, S. & Rank, O. (1925). *The Development of Psychoanalysis*. New York: Nervous and Mental Diseases Publishing [Reprinted, London: Karnac, 1986].

Fierstein, H. (1988). *Torch Song Trilogy*. New York: Signet.

Fonagy, P. (2000, April). A developmental view of rage murder. Paper presented at Ninth Annual Meeting of the International Association for Forensic Psychotherapy, Boston, MA.

Fonagy, P. (2001). *Attachment Theory and Psychoanalysis*. New York: Other.

Fonagy, P. & Target, M. (1995). Towards understanding violence: the use of the body and the role of the father. *International Journal of Psychoanalysis, 76*: 487–502.

Fonagy, P. & Target, M. (1996a). Playing with reality I: theory of mind and the normal development of psychic reality. *International Journal of Psychoanalysis*, 77: 217–233.

Fonagy, P. & Target, M. (1996b). Playing with reality II: the development of psychic reality from a theoretical perspective. *International Journal of Psychoanalysis*, 77: 459–479.

Fonagy, P. & Target, M. (1997). Attachment and reflective function: their role in self-organization. *Development and Psychopathology*, 9: 679–700.

Fonagy, P., Moran, G. S. & Target, M. (1993). Aggression and the psychological self. *International Journal of Psychoanalysis*, 74: 471–485.

Fonagy, P., Gergely, G., Jurist, E. L. & Target, M. (2002). *Affect Regulation, Mentalization, and Development of the Self*. New York: Other.

Freud, S. (1900a). *The Interpretation of Dreams*, S.E., 4, 5. London: Hogarth.

Freud, S. (1905d). Three essays on the theory of sexuality, S.E., 7. London: Hogarth.

Freud, S. (1910a). Five lectures on psychoanalysis, S.E., 2. London: Hogarth.

Freud, S. (1912d). On the universal tendency to debasement in the sphere of love, S,E., 11. London: Hogarth.

Freud, S. (1914c). On narcissism: an introduction, S.E., 14. London: Hogarth.

Freud, S. (1914g). Remembering, repeating and working-through, S.E., 12. London: Hogarth.

Freud, S. (1916a). Criminals from a sense of guilt, S.E., 14. London: Hogarth.

Freud, S. (1916d). Some character-types met with in psycho-analytic work, S.E., 14. London: Hogarth.

Freud, S. (1916–17). *Introductory Lectures on Psycho-Analysis*, S.E., 15, 16. London: Hogarth.

Freud, S. (1917c). On transformations of instinct as exemplified in anal eroticism, S.E., 17. London: Hogarth.

Freud, S. (1917e). Mourning and melancholia, S.E., 14. London: Hogarth.

Freud, S. (1918b). From the history of an infantile neurosis, S.E., 17. London: Hogarth.

Freud, S. (1920g). *Beyond the Pleasure Principle*, S.E., 18. London: Hogarth.

Freud, S. (1923b). *The Ego and the Id*, S.E., 19. London: Hogarth.

Freud, S. (1925j). Some psychical consequences of the anatomical distinction between the sexes, S.E., 20. London: Hogarth.

Freud, S. (1926d). Inhibitions, symptoms and anxiety, S.E., 20. London: Hogarth.

Freud, S. (1930). *Civilization and Its Discontents*. J. Riviere (Trans.). London: Hogarth.

Freud, S. (1932–1936). *New Introductory Lectures on Psycho-Analysis, S.E., 22.* London: Hogarth.

Freud, S. (1934b). *Totem and Taboo and Other Works, S.E., 13.* London: Hogarth.

Freud, S. (1937c). Analysis terminable and interminable, *S.E., 23.* London: Hogarth.

Freud, S. (1953–1974). *The Standard Edition of the Complete Psychological Works of Sigmund Freud,* 24 volumes [English edition]. London: Hogarth.

Gallwey, P. (1978a). Transference utilization in aim-restricted psychotherapy. *British Journal of Medical Psychology, 51*: 225–236.

Gallwey, P. (1978b). Symbolic dysfunction in the perversions (unpublished lecture, British Psychoanalytical Society).

Gallwey, P. (1985). The psychodynamics of borderline personality. In: D. P. Farrington & J. Gunn (Eds.), *Aggression and Dangerousness.* London: Wiley.

Gallwey, P. (1991). Social maladjustment. In: J. Holmes (Ed.), *Textbook of Psychotherapy in Psychiatric Practice.* London: Churchill Livingstone.

Gallwey, P. (1992). The psychotherapy of psychopathic disorder. *Criminal Behaviour and Mental Health, 2*: 159–168.

Gallwey, P. (1995, May). Violence (keynote speech, International Association for Forensic Psychotherapy, Glasgow).

Gallwey, P. (1996). Psychotic and borderline processes. In: C. Cordess & M. Cox (Eds.), *Forensic Psychotherapy.* London: Jessica Kingsley.

Gallwey, P. (1997). Foreword to P. Polledri, Forensic psychotherapy with a potential serial killer. *British Journal of Psychotherapy, 13(4)*: 473–488.

Gallwey, P. (2003). Personal communication.

Gallwey, P. (2008). Personal communication.

Gedo, J. (1979). *Beyond Interpretation: Toward a Revised Theory for Psychoanalysis.* New York: International Universities Press.

Gifford, E. (1958). *The Evil Eye: Studies in the Folklore of Vision.* New York: Macmillan.

Gilligan, J. (1996). Exploring shame in special settings. In: C. Cordess & M. Cox (Eds.), *Forensic Psychotherapy.* London: Jessica Kingsley.

Gilligan, J. (1997). *Violence: Our Deadly Epidemic and Its Causes.* New York: Grosset/Putnam.

Gilligan, J. (2000). *Violence: Reflections on Our Deadliest Epidemic* (Forensic Focus Series, Vol. 18). London: Jessica Kingsley.

Glasser, M. (1996). The assessment and management of dangerousness: the psychoanalytic contribution. *Journal of Forensic Psychiatry, 7*: 271–283.

Glasser, M. (1998). On violence: a preliminary communication. *International Journal of Psychoanalysis, 79*: 887–902.

Glover, E. (1922). The roots of crime. In: E. Glover, *The Roots of Crime: Selected Papers on Psycho-Analysis, Vol. II.* London: Imago, 1960.

Glover, E. (1949). Outline of the investigation and treatment of delinquency in Great Britain, 1912–48. In: E. Glover, *The Roots of Crime: Selected Papers on Psycho-Analysis, Vol. II.* London: Imago, 1960.

Gopnik, A., Meltzoff, A. & Kuhl, P. (1999). *The Scientist in the Crib: What Early Learning Tells Us about the Mind.* New York: Perennial.

Gordon, R. (1993). The drive towards death: a vector of the self. In: *Bridges: Metaphor for Psychic Processes.* London: Karnac.

Green, A. (1996). *On Private Madness* (Classics of Psychoanalysis Series). London: Rebus.

Green, A. (2005). Winnicott at the start of the third millenium. In: L. Caldwell (Ed.), *Sex and Sexuality.* London: Karnac.

Green, A. & Kohon, G. (2005). *Love and Its Vicissitudes.* London: Routledge.

Greenson, R. (1974). Loving, hating and indifference towards the patient. *International Review of Psycho-Analysis, 1*: 259–266.

Grotstein, J. S. (1981). *Splitting and Projective Identification.* New York: Jason Aronson.

Grotstein, J. S. (1983). The significance of Kleinian contributions to psychoanalysis: IV Critiques of Klein. *International Journal of Psycho-Analytic Psychotherapy, 9*: 511–535.

Guntrip, H. (1968). *Schizoid Phenomena, Object-Relations, and the Self.* New York: International Universities Press/London: Hogarth.

Habermas, J. (1979). *Communication and the Evolution of Society.* Boston, MA: Beacon.

Harpold, J. A. & Band, S. R. (1998). Lessons learned: an FBI perspective (School Violence summit). Little Rock, AR: Behavioral Science Unit, FBI Academy.

Hart, S. (2008). *Brain, Attachment, Personality: An Introduction to Neuroaffective Development.* London: Karnac.

Hawkins, J. D., Herronkohl, T., Farrington, D. P., Brewer, D., Catalano, R. F. & Harachi, T. W. (1998). A review of predictors of youth violence. In: E. Loeber & D. P. Farrington (Eds.), *Serious and Violent Juvenile Offenders.* Thousand Oaks, CA: Sage.

Heim, C. & Nemeroff, C. B. (1999). The impact of early adverse experiences on brain systems involved in the psychophysiology of anxiety and affective disorders. *Biological Psychiatry, 46*: 1509–1522.

Heim, C. & Nemeroff, C. B. (2001). The role of childhood trauma in the neurobiology of mood and anxiety disorders: preclinical and clinical studies. *Biological Psychiatry, 49*: 1023–1039.

Hering, C. (1997). Beyond understanding? Some thoughts on the meaning and function of the notion of "evil". *British Journal of Psychotherapy, 14*: 209–219.

Hinshelwood, R. D. (1989). *A Dictionary of Kleinian Thought.* London: Free Association.

Hinshelwood, R. D. (1994). *Clinical Klein*. London: Free Association.

Hobson, R. P. (2002). *The Cradle of Thought*. London: Pan Macmillan.

Holbrook, D. (1971). *Human Hope and the Death Instinct: An Exploration of Psychoanalytical Theories of Human Nature and Their Implications for Culture and Education*. Oxford: Pergamon.

Holland, R. (1990). Scientificity and psychoanalysis: insights from the controversial discussions. *International Review of Psycho-Analysis*, *17*: 133–158.

Hollin, C. R. (1989). *Psychology and Crime: An Introduction to Criminological Psychology*. London: Routledge.

Holmes, J. (1993). Attachment theory: a biological base for psychotherapy? *British Journal of Psychiatry*, *163*: 430–438.

Holmes, J. (1996). *Attachment, Intimacy, Autonomy: Using Attachment Theory in Adult Psychotherapy*. Northville, NJ: Jason Aronson.

Holmes, J. (1997). Commentary on "Autobiography, narrative, and the Freudian concept of life history". *Philosophy, Psychiatry, and Psychology*, *4(3)*: 201–203.

Holmes, J. (1998a). The psychotherapy department and the community mental health team: bridges and boundaries. *Psychiatric Bulletin*, *22*: 729–732.

Holmes, J. (1998b). The changing aims of psychoanalytic psychotherapy: an integrative perspective. *International Journal of Psychoanalysis*, *79*: 227–240.

Hopper, E. (1991). The encapsulated psychosis. *International Journal of Psychoanalysis*, *72*: 607–624.

Hopper, E. (1995). A psychoanalytical theory of drug addiction: unconscious fantasies of homosexuality, compulsions, and masturbation within the context of traumatogenic processes. *International Journal of Psychoanalysis*, *76(6)*: 1121–1142.

Horney, K. (1923). *Feminine Psychology*. New York: W. W. Norton.

Horney, K. (1924). On the genesis of the castration complex in women. *International Journal of Psychoanalysis*, *5*: 50–63.

Horney, K. (1926). The flight from womanhood. *International Journal of Psychoanalysis*, *7*: 323–339.

Horney, K. (1932). The dread of woman. *International Journal of Psychoanalysis*, *13*: 348–360.

Horney, K. (1933). The denial of the vagina. *International Journal of Psychoanalysis*, *14*: 57–70.

Horney, K. (1939). *New Ways in Psychoanalysis*. New York: W. W. Norton.

Horney, K. (1948). The value of vindictiveness. *American Journal of Psychoanalysis*, *8*: 3–12.

Howell, J. C. (1997). *Juvenile Justice and Youth Violence*. Thousand Oaks, CA: Sage.

Hyatt-Williams, A. (1964). The psychopathology and treatment of sexual murders. In: I. Rosen (Ed.), *Psychology and Treatment of Sexual Deviation.* London: Oxford University Press.

Hyatt-Williams, A. (1975). *Rape, Murder, Sexual Behaviour, and the Law.* London: Thomas.

Hyatt-Williams, A. (1998). *Cruelty, Violence, and Murder: Understanding the Criminal Mind.* New York: Jason Aronson/London: Karnac.

Hyatt-Williams, A. (2002). Container and contained: the school of Bion. In: M. Weegmann & R. Cohen (Eds.), *The Psychodynamics of Addiction.* London: Whurr.

Hyatt-Williams, A. & Cordess, C. (1996). The criminal act and acting out. In: C. Cordess & M. Cox (Eds.), *Forensic Psychotherapy.* London: Jessica Kingsley.

Irigaray, L. (1987). *Sexes et parentes.* Paris: Minuit. [Translated as *Sexes and Genealogies.* New York: Columbia University Press, 1993.]

Jacobus, M. (1996). *First Things: The Maternal Imaginary in Literature, Art and Psychoanalysis.* London: Routledge.

Jaffe, D. S. (1968). The masculine envy of women's procreative function. *Journal of American Psychoanalytic Association, 16*: 521–548.

Joffe, W. (1969). A critical review of the status of the envy concept. *International Journal of Psychoanalysis, 50*: 533–545.

Johnson, J. G., Cohen, P., Brown, J., Smailes, E. M. & Bernstein, D. P. (1999). Childhood maltreatment increases risk for personality disorders during early adulthood. *Archives of General Psychiatry, 56*: 600–605.

Joseph, B. (1975). The patient who is difficult to reach. In: P. Giovanni (Ed.), *Tactics and Techniques in Psychoanalytic Therapy, Vol. II: Counter-transference.* New York: Jason Aronson.

Joseph, B. (1982). Addiction to near death. In: M. Feldman & E. Bott Spillius (Eds.), *Psychic Equilibrium and Psychic Change, Selected Papers of Betty Joseph.* London: Routledge, 1989.

Joseph, B. (1985). Transference: the total situation. *International Journal of Psychoanalysis, 66*: 447–454.

Joseph, B. (1986). Envy in everyday life. *Psychoanalytic Psychotherapy, 2(1)*: 13–22.

Jukes, A. (1993). *Why Men Hate Women.* London: Free Association.

Kahr, B. (Ed.) (1996). *D. W. Winnicott: A Biographical Portrait.* London: Karnac.

Kahr, B. (2001). *Exhibitionism: Ideas in Psychoanalysis.* London: Eros.

Kahr, B. (2002). *The Legacy of Winnicott: Essays on Infant and Child Mental Health.* London: Karnac.

Kaplan, L. J. (1993). *Female Perversion: The Temptations of Madame Bovary.* Harmondsworth: Penguin.

Karr-Morse, R. & Wiley, L. (1997). *Ghosts from the Nursery.* New York: Atlantic Monthly.

Kaufman, G. (1992). *Shame: The Power of Caring*. Rochester, VT: Schenkman.

Kermode, F. (2001). *Shakespeare's Language*. London: Penguin.

Kernberg, O. (1969). A contribution to the ego-psychological critique of the Kleinian school. *International Journal of Psychoanalysis*, 50: 317–333.

Kernberg, O. (1972). *Barriers to Being in Love*. Topeka, KS: The Menninger Foundation.

Kernberg, O. (1975). *Borderline Conditions and Pathological Narcissism*. New York: Jason Aronson.

Kernberg, O. (1977). The structural diagnosis of borderline personality organization. In: P. Hartocollis (Ed.), *Borderline Personality Disorders*. New York: International Universities Press.

Kernberg, O. (1992). *Aggression in Personality Disorders and Perversions*. New Haven, CT: Yale University Press.

Kernberg, O. (2006). Perversion, perversity, and normality: diagnostic and therapeutic considerations. In: D. Nobus & L. Downing (Eds.), *Perversion: Psychoanalytic Perspectives*. London: Karnac.

Kestenbaum, C. J. (1984). Pathological attachments and their relationship to affective disorders in adult life. *American Journal of Psychoanalysis*, 44: 33–49.

Khan, M. M. R. (1974). *The Privacy of the Self*. London: Hogarth/The Institute of Psychoanalysis.

King, P. & Steiner, R. (Eds.) (1991). *The Freud–Klein Controversies 1941–45*. London: Tavistock/Routledge.

Kingston, L. & Prior, M. (1995). The development of stable, transient, and school-age onset aggressive behavior in young children. *Journal of the American Academy of Child and Adolescent Psychiatry*, 34: 348–358.

Kittay, E. (1984). Womb envy: an explanatory concept. In: J. Trebilcot (Ed.), *Mothering: Essays in Feminist Theory*. Lanham, MD: Littlefield and Adams.

Kittay, E. (1988). Rereading Freud on "Femininity" or why not womb envy? *Women's Studies International Forum*, 7(5): 385–391.

Kittay, E. (1995). Mastering envy: from Freud's narcissistic wounds to Bettelheim's symbolic wounds to a vision of healing. *Psychoanalytic Review*, 82(1): 125–158.

Klein, M. (1926). The psychological principles of early analysis. In: *Love, Guilt and Reparation and Other Works, 1921–1945*. London: Hogarth, 1975.

Klein, M. (1927). Criminal tendencies in normal children. In: *Love, Guilt and Reparation and Other Works, 1921–1945*. London: Hogarth, 1975.

Klein, M. (1928). Early stages of the Oedipus conflict. *International Journal of Psychoanalysis*, 9: 167–180.

Klein, M. (1930). The importance of symbol formation in the development of the ego. In: *Love, Guilt and Reparation and Other Works, 1921–1945.* London: Hogarth, 1975.

Klein, M. (1931). A contribution to the theory of intellectual inhibition. In: *Love, Guilt and Reparation and Other Works, 1921–1945.* London: Hogarth, 1975.

Klein, M. (1932). *The Psycho-Analysis of Children.* A. Strachey (Trans.). London: Hogarth, 1975.

Klein, M. (1934). On criminality. In: *The Writings of Melanie Klein, Vol. 1.* London: Hogarth, 1975.

Klein, M. (1935). A contribution to the psychogenesis of manic-depressive states. In: *Love, Guilt and Reparation and Other Works, 1921–1945.* London: Hogarth, 1975.

Klein, M. (1936). Weaning. In: *Love, Guilt and Reparation and Other Works, 1921–1945.* London: Hogarth, 1975.

Klein, M. (1937). Love, guilt and reparation. In: *Love, Guilt and Reparation and Other Works, 1921–1945.* London: Hogarth, 1975.

Klein, M. (1940). Mourning and its relation to manic-depressive states. In: *Love, Guilt and Reparation and Other Works, 1921–1945.* London: Hogarth, 1975.

Klein, M. (1945). The Oedipus complex in the light of early anxieties. In: *Love, Guilt and Reparation and Other Works, 1921–1945.* London: Hogarth, 1975.

Klein, M. (1946). Notes on some schizoid mechanisms. In: *Envy and Gratitude and Other Works 1946–1963.* London: Hogarth, 1975.

Klein, M. (1948). On the theory of anxiety and guilt. In: *Envy and Gratitude and Other Works 1946–1963.* London: Hogarth, 1975.

Klein, M. (1950). On the criteria for the termination of a psycho-analysis. In: *Envy and Gratitude and Other Works 1946–1963.* London: Hogarth, 1975.

Klein, M. (1952a). Some theoretical conclusions regarding the emotional life of the infant. In: *Envy and Gratitude and Other Works 1946–1963.* London: Hogarth, 1975.

Klein, M. (1952b). On observing the behaviour of young infants. In: *Envy and Gratitude and Other Works 1946–1963.* London: Hogarth, 1975.

Klein, M. (1955). On identification. In: *Envy and Gratitude and Other Works 1946–1963.* London: Hogarth, 1975.

Klein, M. (1957). Envy and gratitude. In: *Envy and Gratitude and Other Works 1946–1963.* London: Hogarth, 1975.

Klein, M. (1958). On the development of mental functioning. In: *Envy and Gratitude and Other Works 1946–1963.* London: Hogarth, 1975.

Klein, M. (1959). Our adult world and its roots in infancy. In: *Envy and Gratitude and Other Works 1946–1963.* London: Hogarth, 1975.

Klein, M. (1960a). On mental health. In: *Envy and Gratitude and Other Works 1946–1963.* London: Hogarth, 1975.

Klein, M. (1960b). A note on depression in the schizophrenic. In: *Envy and Gratitude and Other Works 1946–1963.* London: Hogarth, 1975.

Klein, M. (1961). *Narrative of a Child Analysis: The Conduct of the Psycho-Analysis of Children as Seen in the Treatment of a Ten Year Old Boy.* London: Hogarth.

Klein, M. (1963). On the sense of loneliness. In: *Envy and Gratitude and Other Works 1946–1963.* London: Hogarth, 1975.

Klein, M. (1975). *Collected Works of Melanie Klein.* London: Hogarth/The Institute of Psychoanalysis.

Knight, J. A. (1971). Unusual case: false pregnancy in a male. *Medical Aspects of Human Sexuality*, March: 58–67.

Kohon, G. (Ed.) (2001). *The Dead Mother: The Work of André Green.* London: Brunner-Routledge.

Kohut, H. (1971). *The Analysis of the Self.* New York: International Universities Press.

Kohut, H. (1972). Thoughts on narcissism and narcissistic rage. *The Psychoanalytic Study of the Child*, 27: 360–399.

Kohut, H. (1977). *The Restoration of the Self.* New York: International Universities Press.

Kohut, H. (1984). *How Does Analysis Cure?* Chicago, IL: University of Chicago Press.

Kumin, I. (1996). *Pre-Object Relatedness: Early Attachment and the Analytic Situation.* New York: Guilford.

Laing, R. D. (1960). *The Divided Self: An Existential Study in Sanity and Madness.* Harmondsworth: Penguin.

Laing, R. D. (1965). Practice and theory: the present situation. In: M. Pines & T. Spoerri (Eds.), *Proceedings of 6th International Congress of Psychotherapy.* New York: Karger.

Laing, R. D. & Esterson, A. (1964). *Sanity, Madness and the Family: Families of Schizophrenics.* London: Penguin.

Lansky, M. & Morrison, A. (1997). *The Widening Scope of Shame.* Hillsdale, NJ: The Analytic Press.

Laplanche, J. (1976). *Life and Death in Psychoanalysis.* J. Melham (Trans.). Baltimore, MD: Johns Hopkins University Press.

Laplanche, J. (1989). *New Foundations for Psychoanalysis.* D. Macey (Trans.). Oxford: Blackwell.

Laplanche, J. (1999a). *Essays on Otherness.* London: Routledge.

Laplanche, J. (1999b). The so-called death drive: a sexual drive. In: R. Weatherill (Ed.), *The Death Drive: New Life for a Dead Subject?* (*Encyclopaedia of Psychoanalysis, Vol. 3*). London: Rebus.

Lashley, K. (1951). The problem of serial order in behavior. In: L. A. Jefress (Ed.), *Cerebral Mechanisms in Behavior*. New York: Wiley.

LeDoux, J. E. (1994). Emotion, memory, and the brain. *Scientific American*, 270: 32–39.

Lerner, H. (1974). The hysterical personality: a woman's disease. *Comprehensive Psychiatry*, 15(2): 157–164.

Levin, S. (1971). The psychoanalysis of shame. *International Journal of Psychoanalysis*, 52: 355–362.

Lewis, H. B. (1979). Shame in depression and hysteria. In: C. E. Izard (Ed.), *Emotions in Personality and Psychopathology*. New York: Plenum.

Likierman, M. (2001). *Melanie Klein: Her Work in Context*. London: Continuum.

Limentani, A. (1989). *Between Freud and Klein*. London: Free Association.

Lloyd-Owen, D. (2003). Perverse females: their unique psychopathology. *British Journal of Psychotherapy*, 19(3): 285–296.

Lochman, J. & Dodge, K. (1994). Social cognitive processes of severely violent, moderately aggressive, and nonaggressive boys. *Journal of Consulting and Clinical Psychology*, 62: 366–374.

Loeber, R. & Farrington, D. P. (1998). Executive Summary, *Serious and Violent Juvenile Offenders*. Thousand Oaks, CA: Sage.

Loeber, R. & Stouthamer-Loeber, M. (1998). Development of juvenile aggression and violence: some common misconceptions and controversies. *American Psychologist*, 53: 242–259.

London, J. (1967). *Martin Eden*. London: Arcol/Penguin.

Long, S. (2008). *The Perverse Organization and its Deadly Sins*. London: Karnac.

Lopez-Corvo, R. (1992). About interpretation of self envy. *International Journal of Psychoanalysis*, 73: 719–728.

Lopez-Corvo, R. (1994). *Self Envy*. Northvale NJ: Jason Aronson.

Lorenz, K. (1935). Companionship in bird life. C. Schiller (Trans.). In: C. Schiller (Ed.), *Instinctive Behavior*. New York: International Universities Press, 1957.

Lyons-Ruth, K., Connell, D. B., Grunebaum, H. U. & Botein, S. (1990). Infants at social risk: maternal depression and family support services as mediators of infant development and security of attachment. *Child Development*, 61(1): 85–98.

McDougall, J. (1988). Perversions in psychoanalytic attitude. In: G. I. Fogel & W. A. Myers (Eds.), *Perversions and Near Perversions in Clinical Practice: New Psychoanalytic Perspectives*. New Haven, CT: Yale University Press.

McDougall, J. (1989). *Theaters of the Body: A Psychoanalytic Approach to Psychosomatic Illness*. New York: W. W. Norton.

McDougall, J. (1992). *Plea for a Measure of Abnormality* (revised edition). New York: Brunner-Mazel.

McDougall, J. (1995). *The Many Faces of Eros: A Psychoanalytic Exploration of Human Sexuality*. London: Free Association.

McDougall, J. (2004). *Théâtres du Je* (Folio Essais). Paris: Gallimard.

McGilchrist, I. (2009). *The Master and His Emissary*. New Haven, CT: Yale University Press.

Mahler, M. S. (1979). Notes on the development of basic moods: the depressive affect. In: *Selected Papers of Margaret Mahler*. New York: Jason Aronson.

Main, M. & Hesse, E. (1990). Parents' unresolved traumatic experiences are related to infant disorganized attachment status: is frightened and/or frightening parental behavior the linking mechanism? In: M. T. Greenberg, D. Cicchetti, & E. M. Cummings (Eds.), *Attachment in the Preschool Years*. Chicago, IL: University of Chicago Press.

Main, M. & Solomon, J. (1986). Discovery of an insecure-disorganized/ disoriented pattern. In: T. B. Brazelton & M. Yogman (Eds.), *Affective Development in Infancy*. Norwood, NJ: Ablex.

Main, M. & Solomon, J. (1990). Procedures for identifying infants as disorganized/disoriented during the Strange Situation. In: M. T. Greenberg, D. Cicchetti, & E. M. Cummings (Eds.), *Attachment in the Preschool Years*. Chicago, IL: University of Chicago Press.

Mann, D. (1995). *Psychotherapy: An Erotic Relationship*. London: Brunner-Routledge.

Martin, G. & Clark, R. (1982). Distress crying in neonates: species and peer specificity. *Developmental Psychology*, 18: 3–9.

Masterson, I. (1999). Life or death? An even choice. In: R. Weatherill (Ed.), *The Death Drive: New Life for a Dead Subject?* (*Encyclopaedia of Psychoanalysis, Vol. 3*). London: Rebus.

Mead, G. H. (1934). *Mind, Self and Society*. Chicago, IL: University of Chicago Press.

Meissner, W. W. (1980). A note on projective identification. *Journal of the American Psychoanalytic Association*, 28: 43–65.

Meloy, R. J. (1992). *Violent Attachments*. Northvale, NJ: Jason Aronson.

Meltzer, D. (1975). *Explorations in Autism: A Psycho-Analytical Study*. Strath Tay, Perthshire: Clunie.

Menninger, K., Mayman, M. & Pruyser, P. (1963). *The Vital Balance: The Life Process in Mental Health and Illness*. New York: Viking.

Midgely, M. (1984). *Wickedness*. London: Routledge & Kegan Paul.

Migone, P. (1995). Expressed emotion and projective identification. *Contemporary Psychoanalysis*, 31: 617–640.

Miller, S. (1996). *Shame in Context*. Hillsdale, NJ: The Analytic Press.

Minsky, R. (1995). Reaching beyond denial-sight and in-sight, a way forward? *Free Association*, *35(3)*: 326–351.

Minsky, R. (1999). "Too much of a good thing": control or containment in coping with change. *Psychoanalytic Studies*, *1(4)*: 391–405.

Mitchell, J. (1986). *The Selected Melanie Klein*. Harmondsworth: Penguin.

Mitchell, J. (2001). Sexuality, psychoanalysis and social change. In: A. Molino & C. Ware (Eds.), *Where Id Was*. London: Continuum.

Modell, A. H. (2001). The dead mother syndrome and the reconstruction of trauma. In: G. Kohon (Ed.), *The Dead Mother: The Work of André Green*. London: Brunner-Routledge.

Mollon, P. (2002). *Shame and Jealousy: The Hidden Turmoils*. London: Karnac.

Monahan, J. (1992). Mental disorder and violent behaviour: perceptions and evidence. *American Psychologist*, *47*: 511–521.

Money-Kyrle, R. (1955). Psychoanalysis and ethics. In: M. Klein, P. Heimann, & R. Money-Kyrle (Eds.), *New Directions in Psychoanalysis*. London: Tavistock. [Reprinted in *The Collected Papers of Roger Money-Kyrle*. Strath Tay, Perthshire: Clunie, 1978].

Morrison, A. (1984). Working with shame in psychoanalytic treatment. *Journal of American Psychoanalytic Association*, *32*: 479–505.

Morrison, A. (1989). *Shame: The Underside of Narcissism*. Hillsdale, NJ: The Analytic Press.

Nakamura, K., Kawashima, R., Sugiura, M., Kato, T., Nakamura, A., Hatano, K., Nagumo, S., Kubota, K., Fukuda, H. & Kojima, S. (1999). Activation of the right inferior frontal cortex during assessment of facial emotion. *Journal of Neurophysiology*, *82*: 1610–1614.

Nathanson, D. L. (1987). A timetable for shame. In: D. L. Nathanson (Ed.), *The Many Faces of Shame*. New York: Guilford.

Nathanson, D. L. (1992), *Shame and Pride: Affect, Sex, and the Birth of the Self*. New York: W. W. Norton.

Nobus, D. & Downing, L. (Eds.) (2006). *Perversion: Psychoanalytic Perspectives*. London: Karnac.

Nussbaum, M. C. (2004). *Hiding from Humanity: Disgust, Shame, and the Law*. Princeton, NJ: Princeton University Press.

Ogden, T. (1979). On projective identification. *International Journal of Psychoanalysis*, *60*: 357–373.

Ogden, T. (1982). *Projective Identification and Psychotherapeutic Technique*. New York: Jason Aronson.

Ogden, T. (1990). *The Matrix of the Mind*. Northvale, NJ: Jason Aronson.

Ogden, T. (1994). *The Analytic Third: Working with Inter-Subjective Clinical Facts*. London: Karnac.

Parker, R. (1993). *Torn in Two: The Experience of Maternal Ambivalence*. London: Virago.

Perelberg, R. (1999). *Psychoanalytic Understanding of Violence and Suicide.* London: Routledge.

Perry, B. (1996). Childhood trauma, the neurobiology of adaptation, and "use dependent" development of the brain: how "states" become "traits". *Infant Mental Health Journal, 16*: 271–291.

Petot, J. M. (1991). *Melanie Klein.* Madison, CT: International Universities Press.

Pines, M. (1987). Shame: what psychoanalysis does and does not say. *Group Analysis, 20*: 16–31.

Pines, M. (1995). The universality of shame: a psychoanalytic approach. *British Journal of Psychotherapy, 11(3)*: 346–357.

Polledri, P. (1995, May). Acting on the urge to kill (lecture, International Association for Forensic Psychotherapy, Glasgow).

Polledri, P. (1996). Munchausen Syndrome by Proxy and perversion of the maternal instinct. *Journal of Forensic Psychiatry, 7(3)*: 561–562.

Polledri, P. (1997). Forensic psychotherapy with a potential serial killer. *British Journal of Psychotherapy, 13(4)*: 473–488.

Polledri, P. (1998, April). Latent murderousness. Paper presented at the International Psychoanalytical Association and UNESCO Conference: En el Umbral del Milenio: Cultura–Ecologica–Genero–Violencia, Lima, Peru.

Polledri, P. (1999). Latent murderousness. *The Psychotherapy Review, 1(1)*: 10–15.

Polledri, P. (2003). Envy revisited. *British Journal of Psychotherapy, 20(2)*: 195–218.

Polledri, P. (2012, March). Which version of perversion is womb envy? Paper, 21 st International Association of Forensic Psychotherapy Conference, Venice.

Pritchard, H. A. (1950). *Knowledge and Perception.* Oxford: Clarendon.

Rapaport, D. (1960). *The Structure of Psychoanalytic Theory: A Systematizing Attempt.* New York: International Universities Press.

Raphael-Leff, J. (1996). Primary maternal persecution. In: B. Kahr (Ed.), *D. W. Winnicott: A Biographical Portrait.* London: Karnac.

Raphael-Leff, J. (2000). *Spilt Milk: Perinatal Loss and Breakdown.* London: The Institute of Psychoanalysis.

Reik, T. (1925). The compulsion to confess: on the psychoanalysis of crime and punishment. In: J. Farrar (Ed.), *The Compulsion to Confess and the Need for Punishment.* New York: Farrar, Straus, and Cudahy, 1959.

Revitch, E. & Schlesinger, L. B. (1981). *Psychopathology of Homicide.* Springfield, IL: Charles Thomas.

Rich, A. (1977). *Of Woman Born.* London: Virago.

Riley, D. (1983). *War in the Nursery: Theories of the Child and Mother.* London: Virago.

Riviere, J. (1936). On the genesis of psychical conflict in earliest infancy. *International Journal of Psychoanalysis, 17*: 395–422.

Rizzutto, A. M. (1991). Shame in psychoanalysis. *International Journal of Psychoanalysis, 72*: 297–312.

Roazen, P. (2000). *Oedipus in Britain: Edward Glover and the Struggle over Klein*. New York: Other.

Robson, K. (1967). The role of eye-to-eye contact in maternal-infant attachment. *Journal of Child Psychiatry, 8*: 13–25.

Rose, J. (2003). On shame. In: J. Rose (Ed.), *On Not Being Able to Sleep*. London: Chatto & Windus.

Rosenfeld, H. (1971). A clinical approach to the psychoanalytic theory of the life and death instincts: an investigation into the aggressive aspects of narcissism. *International Journal of Psychoanalysis, 52(2)*: 169–178.

Rosenfeld, H. (1987). *Impasse and Interpretation*. London: Tavistock.

Roth, P. & Lemma, A. (Eds.) (2008). *Envy and Gratitude Revisited*. London: Karnac.

Rowan, J. (1990). *The Horned God*. London: Routledge.

Ruotolo, A. K. (1968). Dynamics of sudden murder. *American Journal of Psychoanalysis, 28*: 162–176.

Ruszczynski, S. & Morgan, D. (Eds.) (2007). *Lectures on Violence, Perversion, and Delinquency*. London: Karnac.

Rycroft, C. (1968). *A Critical Dictionary of Psychoanalysis*. Harmondsworth: Penguin.

Salgado, G. & Salgado, F. (1985). *Shakespeare: Othello*. London: Penguin.

Salovay, P. (Ed.) (1991). *The Psychology of Jealousy and Envy*. New York: Guilford.

Sandell, R. (1993). Envy and admiration. *International Journal of Psychoanalysis, 74*: 1221–1223

Sandler, J. (1976). Countertransference and role-responsiveness. *International Review of Psycho-Analysis, 3*: 43–47.

Sands, S. (1997). Self psychology and projective identification—whither the two shall meet? *Psychoanalytic Dialogue, 7*: 651–668.

Sartre, J.-P. (1956). *Being and Nothingness* (originally published as *L'Être et le néant*, 1943). H. Barnes (Trans.). New York: Simon & Schuster.

Scarfone, D. (2008). The analyst at work: a psychoanalytic exchange for sharing our experience and learning from our differences. *International Journal of Psycho-Analysis, 89*: 5–7.

Schafer, R. (1968). *Aspects of Internalization*. New York: International Universities Press.

Schoeck, H. (1969). *Envy: A Theory of Social Behaviour*. New York: Harcourt Brace. [Reissued, Indianapolis, IN: Liberty, 1987].

Schore, A. N. (1991). Early superego development: the emergence of shame. *Psychoanalysis and Contemporary Thought, 14*: 187–250.

Schore, A. N. (1994). *Affect Regulation and the Origin of the Self: The Neurobiology of Emotional Development*. Hillsdale, NJ: Lawrence Erlbaum.

Schore, A. N. (1996). The experience-dependent maturation of a regulatory system in the orbital prefrontal cortex and the origin of developmental psychopathology. *Development and Psychopathology*, 8: 59–87.

Schore, A. N. (2001). Minds in the making: attachment, the self-organizing brain, and developmentally-oriented psychoanalytic psychotherapy. *British Journal of Psychotherapy*, 1(3): 229–328.

Schore, A. N. (2002). The neurobiology of attachment and early personality organization. *Journal of Prenatal and Perinatal Psychology and Health*, 16: 249–263.

Schore, A. N. (2003a). *Affect Dysregulation and Disorders of the Self*. New York: W. W. Norton.

Schore. A. N. (2003b). *Affect Regulation and the Repair of the Self*. New York: W. W. Norton.

Scott, W. C. (1975). Self envy of dreams and dreaming. *International Review of Psycho-Analysis*, 2(3): 333–338.

Segal, H. (1957). Notes on symbol formation. *International Journal of Psychoanalysis*, 38: 391–397. [Reprinted in *The Work of Hanna Segal*. London: Free Association, 1981].

Segal, H. (1966). Discussion of "From Gravida to the Death Instinct" by Lawrence J. Friedman. *Psychoanalytic Forum*, 1: 55–58.

Segal, H. (1979). *Melanie Klein*. New York: Viking.

Segal, H. (1988). *Introduction to the Work of Melanie Klein*. London: Hogarth/ The Institute of Psychoanalysis.

Segal, H. (1991). *Dream, Phantasy and Art*. London: Routledge.

Segal, H. (1993). On the clinical usefulness of the death instinct. *International Journal of Psychoanalysis*, 74: 55–61.

Segal, H. (1997). *The Uses and Abuses of Counter-Transference: Psychoanalysis, Literature and War*. London: Routledge.

Seymour Report (1985, November). Tavistock and Portman Clinic Review. Independent Review Group set up by the Minister of State for Health (unpublished).

Shane, M. (1985). Summary and discussion of Kohut's "The Self Psychological Approach to Defense and Resistance". In: A. Goldberg (Ed.), *Progress in Self Psychology, Vol. 1*. New York: Guilford.

Siegel, D. J. (1999). *The Developing Mind: How Relationships and the Brain Interact to Shape Who We Are*. New York: Guilford.

Siegel, D. J. (2006). An interpersonal neurobiology approach to psychotherapy: awareness, mirror neurons, and neural plasticity in the development of well-being. *Psychiatric Annals*, 36(4): 247–258.

Siegel, D. J. (2007). *The Mindful Brain*. New York: W. W. Norton.

Siegel, D. J. (2011, April). Why psychotherapy works (lecture, Royal College of Physicians, London Confer Conference).

Silver, C. B. (2007). Womb envy: loss and grief of the maternal body. *Psychoanalytic Review, 94(3)*: 409–430.

Singer, J. & Fagen, J. (1992). Negative affect, emotional expression, and forgetting in infants. *Developmental Psychology, 28*: 48–57.

Smith, C. & Thomberry, T. P. (1995). The relationship between child maltreatment and adolescent involvement in delinquency. *Criminology, 33*: 451–477.

Sohn, L. (1997). Unprovoked assaults: making sense of apparently random violence. In: D. Bell (Ed.), *Reason and Passion: A Celebration of the Work of Hanna Segal*. London: Duckworth.

Spence, D. P. (1982). *Narrative Truth and Historical Truth: Meaning and Interpretation in Psychoanalysis*. New York: W. W. Norton.

Spillius, E. Bott (1988). *Melanie Klein Today, Vols. 1 and 2*. London: Routledge.

Spillius, E. Bott (1993). Varieties of envious experience. *International Journal of Psychoanalysis, 74*: 1199–1212.

Spitz, R. A. (1965). *The First Year of Life*. New York: International Universities Press.

Steedman, C. (1986). *Landscape for a Good Woman*. London: Virago.

Steiner, J. (1981). Perverse relationships between parts of the self: a clinical illustration. *International Journal of Psychoanalysis, 62*: 241–245.

Steiner, J. (1993). *Psychic Retreats*. London: Routledge.

Steiner, J. (2008). The repetition compulsion, envy, and the death instinct. In: P. Roth & A. Lemma (Eds.), *Envy and Gratitude Revisited*. London: Karnac.

Stephen, K. (1941). Aggression in early childhood. *British Journal of Medical Psychology, 18*: 179–190.

Stern, D. (1974). Mother and infant at play: the dyadic interaction involving facial, vocal, and gaze behaviors. In: M. Lewis & L. Rosenbaum (Eds.), *The Effect of the Infant on its Caregiver*. New York: Wiley.

Stern, D. (1985). *The Interpersonal World of the Infant: A View from Psychoanalysis and Developmental Psychology*. New York: Basic.

Stern, D. (1990). *Diary of a Baby*. New York: Basic.

Stern, D. (1994). One way to build a clinically relevant baby. *Infant Mental Health Journal, 15(1)*: 9–25.

Stoller, R. J. (1975). *Perversion: The Erotic Form of Hatred*. London: Maresfield, 1986.

Stoller, R. J. (1985). *Observing the Erotic Imagination*. New Haven, CT: Yale University Press.

Stoller, R. J. (1991). The term perversion. In: G. I. Fogel & W. A. Myers (Eds.), *Perversions and Near Perversions in Clinical Practice: New Psychoanalytic Perspectives*. New Haven, CT: Yale University Press.

Stone, A. A. (1993). Murder with no apparent motive. *The Journal of Psychiatry and Law, 21*: 175–190.

Styron, W. (1991). *Darkness Visible: A Memoir of Madness*. London: Jonathan Cape.

Tanay, E. (1969). Psychiatric study of homicide. *American Journal of Psychiatry, 175*: 1252–1258.

Teti, D. M., Gelfand, C. M., Messinger, D. S. & Isabella, R. (1995). Maternal depression and the quality of early attachment: an examination of infants, pre-schoolers, and their mothers. *Developmental Psychology, 31*: 364–376.

Tinbergen, N. (1952, December). The curious behaviour of the stickleback. *Scientific American, 187*: 22–26.

Tomkins, S. (1962). *Affect, Imagery, Consciousness. Volume 1: The Positive Affects*. New York: Springer.

Tomkins, S. (1963). *Affect, Imagery, Consciousness. Volume 2: The Negative Affects*. New York: Springer.

Tomkins, S. (1987). Shame. In: D. L. Nathanson (Ed.), *The Many Faces of Shame*. New York: Guilford.

Torok, M. (1994). The meaning of penis envy in women. In: N. Abraham & M. Torok, *The Shell and the Kernel*. Chicago, IL: University of Chicago Press.

Totton, N. (2006). Birth, death, orgasm, and perversion. In: D. Nobus & L. Downing (Eds.), *Perversion: Psychoanalytic Perspectives*. London: Karnac.

Tournier, P. (1962). *Guilt and Grace: A Psychological Study*. New York: Harper.

Trowell J. & Etchegoyen, A. (2002). *The Importance of Fathers*. London: Brunner-Routledge.

Tustin, F. (1972). *Autism and Childhood Psychosis*. London: Hogarth.

Tustin, F. (1981). *Autistic States in Childhood*. London: Hogarth.

Tustin, F. (1987). *Autistic Barriers in Neurotic Patients*. London: Karnac.

Tustin, F. (1992). *Autistic States in Children*. London: Tavistock/Routledge.

Tzourio-Mazoyer, N., De Schonen, S., Crivello, F., Reutter, B., Aujard, Y. & Nazoyer, B. (2002). Neural correlates of woman face processing by 2-month-old infants. *Neuroimage, 15*: 454–461.

Ulanov, A. B. & Ulanov, B. (1983). *Cinderella and Her Sisters: The Envied and the Envying*. Philadelphia, PA: Westminster.

Van Velsen, C. & Welldon, E. (Eds.) (1997). *A Practical Guide to Forensic Psychotherapy*. London: Jessica Kingsley.

Villejo, R. E. (1997). Insights on envy: a Kleinian analysis of Shakespeare's *Othello*. *Journal of Melanie Klein and Object Relations, 15(3)*: 467–474.

Waldron-Skinner, S. (1986). *Dictionary of Psychotherapy*. London: Routledge & Kegan Paul.

Weatherill, R. (Ed.) (1999). *The Death Drive: New Life for a Dead Subject?* (*Encyclopaedia of Psychoanalysis, Vol. 3*). London: Rebus.

Weiss, J., Lamberti, J. & Blackman, N. (1960). The sudden murderer: a comparative analysis. *Archives of General Psychiatry, 2*: 669.

Welldon, E. (1988). *Mother, Madonna, Whore: The Idealization and Denigration of Motherhood*. London: Free Association.

Welldon, E. (1996). Perverse men and perverse women? *British Journal of Psychotherapy, 12(4)*: 485–500.

West, M. (2010). Envy and difference. *The Journal of Analytical Psychology, 55*: 459–484.

Williams, P. J. (1991). *The Alchemy of Race and Rights*. Cambridge, MA: Harvard University Press.

Winnicott, C., Shepard, R. & Davis, M. (Eds.) (1989). *Psychoanalytic Exploration*. Cambridge, MA: Harvard University Press.

Winnicott, D. W. (1956). Mirror role of mother and family in child development. In: D. W. Winnicott, *Playing and Reality*. London: Tavistock, 1971.

Winnicott, D. W. (1958). The capacity to be alone. In: D. W. Winnicott (Ed.), *The Maturational Processes and the Facilitating Environment*. London: Hogarth, 1965.

Winnicott, D. W. (1960). The theory of the parent–infant relationship. *International Journal of Psychoanalysis, 41*: 585–595.

Winnicott, D. W. (1962). Ego integration in child development. In: D. W. Winnicott (Ed.), *The Maturational Processes and the Facilitating Environment*. London: Hogarth, 1965.

Winnicott, D. W. (1963). Communicating and not communicating leading to a study of certain opposites. In: D. W. Winnicott (Ed.), *The Maturational Processes and the Facilitating Environment*. London: Hogarth, 1965.

Winnicott, D. W. (Ed.) (1965). *The Maturational Processes and the Facilitating Environment*. London: Hogarth.

Winnicott, D. W. (1971). *Playing and Reality*. London: Tavistock.

Winnicott, D. W. (1974). Fear of breakdown. *International Review of Psycho-Analysis, 1*: 103–107.

Winnicott, D. W. (1984). *Deprivation and Delinquency*. London: Tavistock.

Winnicott, D. W. (1992). Primitive emotional development. In: D. W. Winnicott, *Through Pediatrics to Psychoanalysis: Collected Papers*. New York: Brunner-Mazel.

Wittling, W. (1957). The right hemisphere and the human stress response. *Acta Physiologica Scandinavaca, 640*: 55–59.

Wright, K. (1991). *Vision and Separation between Mother and Baby*. London: Free Association.

Wurmser, L. (1987). Shame: the veiled companion of narcissism. In D. L. Nathanson (Ed.), *The Many Faces of Shame*. New York: Guilford.

Wurmser, L. (1997). *The Mask of Shame*. Baltimore, MD: Johns Hopkins University Press.

Zilboorg, G. (1944). Masculine and feminine. *Psychiatry*, 7: 290.

Zulueta, F. de (1996). Theories of aggression and violence. In: C. Cordess & M. Cox (Eds.), *Forensic Psychotherapy*. London: Jessica Kingsley.

Zulueta, F. de (2000). *From Pain to Violence*. London: Whurr.

# INDEX

abandonment 150–151
Abraham, Karl 9, 11–12, 134
    genetic model 12–13
    on sadism 138–139
Abraham, Nicolas xxx, 112–113
acting out 3–4, 61–62, 115, 130
affect dysregulation 39, 81–82
aggression
    and the death instinct 21–23,
        157–158
    and womb envy 138, 145,
        148–149, 151
    Freud's theory 22–23, 34
    Klein's views 13–15, 62, 94
    neurobiological perspective
        39–40
    Schore's research 39
    see also violence
    versus destructive hatred 23
    Winnicott on 20, 29
Alexander, Richard 117–118

ambivalence
    and sexuality 140–141
    maternal 16, 22, 117
anal sadism, Klein 9–10, 29
antisocial behaviour
    and resistance to change 81, 156
    delinquency 57–61
anxiety
    and death instinct, Klein 16, 22
    and greed, Klein 13–14
    and nameless dread 55–56
    and perversion 151
    blank, Green 103, 110
    fear of death as ultimate 56–57,
        81
    separation, Bowlby 35, 62
Apter, Emily 132
attachment (relationship) xix
    and eye contact 87, 89
    envy embedded in failure of
        xxv

innate predisposition 7
shaping maturation of right brain
    38–40
attachment theory and
    psychoanalysis 24–28
Gallwey's model linking 49–60
attunement 37–38, 82
    lack of leading to shame 90, 92,
    96
autism 53–56, 80
    and affect dysregulation 81–82
    case history 66–78
Ayers, M. xxix, 88–90

bad behaviour, causes of 60–61
Barford, D. 18, 20–21
Barth, Diane 93–94
Bateson, G. xxxiii–xxxiv
Beebe, B. 30–32, 38, 86, 109
Berke, Joseph 53, 83–85, 101, 118–119,
    142, 148–149
Berman, E. 98–99
Bettelheim, Bruno 18, 140–141
Bick, Esther 52, 70
Bion, Wilfred xxxi, xxxiv, 35, 63,
    65, 124
    containment theory 42–44, 48,
        55–56, 117
    mother–infant adjustment 47
    psychotic and non-psychotic
        parts of the mind 98–99
Blake, William 125
blank anxiety/mourning 103, 110
body image 52
Bowlby, John 24–28, 36, 39, 95,
    111
brain development xxvii, 32, 36–40
breast, innate envy of, Klein xiv, xxi,
    xxii, 10–11, 18–19, 94
Butler Report 2
Butterworth, G. 31

"Caroline" (case study) 120–124
case studies xxvi–xxvii
    denied envy 142–145
    primary linking, failure in 66–78
    self envy 101–105, 120–124
castration complex 9
Chasseguet-Smirgel, Janine 85,
    148
childhood trauma see traumatic early
    experiences
Clark, R. 30
clinical material xxxi–xxxiii
    see also case studies
    use of xxx–xxxi
Colman, W. 15, 106
constitutional envy, Klein xxiii,
    9–12
containerlessness see encapsulated
    containerlessness
containment, Bion's theory of 43–44,
    48, 55–56, 117
controversies in forensic
    psychotherapy 5
Cordess, C. xxxiii, 4–5
countertransference xxiv, 42, 81, 104,
    116, 144
criminality
    and frustration, Klein 12
    forensic psychotherapy 1–3
    Gallwey's views 60–62
    psychoanalytic models of 3–4

Damasio, A. R. 38
Darwin, Charles xxiv
dead mother syndrome xxxiii,
    108–112
    case study example 120–124
death
    fear of 15, 56–57, 62–64, 81
    symbolic 57, 103
death instinct 8, 18

alternative perspective xviii–xix, 153
and envy 50, 65, 105, 107
counter-arguments to 20–24, 157–158
Freud's ideas xiii, xvi, xxii, 34, 134
Klein's theory of xxiii, 11–12, 17, 19, 94
versus fear of death 15–17
Winnicott's critique 34
De Casper, A. 31
defence mechanisms 10, 40–45, 92–95
delinquency 57–61
De Paola, H. 9
depression
and dead mother syndrome 108–112
and self envy 100, 110, 120–122
infantile 112, 118
maternal 25, 35, 53–54, 108, 111, 1 20
deprivation xxiii, xxiv
and delinquency 58–59
Klein's concept of 12–13, 94, 133
maternal xvii, 35–36, 39, 57, 94
De Shazer, S. xxxiii–xxxiv
despair 117–120
destructive envy 53, 64–65, 119, 151–153
case study 120–124
destructiveness 34–35
against the self (self envy) 107, 114, 128–129
against the therapist 123
and denied envy, case study 142–145
causal factors 38
Klein's theories 7, 11, 22
see also death instinct
versus aggression 16, 22–23

devaluation 53, 106, 121–122, 142, 148
de Zulueta, F. 82
disorganized attachment 25, 110–111
Downing, L. 131–132
dreams 55, 72–73, 121–122
dysmorphophobias 52, 76

Eagle, Morris 27
Eissler, M. J. 17
emotional development, role of right brain 46–47
emptiness, problem of 103–104, 110
encapsulated containerlessness 49–60
case study 66–78
comparison of Gallwey with other researchers 60–66
envious superego 80, 101
environmental influences, infant development xxiii, xxiv, xxxi, 17, 29–32
Envy and Gratitude (Klein) 8, 10, 17, 18, 133
Winnicott's criticism of 28–29
ethical challenges, perversion 131–132
eye contact
and shame 87–89, 103
role in parent-infant attachment 112

facial mirroring 90–91
Fagen, J. 32
Fairbairn, Ronald xvii, 16–17, 24, 32–33, 62–63, 85, 135–136
false self/existence, Winnicott 35, 57
fantasy see phantasy
"Fear of Breakdown" (Winnicott) 103, 105
fear of death 15, 56–57, 62–64, 81
fear, lack of capacity to experience 93

Feldman, E. 9
female perversion 132
femininity, Freud's theory of 149–150
Fenichel, Otto 21, 103
Fifer, W. 31
Fonagy, P. 25–28, 96, 110–111
forensic psychotherapy
    difficulties encountered in 3–5
    historical background 1–3
    see also criminality
Freud, Sigmund xiii, xvii, xxv
    and female sexuality 140–141,
        149–150
    and gender envy 148–149
    and Klein's position 19
    and perverse relationships 126, 134
    and the death instinct 18, 21–24,
        34, 107
    and the unconscious 26–27
    avoidance of clinical observation
        xiv–xv
    castration complex 9
    guilt and illness 79–80
    on aggression 22–23, 34
    on crime and guilt 4
    on love 150
    on shame 92–93
    omnipotent phantasy xxii–xxiii
    over-severe superego 101
    penis envy 145–146
    psychosexual development 30–31
    theory on acting out 61–62
frustration, Klein's theory of 12–13

Gallwey, Patrick xxiv, xxv–xxvi,
    xxviii–xxix, xxxiv, 6, 20, 48
    and Klein and post-Kleinian
        views 62–66
    and perverse psychopathology
        128
    and self-envy 114–115, 119
    and Winnicott's model 60–62

antisocial behaviour and
    profound resistance to change
    81, 156
clinical application of work 66–78
encapsulated containerlessness
    model 49–60
implications for treatment 79–80
gender envy, Freud 148–149
Gilligan, James 23, 93, 96–97, 157–158
Glover, Edward 2, 5
"good-enough" mother(ing) 17, 34,
    147
Gordon, Rosemary 15–16
gratification, Klein 12–13, 94
greed, Klein's theory of 11, 13–15,
    133
Green, Andre xxix–xxx, xxxiii, 34–35,
    103, 108–112
Grotstein, J. S. 43
guilt 4, 79–80, 93, 103
Guntrip, H. 19, 63

Hart, S. 24
hatred of women, womb envy
    138–140, 148, 152–153
healthy child development xvii–xviii,
    33–34, 158
Heim, C. 39
helplessness of infant xix
Hesse, E. 25, 36
Hinshelwood, R. D. 28, 32–33, 44
holding on, linking function 51–52
Holmes, Jeremy 26–28
Horney, Karen 79–80, 130–131, 146
humiliation 85–86, 93–96, 133,
    148–149
Hyatt-Williams, Arthur xxxiii, 6, 131

ideology, and perversion 131–132
imagination
    and symbol formation 64, 82
    see also phantasy

*Impasse and Interpretation* (Rosenfeld) 76–77, 79, 99–100
infant development
    environmental influences xxiv, xxvii, 38–40
    of sense of self 29–32
insecure attachment 27, 40, 47, 110
instinct
    and violent men 96–97
    Klein's theory of 12–14
    mistranslation of impulse 18
    *see also* death instinct
    uses/misuse of term xiv–xv, xxiii
International Association of Forensic Psychotherapy 2–3
introjective identification xxix, 14–15, 63, 65

Joseph, B. 110
Jukes, A. 138

Kaplan, Louise 132
Karr-Morse, R. 38, 114
Kaufman, G. 109
Kernberg, Otto xxviii, 4, 65, 85, 148, 153
Kittay, Eva 138, 140
Klein, Melanie xxi
    and attachment 27
    and death drive/instinct 15–18, 22
    and Freud's death instinct xxii, xxiii
    and primary envy 18–20
    constitutional/inborn envy xxv, 9–12
    frustration, deprivation and gratification 12–15
    influence of 28–29
    object relations theory 19–20, 32–33
    on anxiety and aggression 62

projective identification xxviii, 40–41, 45–46, 48
    use of word "instinct" xxiii, 33
knowledge, perception of xxxiv
Kohut, Heinz 4, 64, 91, 93

Lachmann, F. M. 30–32, 38, 86, 109
Laing, R. D. 35
Laplanche, J. 18
learning difficulties, failure in linking functions 53
LeDoux, J. E. 38
Lewis, H. B. 92
libido 13–14, 30–31
linking functions *see* primary linking functions
links, attachment bond, Bion 47
Lloyd-Owen, Dorothy 151
London, Jack 65
Long, S. 140, 152
Lopez-Corvo, R. 100
Lorenz, Konrad 28
loss 60, 150–151
love 23, 34–35, 150
    withholding of 134–135

Mahler, M. S. 92
Main, M. 25, 36
*Many Faces of Eros, The* (McDougall) 136
*Martin Eden* (London) 65
Martin, G. 30
masculine protest 9, 149
masochism 21, 85, 105, 134, 149
Masterson, Ingrid 16, 19–20, 22, 34
maternal depression 25, 35, 53–54, 108, 111
maternal deprivation xvii, 35–36, 39, 94
McDougall, Joyce 16, 136

Meissner, W. W. 44
mental illness
    and guilt, Freud 79
    maternal 102–104
    PTSD leading to 59
"micro-depression" of infant 112
Midgely, Mary 21–23
mind, definition of 36
Minsky, R. 146–147
mirroring mother 43, 88–91
misattunement and shame 90, 92, 96
Modell, A. H. xxxiii, 105, 108–109
Mollon, Phil 91, 122
Morrison, Andrew 84, 86, 95
murderousness xix, 68–69, 74–75,
    153

nameless dread 55–56
narcissism 84–87, 93–94
    and perversion 127–130, 133–135
    destructive 35, 59, 64–65, 106–108
Nathanson, Donald 26, 30–31, 84–87
negative attachment, delinquency
    arising from 58–59
negative narcissism 35, 107
negative therapeutic reaction 79–80,
    119, 123
    as an impasse in treatment 111,
        130
    as defence against shame
        of therapy 100
    self envy case study 104, 106–107
Nemeroff, C. B. 39
neurobiology 36–40
neuroplasticity 36, 38
neuroscientific research xxiv–xxv, 40
"Nicola" (case study) 142–145
night terrors 55, 72–73
Nobus, D. 131–132
"non-existence" 16, 57, 103, 117
non-psychotic part of personality,
    Bion 77, 99, 124

object relations theory
    and projective identification
        43–44, 47
    and shame 94
    Fairbairn's views 16–17, 32–33
    Klein 11, 19–20, 32–33, 95, 142
    modern feminist 147
    Winnicott 35–36, 95
Oedipus complex xv, xvi, 19, 100
offenders, therapy for 2–5, 58, 61–62
Ogden, Thomas 41–45, 47–48
omnipotent phantasies xxii–xxiii,
    xxv, xxix, 6–7, 14, 59, 63, 65
oral sadism, Klein 10, 14, 29
over-severe superego 101

"paranoid-schizoid position", Klein
    xxii, xxiii, 41
Parker, Rozsika 117
penis envy 9, 145–151
Perelberg, R. 117
perverse relationships 126–129
    furthering understanding
        of 133–136
    history, ideology, and ethics
        131–132
perversion and womb envy 137–138
Petot, J. M. 14
phantasy/phantasies
    objects, Klein 19–20
    omnipotent xxii–xxiii, xxv, xxix,
        6–7, 14, 59, 63, 65
    primary 54, 157
    secondary 54–55, 57–58, 60,
        64–65
    sexual 150–151
    unconscious 11, 26, 33, 46, 117
phantomatic haunting 112–114
philosophy xxxi–xxxiii
Plath, Sylvia 89
Polledri, P. xviii–xix
pornography 135, 145

Portman Clinic 1–3
post-traumatic stress disorder 59
pregnancy, male hostility towards
    138–139, 143, 145, 148–149,
    152
primary envy, Klein 18–20
primary identification 33, 50–51, 64,
    81
    effect of deficits in 57–58
primary linking functions/
    functioning 47, 50–54
    failure in xxv, xxvi, xxviii, 66–78,
    81, 124
primary maternal preoccupation 44,
    51
primary phantasies 54, 157
primitive autism 53, 56
primitive hatred 152–153
Pritchard, H. xxxi
privation, Klein 13–14
projective identification xxi–xxii,
    xxviii, 40–45
    and brain development 38
    and perversion 131, 151
    and symbol formation, Segal 64,
    127
    Bion's theories 47, 55–56, 64–65,
    99
    Gallwey on 49–50, 55, 66
    Kernberg's views 65
    Klein's theory of 11, 15
    psychoneurobiological model
    of 45–48
prospective linking 51
"psychical holes" 110
Psycho-Analysis of Children,
    The (Klein) 12
psychoanalytic models xxi–xxiii
psychobiological perspective 46–47
psychopaths, lack of fear in 93
psychopoesis, Gallwey 58
psychotic process, Bion 124

Rapaport, D. 30
reflective mirroring, mother–infant
    44, 87–90
revenge 12–13, 61, 116, 134, 138
Rich, Adrienne 150
right brain xxvii, 38–40, 47–48, 90
Riviere, Joan 80
Robson, Kenneth 91–92, 112
"Rose" (case study) 101–105,
    114–117
Rose, Jacqueline 97
Rosenfeld, Herbert 116, 123, 130, 133,
    158
    negative narcissism 107–108
    on hostility towards analyst 75
    on negative therapeutic reactions
    79, 99–100, 106, 111
    on the therapeutic relationship
    76–77
Rycroft, Charles 87

sadism 134–135, 138–139, 144
    Klein 10, 12–15, 19, 29
"Sally" (case study) 66–78
Scarfone, Dominique xxxi–xxxii
Schore, A. N. xxx, 32, 37–40, 45–47,
    90–92, 109, 114
secondary phantasies 54–55, 57–58,
    60, 64–65
secure attachment 24–25, 38, 47
Segal, Hanna 44–45, 64–65, 73, 101,
    127
self-destructiveness 23–24, 35, 107,
    128–129
    and self envy 114–115, 120–122
    and shame 95–96
self envy 98–101
    and despair 117–119
    case studies 101–105, 120–124
    dead mother syndrome 108–112
    suicidality, understanding
    114–117

transgenerational phantom
112–114
treatment implications 105–108
self-esteem 94, 130–131
self in relation to other 29–32
self-loathing and shame 95–96, 106
sense of self, development of 33–36
separation anxiety 62
sexual abuse xiv–xv
sexual perversion 5, 59–60, 129, 132
Seymour Report 2
shame 83–84
    and eye contact 86–92, 103
    and male violence 96–97
    as a primary affect 84–86
    case study 102, 105–106
    defences against 92–95
    Steiner's clinical example 129
Shell and the Kernel, The (Abraham
    and Torok) 112
Siegel, Daniel 36–38
Singer, J. 32
social interaction 24, 30–31
Sohn, Leslie 60
Spence, M. 31
Spillius, E. 57
splitting 41, 101, 107–108, 127
Steiner, John 127–130, 148–149
Stephen, Karin 55
Stern, Daniel 28, 89, 112
Stoller, Robert 132, 135, 137–138,
    150–151
stress 38–40, 59, 62, 109
Styron, W. 100
substantive linking 52–54
suicidality 35, 57, 85
    case studies 67–72, 101–105,
        114–115, 118–119
symbol formation 64, 82
    absence of, autism 55
    and the perversions 127–128

symbolic death, sources of 57
Symbolic Wounds (Bettelheim)
    140–141

therapy
    and self envy 105–109, 123, 130
    countertransference xxiv, 42, 81,
        104, 116, 144
    for offenders 2–5, 58, 61–62
    see also negative therapeutic
        reaction
Tomkins, Silvan 26, 85–86, 92
Torok, Maria 112–114, 145–146
transference xv–xvi, 3–5, 42, 123
transference depression 110
transgenerational phantom xxx,
    112–114
"transitional space", Winnicott 147
traumatic early experiences xiv–xv,
    xxv
    and capacity to form
        relationships 82
    effect on right brain structure
        xxvii, 38–40
    in maternal relatedness 35, 99,
        108–109
    link to adult violence 38, 96
    primitive defences used to cope
        with 49–60
truth xxxiii–xxxiv
Tustin, Frances 78, 80

Van Velsen, Cleo 3
violence 6–7
    and phantasy, Stoller 150–151
    as biological drive 157–158
    in men, hiding behind "instinct"
        96–97
    in women, directed inwards
        118–119
    link to childhood trauma 38, 96

*see also* aggression
shame as precondition for 93
usefulness of instinct idea 96–97
visual contact and shame 91, 112
vital concept 50, 76, 115–116, 155

Welldon, Estela 2–3, 126
Wiley, L. 38, 114
Winnicott, D. W. xxviii–xxix, xxxiii,
    6–7, 15, 17, 20
    criticism of Freud's "death
        instinct" 34
    criticism of Klein 28–29
    deprivation and delinquency
        60–61
    false self/existence 35, 57
    "good-enough" mother xxxiii, 17,
        34, 36, 147

infant's sense of self 31–32, 34
mother–infant unity 33–36
on adult psychopathy 57
on primary identification 33
primary maternal preoccupation
    44
"transitional space" 147
Wolf Man case study, Freud 141
womb envy xviii–xix
    and penis envy 145–151
    and primitive hatred 152–153
    case study 142–145
    perverse aspects of 151–152

Zilboorg, Gregory 141